Understanding
HEALTH CARE
REFORM

**Bridging the Gap
Between Myth and Reality**

Understanding HEALTH CARE REFORM

Bridging the Gap Between Myth and Reality

Arthur M. Feldman, MD, PhD

CRC Press
Taylor & Francis Group
Boca Raton London New York

CRC Press is an imprint of the
Taylor & Francis Group, an **informa** business

A PRODUCTIVITY PRESS BOOK

CRC Press
Taylor & Francis Group
6000 Broken Sound Parkway NW, Suite 300
Boca Raton, FL 33487-2742

© 2012 by Taylor & Francis Group, LLC
CRC Press is an imprint of Taylor & Francis Group, an Informa business

No claim to original U.S. Government works

Printed in the United States of America on acid-free paper
Version Date: 20111107

International Standard Book Number: 978-1-4398-7948-1 (Hardback)

This book contains information obtained from authentic and highly regarded sources. Reasonable efforts have been made to publish reliable data and information, but the author and publisher cannot assume responsibility for the validity of all materials or the consequences of their use. The authors and publishers have attempted to trace the copyright holders of all material reproduced in this publication and apologize to copyright holders if permission to publish in this form has not been obtained. If any copyright material has not been acknowledged please write and let us know so we may rectify in any future reprint.

Except as permitted under U.S. Copyright Law, no part of this book may be reprinted, reproduced, transmitted, or utilized in any form by any electronic, mechanical, or other means, now known or hereafter invented, including photocopying, microfilming, and recording, or in any information storage or retrieval system, without written permission from the publishers.

For permission to photocopy or use material electronically from this work, please access www.copyright.com (http://www.copyright.com/) or contact the Copyright Clearance Center, Inc. (CCC), 222 Rosewood Drive, Danvers, MA 01923, 978-750-8400. CCC is a not-for-profit organization that provides licenses and registration for a variety of users. For organizations that have been granted a photocopy license by the CCC, a separate system of payment has been arranged.

Trademark Notice: Product or corporate names may be trademarks or registered trademarks, and are used only for identification and explanation without intent to infringe.

Visit the Taylor & Francis Web site at
http://www.taylorandfrancis.com

and the CRC Press Web site at
http://www.crcpress.com

This book is dedicated to my patients who have taught me, the doctors who have cared for me, my daughters Emily Kate and Elizabeth Willa who make everything worth doing, and my wife Susan who has supported me through thick and thin.

Special thanks go to Marianne LaRusso for preparing the manuscript, Emily K. Feldman for her excellent editing, to Kristine Mednansky, and all of the staff at Taylor & Francis.

Contents

Preface xi
Introduction xv

1 Reforming the Private Insurance Industry 1
    Private Insurance Industry in the United States 3
    Reforming the Private Insurance Industry 4
    Flaws in the Patient Protection and Affordable Care Act 8
    Strengthening the Health Care Reform Legislation 15
    Notes 17

**2 How Will Health Care Reform Affect the Medicare and
Medicaid Populations?** 19
    About Medicare 21
    How Does the Health Care Reform Legislation Change Medicare
    and Medicaid? 24
        Independence at Home Program 25
        Medical Homes 25
        Accountable Care Organizations 27
        Extension Program Hub 31
        Community Health Centers 32
    Lowering Medicare and Medicaid Costs 33
        State Governments and Medicaid–Medicare Reform ... 34
        Lowering Health Care Costs through Health Care Reform 35
    Notes 38

3 Can We Lower Health Care Costs by Eliminating Waste? ... 41
    Medical Waste and Economic Waste 43
    Cost–Benefit Analysis 45
    Controlling Medical and Economic Waste 46
        Medical Spending during the Last Days of Life 47
        Patient Protection and Affordable Care Act and Waste 49

vii

Placing the Burden of Cost Control on the Patient 49
Placing Responsibility for Decreasing Waste on Hospitals 50
Unintended Consequences of Attempts to Eliminate Waste 51
Developing a Rational and National Strategy to
Reduce Waste 51
Notes 55

4 Role of Disease Prevention in Health Care Reform 57
Prevention and Wellness Programs in the Patient Protection and
Affordable Care Act 60
Section 2705 of the Patient Protection and Affordable Care
Act—Legislating Wellness! 61
U.S. Preventive Services Task Force: Another Potential Flaw
in the Patient Protection and Affordable Care Act 62
Prevention Doesn't Lower Health Care Costs—It Might
Actually Increase Them! 63
Addressing the Epidemic of Obesity—and Health
Care Reform 65
Complex Social and Economic Issues of the
Obesity Epidemic 65
Individuals Must Often Support the Costs of Prevention 67
Steps to Ensure Prevention and Wellness 68
Notes 70

**5 How Will Health Care Reform Affect the Medically
Underserved and the Safety Net Hospitals That Care
for Them?** 73
Health Care Safety Net 76
History of Safety Net Hospitals 77
Disproportionate-Share Hospital Payments 79
Safety Net Hospitals Falter When DSH Funds Are
Redirected to Pay for Health Insurance 80
Patient Protection and Affordable Care Act Threatens the
Country's Safety Net 80
Pay-for-Performance Can Also Threaten Safety
Net Hospitals 81
Health Care Exchange 82
Will the Exchanges Work? 84
Some States Are ahead of the Curve—Others behind It 86
Health Care Reform in Massachusetts: A Template for
Health Care Exchanges? 87

How Can the Patient Protection and Affordable Care Act Be
Modified to Protect the Safety Net?.. 88
Notes 90

**6 How Can We Improve the Quality of Care in the
United States?** **93**
The Cost–Quality Conundrum 95
The *Dartmouth Atlas* and Health Care Reform 97
Measuring Quality of Care 100
    Measuring Quality of Care: The Health Care Reform
    Legislation 101
    Pay-for-Performance 102
    Electronic Health Record 103
    Value-Based Purchasing.. 103
Substantive Steps Taken by the Patient Protection and Affordable
Care Act... 104
What Additional Steps Should Congress Take to Ensure Quality
of Care?.. 106
Notes 109

**7 Will There Be Enough Doctors to Care for 35 Million New
Patients?** **113**
How Does the Patient Protection and Affordable Care Act
Address the Workforce Crisis?... 116
The 1997 Balanced Budget Act and the Health Care Workforce
Crisis.. 118
    Changing Demographics of the Physician Workforce................119
    Workforce Crisis Is Not in Primary Care Alone 120
    Lessons from Massachusetts 121
How Have We Approached the Need to Increase the Number of
Practicing Physicians in the United States? 121
Danger around the Corner 124
What Should We Do to Increase the Size of the Health Care
Workforce?... 125
Notes 128

8 Can Research Guide Us to Improved Care at Lower Costs?.......... **131**
Why Comparative–Effectiveness Research Has Become a
Lightning Rod in the Health Care Debates 134
Patient Protection and Affordable Care Act and Comparative-
Effectiveness Research... 135
Potential Value of Comparative-Effectiveness Research 136

Can Comparative-Effectiveness Research Lower Costs?..................... 138
Limitations of Comparative-Effectiveness Studies............................ 140
Using Comparative-Effectiveness Research 142
Notes 144

9 How Will Health Care Reform Change the Way We Practice Medicine?.. 147
Physician Compensation 149
Sustainable Growth Rate 150
How Did the Patient Protection and Affordable Care Act Change the Way Doctors Are Paid? 151
    Pay-for-Performance 152
    Payment Bundling 153
    Global Payment 154
    Electronic Health Records 156
    Multispecialty Group Practices 159
    The Independent Payment Advisory Board 160
How Can the Patient Protection and Affordable Care Act Be Improved? 161
Notes 163

10 Will We Ever See Tort Reform in the United States?..................... 165
Current Tort System 167
Malpractice Caps 170
Patient Protection and Affordable Care Act Failed to Address Tort Reform 171
Medical Malpractice—A Silent Disease 172
Employment Law and the Health Professions 173
It Is Not Too Late—Novel Strategies for Reforming Our Tort System 174
Notes 176

11 Conclusion.. 179
Surviving Health Care Reform 186
Notes 188

Index 189

Preface

A Cure? Understanding the Patient Protection and Affordable Care Act

America's health care system is broken. Our health care costs are higher than in any developed country, yet we rank twenty-seventh in the world in life expectancy. Increasing premium costs force middle-income families to purchase benefits packages that are so skimpy that a serious medical problem could wipe out their savings. Thousands die and millions declare bankruptcy each year because they have no health insurance at all. In March 2010, after nearly a year of debate, Congress passed and the president signed the omnibus Patient Protection and Affordable Care Act to reform this nation's health care system and to provide insurance coverage for 35 million of the 50 million Americans who are uninsured. The most significant social legislation since the civil rights legislation and the creation of Medicare and Medicaid in the 1960s, the bill's passage has been met with great controversy.

People on the left of the political spectrum bemoan the fact that the bill does not include a government-run single-payer universal health care system while those on the right view the bill as socialized medicine that is being foisted on an unaware public. The majority of those in the middle of the political spectrum find that the nearly 1,000-page bill is difficult to understand. Many Americans have left the interpretation of the bill to the political pundits, politicians, health care economists, and policy analysts who have filled the airwaves and the lay press with their opinions. Even the many articles that have appeared in prestigious medical journals have been in large part authored by nonphysicians. Little has been heard from those who have the most invested in health care delivery reform—patients and their doctors.

During my medical career, I have been fortunate to care for patients, teach students, and pursue research at some of America's foremost hospitals and medical schools. I have served as a division chief, a department chair, the president of two professional organizations, a college trustee, the editor of a medical journal, and the founder and director of a biotechnology company. These activities have taken me to academic medical centers and teaching hospitals in thirty different states and fifteen different countries, to the Food and Drug Administration, and to the Centers for Medicare and Medicaid Services. I have seen health care delivered in towns as small as Haynesville, Louisiana, and Clarksburg, West Virginia, and in cities as large as Baltimore and Philadelphia. While all of these experiences have informed my opinions on our health care system and on the need for health care reform, no experience has been as instructive as becoming a patient. In November 2009, in the midst of the congressional health care debate, I was diagnosed with prostate cancer. Being a patient in this health care system has transformed my thinking about health care reform in ways that I could not have imagined. It was the dual perspective of patient and physician that led me to write this book.

Health care reform was designed to be a work in progress. The Patient Protection and Affordable Care Act states that the "secretary [of Health and Human Services] shall" or the "secretary may" establish a variety of institutes, centers, regulations, demonstration projects, pilot projects, and oversight bodies in 1,000 different places. It is these groups and programs that were given the task of creating new policies. In many cases the law stipulated that it would be the state legislatures and not the federal government that would develop new rules and regulations governing the health care industry. Because it will take over a decade for all of these pieces of reform to come together, it was generally assumed that there would be numerous opportunities for informed voters to provide meaningful input.

The mid-term elections of 2010, seen by many as a referendum on health care reform, created enormous uncertainty as to what reform would actually look like as key elements of the legislation were placed in jeopardy. The bill authorizes health care spending by federal agencies. However, the funds to be spent must be separately appropriated by the Congress each year. The Republican majority in the House of Representatives could make appropriations for health care reform problematic. Furthermore, victories by antireform governors and state legislatures may have crippled the ability of some states to carry out effectively their share of the financial and regulatory burden of new programs. Attorneys general in over half of the states are in fact challenging the constitutionality of critical elements of the new bill, placing its mandates at further risk, while the voters of some states have opted out of health care reform altogether.

My goal is to provide you with the information you need to make informed decisions and to help counter the bias of political pundits and the influence of the for-profit health care industry. I will do this by introducing you to a group of dedicated doctors, administrators, and interesting patients whose experience with our health care system will illustrate the strengths and weaknesses of the health care reform legislation. I will tell you about a talented health care administrator who tried unsuccessfully to turn around a safety net hospital in one of America's most economically deprived areas. You will meet a young physician who was diagnosed with cancer of the lung and learn about a new and exciting treatment for which insurance company refused payment. The story of a physician who has worked tirelessly to stem the epidemic of obesity and hypertension in inner-city Philadelphia will illustrate why preventing chronic disease is both expensive and difficult. You'll visit a community on the Louisiana–Arkansas border and learn how dedicated doctors and nurses face the challenges of delivering care in rural areas and how the Patient Protection and Affordable Care Act will affect their practices. And I will tell you about my own experiences with our health care system and the experiences of my patients—to illustrate both the strengths and the weaknesses of the health care reform legislation and why our current health care structure is unsustainable without reform.

Many excellent books have been written on our health care system, most of which have been authored by health care economists, social scientists, and health policy analysts. I am writing as a doctor and as a patient for anyone interested in contemplating the practical issues associated with our new health care reform legislation. This book is not about what is right or wrong with our system. It is focused on providing an understanding of the strengths and weaknesses of the health care reform legislation, explaining how doctors, patients, and families can determine the success or failure of the legislation over time, describing what we need to do to ensure that this landmark legislation succeeds in achieving its goals, and providing an accounting of steps that our elected representatives can take to improve the bill—and how ill-advised actions could threaten your ability to obtain high-quality and timely care. This book cuts through the political rhetoric and focuses the reader on the core question—what do we need to do to preserve our ability to provide the best possible care for our population and to fulfill our societal mission of providing care for our citizens independent of their financial means?

You may agree or disagree with me. But if I have encouraged you to think creatively about how you will play a role in creating a better system of health care in America, then I have fulfilled my goal in writing this book and you will become a good steward of our health care system.

Introduction

America's health care system is neither healthy, caring, nor a system.

Walter Cronkite

The Patient Protection and Affordable Care Act was signed into law on March 26, 2010. This landmark bill is the most significant piece of social legislation since the civil rights legislation and the establishment of Medicare and Medicaid in the 1960s. Yet unlike the earlier social legislation that had bipartisan support, health care reform has been met with controversy. Not a single Republican supported the bill in either the House of Representatives or the Senate, and a substantial number of Democratic representatives crossed party lines to oppose it. Thirty-three percent of Americans "strongly opposed" health care reform according to a Kaiser Family Foundation poll taken in March 2010.[1] A year later, the poll numbers had not significantly changed—with a near split between those who favor health care reform and those who still oppose it. Like the votes in the Senate and the House, public opinion has been split along party lines. I believe that the health care reform bill is a single step over the enormous chasm that separates our current system of spiraling costs and inequality from a restructured system with fair and cost-effective health care, but we face a real threat. The misleading hype, the biased influence of the health care industry, and the failure of the leadership of our political parties to seek compromise threaten to leave us in a position of straddling the chasm of health care with the threat that we will eventually fall into an abyss.

The vast majority of Americans recognize that our health care system doesn't work.[2] We spend more for health care than any other industrialized country, yet we rank thirty-ninth for infant mortality, forty-third for adult female mortality, forty-second for adult male mortality, and thirty-sixth for life expectancy.[3] We spend 16 percent of our gross domestic product on health care—the highest level of any industrialized nation.[4] This level of spending is estimated to increase to 25 percent of the gross domestic product by 2025—a level that will make it difficult for the federal government to fund important social programs and critical infrastructure projects. The United States, Turkey, and Mexico are the only developed countries without universal health coverage.[5] Fifty million Americans are uninsured. Middle-class families are also adversely affected by rising health care costs.[6] Costs for insurance premiums increased 131 percent for an average family between 1999 and 2009 and are expected to double again in the next 10 years.[7] This increase results in many families purchasing skimpy lower-cost health insurance, recognizing that a serious illness could wipe out their savings.[8] Increases in co-payments and out-of-pocket expenses make health care unaffordable for other families.[9]

If our health care system doesn't work, why has there been so much opposition to reform? I suggest that the great amount of discontent is due to uncertainty about how reform might change the quality of our health care and our personal finances. This uncertainty was due in part to the fact that the process for creating reform had flaws. The debates on Capitol Hill were, in large part, closed to the public, and the bill was crafted without adequate input from doctors, patients, and individuals with hands-on experience in the health care delivery system. Lobbyists spent over $1.7 billion since 2006 and a half-billion dollars in 2009 alone in an attempt to influence the votes of Congress.[10] In fact, there were so many health care lobbyists camped out in Washington, DC during the congressional debates that the ratio of lobbyists to congressional members was 6 to 1. For-profit hospitals, health insurance companies, and the pharmaceutical and device industries had far more influence over the crafting of health care reform than doctors or patients. Important opportunities were lost because of the lobbying efforts of the health care industries. We received information from political pundits and media analysts, not from those who were crafting the bill or from health care experts. We heard more about "death panels" and "rationing" and less about substantive issues, and not surprisingly, there is an enormous gap between the beliefs of health care experts and the beliefs of the public regarding key issues in health care reform.[11]

There has been little agreement about the cause of the increase in health care costs, although new technology and prescription drugs, increased numbers of individuals with chronic disease, the aging of the population, and high administrative costs certainly participate. Victor Fuchs, a Nobel laureate in economics, suggested that the high costs in the United States when compared with other high-income countries were attributable to higher administrative costs, a higher ratio of specialists to primary care physicians, more standby capacity (expensive equipment and personnel not used efficiently), open-ended funding (there is no fixed budget for health care), more malpractice claims, less social support for the poor, higher drug prices, and higher physician incomes (although he did not factor in the larger debt of American students).[12] He posited that "only large-scale reform of the way the country funds health insurance and organizes and pays for care will make a substantial, sustainable difference in the level of spending."

In September 2009 I wrote an op-ed for the *Washington Post* that appeared three days before the president addressed a joint session of Congress to present his plans for reform. The article was titled "The Ten Things I Hate about Health Care Reform." I raised a group of issues that I felt had been left out of the health care debate at that point in time. I received over 500 e-mails the next day. They reflected the wide variation in opinions about health care reform but also some gross misconceptions. A reader from Alamo, California, who had chronic heart disease, wrote: "Like most people who are against ObamaCare, I JUST WANT TO BE LEFT ALONE! Why can't liberals accept that I do not want them telling me what to do? Buy insurance for the uninsured but leave me out of it." Many writers expressed pessimism that America would be able to reform a broken health care system. A man who grew up in Canada wrote: "I have come to the reluctant conclusion that the 'Canadian' system or anything like it will never be implemented in this country because of the inherent nature of Americans whose antipathy to government action is, I think, hard wired in the womb." Some of the most vitriolic comments were directed at doctors. An unidentified reader wrote: "It is obvious from your piece that your main concern is your own greed—making sure that your bottom line is enhanced by any reform. You are a pathetic loser. I hope that real reform passes, to help the people of the nation. Your greed and lust for money should take a backseat to that reform."

My op-ed was based on my experiences as a doctor, but my perspective was dramatically changed in November 2009 when I was diagnosed with prostate cancer and became a full-time patient in our health care system. I was shocked to learn that there was a paucity of comparative studies that could adequately inform me regarding how to treat my disease despite the fact that prostate cancer is the most common cancer diagnosed in men. If I changed jobs, would I still be able to get insurance, or would my "preexisting condition" make private insurance unaffordable? Since my health insurance was part of a "preferred provider organization" or PPO, how large would my out-of-pocket costs be if I elected to have my surgery performed by a surgeon who was not part of my network? And why was my insurance company unwilling to pay for a second opinion on both my condition and the biopsy on which the diagnosis was made? The questions patients struggle with in our health care system and the concerns about how health care reform would change the cost or quality of care were no longer abstract ideas to me.

When the health care reform bill became law in March 2010, my recent experience with the U.S. health care system and my communications with people from across the country raised questions and concerns—few of which were addressed by the politicians and pundits who filled the media with their opinions. Even reading the bill was only partially helpful in addressing a lot of my questions. It was clear that private insurance companies would no longer be able to deny me insurance because of my preexisting condition and they could not cap my health care costs over the course of a year or my lifetime. The bill did not guarantee that my health care premium will not increase, nor did it give me confidence that my benefits or my out-of-pocket expenses would remain unchanged. I also couldn't discern whether there would be enough funding to support studies comparing the various treatments for a variety of diseases—including prostate cancer—and I wondered what Medicare would look like when I turn sixty-five.

I realized that some of the most important questions I had wouldn't be answered for three or four years. More than forty important provisions of the law require or permit existing governmental agencies to issue rules—the language of which will have an enormous effect on the impact of the law. Many of these rules will be crafted by new advisory panels and institutes created by the legislation. Some changes will be based on the results of pilot studies and demonstration projects. In some cases the oversight for these activities will come from the secretary of the Department of Health and Human Services (HHS) or from Congress while in other cases it will come from independent panels composed of citizens including patients and caregivers. Will the members of the new panels and institutes bring a broad knowledge and personal experience to their jobs? It is too early to tell.

The federal government will be just one player in health care reform. Individual states through their state health departments, offices of the attorneys general, and state legislatures will play a pivotal role in crafting health care reform as many of the key components of the reform legislation will need to be carried out at the state level. And there's the rub. Most states, unlike the federal government, must balance their budgets each year—they can't incur debt. I worry that many states, burdened by budget deficits, will not be able to afford to implement costly changes in health care. Some states may not want even to participate in health care reform. Nearly half of the attorneys general have already filed motions to declare parts of the bill unconstitutional. They allege that the law represents an unconstitutional violation of the limits of congressional powers. They point to the fact that it is unconstitutional for the government to mandate that individuals purchase health insurance. Some states have even elected to opt out of key elements of the law.

The midterm elections of 2010 served for many as a mandate on health care reform. Indeed, in its first vote of the New Year, the House of Representatives passed legislation "repealing" the Patient Protection and Affordable Care Act. This vote was mostly political posturing as the repeal bill was not brought before the Senate for a vote. It does, however, raise serious concerns. The health care reform legislation "authorizes" the Department of Health and Human Services and other federal departments to spend the necessary sums between 2010 and 2019 to accomplish specific tasks outlined in the bill. These funds must be separately "appropriated" by the House of Representatives. The implementation of the health care reform legislation will be problematic without these appropriations. The president could veto an appropriation bill that fails to allocate money for health care reform or that bars the use of staff time or personnel for writing or issuing regulations required by the bill, but to do so could close down the federal government. Henry Aaron of the Brookings Institute pointed out that a political tactic aimed at crippling the implementation of health care reform would leave the nation with "zombie legislation, a program that lives on but works badly, consisting of poorly funded and understaffed state health exchanges that cannot bring needed improvements to the individual and small group insurance markets, clumsily administered subsidies that lead to needless resentment and confusion, and mandates that are capriciously enforced."[13] If, on the other hand, the Republicans win the White House and both houses of Congress in 2012, the legislation could be dead. It is therefore imperative that we understand the key elements of the health care reform legislation and recognize those areas that must still be clarified and crafted before casting our votes for or against health care reform.

Instead of focusing on what has gotten us to the edge of a precipice, I will focus on the future of health care—how the health care reform act may shape our day-to-day lives and that of the doctors and nurses who care for us. I will focus on both the strengths and the weaknesses of the bill and point out those elements of the bill that must still be defined or refined. The health care reform act encompasses 1,000 pages of public policy that is both complex and arcane. I will put the health care reform bill in perspective by exploring ten critical areas that we each must understand to effectively appreciate the benefits and limitations of health care reform. If we can understand the bill and ask the right questions of our elected officials, we will be able to serve as good stewards of our health care system in the years ahead.

1. **Can we reform the private insurance industry?** This question is at the heart of the health care debate. I will describe how the health care reform legislation will eliminate some of the most egregious and capricious practices of the health insurance industry including refusing to insure people with preexisting conditions, rescinding insurance from people who develop disease, and placing caps on yearly or lifetime coverage. The importance of these changes in our health care laws will be illustrated by describing the plight of one of my colleagues who was diagnosed with a not uncommon form of cancer and who had to battle his insurance company to get the

treatment he needed. The health care reform bill also mandates a number of consumer protections and cost controls. But the new legislation is not a panacea. It fails to set specific limits on increases in the cost of insurance premiums, it forces healthy people who live in areas with a high incidence of chronic disease to support the care of the sick, and it allows insurers to pass new costs down to employers and employees. We will see how our elected officials and representatives can refine the reform bill through new rules and regulatory decisions to provide additional protection for patients and their families.

2. **Health care reform of Medicare and Medicaid:** My purpose in this chapter is to argue that the initiatives that will be undertaken to improve care in the Medicare and Medicaid populations have the greatest potential for reforming health care in America, although there will be formidable obstacles to their success. The health care reform bill gives the secretary of HHS the authority to undertake innovative pilot projects and demonstration projects including those that will evaluate efforts to improve access to care through a Medical Home program; provide in-home care through an Independence at Home program; link hospitals and caregivers in the community with Accountable Care Organizations; and provide incentives for collaborations among various specialties and cost controls through new payment methods. You will learn about some of the formidable obstacles that may inhibit the success of the legislation, and I will describe concrete steps that federal regulators should take to mitigate these potential problems.

3. **Can we lower health care costs by eliminating waste?** An underlying principle of health care reform is that the dramatic increases in health care costs can be reined in by eliminating the three types of health care waste: overutilization, high administrative fees, and fraud. The discussion focuses on overutilization because that is the form of waste that utilizes the most dollars and one that both doctors and patients can control. My own experiences in caring for patients in the current reimbursement system help illustrate how challenging it is to remove waste in a fee-for-service reimbursement system that rewards both doctors and hospitals for doing more and that has few built-in oversights. Patients also drive up the cost of care because they erroneously believe that having more tests and procedures equates with getting better care. Some health care economists have suggested that waste can be eliminated by increasing the portion of costs of care subsumed by patients so that they decrease their utilization and shop for the best price. I suggest that this approach is not valid. My purpose here is to convince you that to eliminate waste we must educate the public about the need for cost controls, train our young doctors in

ethically based medicine, and take steps to police overutilization while rewarding collaborative and high-quality care.

4. **The role of disease prevention in health care reform:** A second underlying principle of health care reform is that we can lower health care costs by preventing disease through early detection and lifestyle modifications. The new regulations established by the health care reform act provide a start to improving the nation's wellness. They require health plans to provide coverage without cost sharing for prevention services, recommended immunizations and preventive care for children, infants, and adolescents, and additional preventive care and screenings for women. They also permit employers to offer their employees modest rewards and incentives for participating in wellness programs. There are enormous challenges, however, to lowering health care costs through prevention and wellness. I will describe the career of a doctor who has spent over thirty-five years trying to stem the epidemics of obesity and hypertension in underserved areas of Philadelphia to illustrate the point that disease prevention is neither easy nor inexpensive. Maintaining a healthy diet and an exercise program is difficult and often not realistic for people in underserved areas. I will make several suggestions for how we can look more realistically at the goals of prevention and wellness programs and how we can target those programs to have the largest possible effect on the nation's health.

5. **Caring for the underserved—the health care "safety net":** The nation's poor have received care at America's so-called safety net hospitals for over a century. These safety net hospitals are often teaching hospitals associated with some of America's most outstanding medical schools. They are often located in underserved urban or rural areas and provide both outpatient and inpatient care for the populations they serve. The very existence of this safety net is threatened by health care reform. We will visit Braddock, Pennsylvania, one of America's most impoverished communities, meet a highly experienced hospital administrator, and learn how, despite outstanding leadership and a large infusion of financial support, our current health care system could not prevent the closing of this safety net hospital. We will see that the Patient Protection and Affordable Care Act may result in the closure of even more safety net hospitals. I will try to convince you that the reform act's mandate to decrease funding to safety net hospitals will adversely affect the health of America's underserved and the communities in which they live. I will describe substantive steps that must be taken to ensure that America's health care safety net does not collapse.

6. **Improving the quality of care in the United States:** We lead the world in health care costs—but we certainly don't lead the world in quality of care. I will describe the care of some patients I have met recently and use

these experiences to illustrate how our health care system fails to insure a high level of care for the nation's population. I will try to dispel the myth that pervades the health care reform debate: that higher costs equate with poor quality of care while low costs are associated with excellent quality of care. I will hopefully convince you that increasing the quality of care will be one of the best ways of lowering health care costs and describe several features of the health care reform bill that will actually point the way to greater quality of care, particularly for Medicare and Medicaid beneficiaries. Finally, I will describe several important steps that must be taken by federal and state legislatures to ensure high quality of care for all Americans.

7. **Will there be enough doctors to care for 35 million new patients?** The United States faces a workforce crisis—one that will get progressively worse as 35 million new people become insured and our population ages. We will visit with a young woman who practices in a suburban community in New Jersey and see how the practice of medicine has changed for many recent medical school graduates. We will also see that the health care reform legislation does not provide adequate incentives for students to pursue careers in primary care. I will also describe how some new medical schools in the United States are taking shortcuts to train primary care doctors more quickly and to increase the number of primary care physicians in the United States. The relatively few actions taken in the health care reform legislation to increase the physician workforce in the United States will only serve as a Band-Aid on the gaping wound in the health care worker pipeline. I will address the steps that Congress must take in order for us to be able to train enough doctors to care for an increasing number of patients, to encourage young trainees to pursue careers in primary care and in underserved urban or rural areas, and to break the logjam in the training pipeline.

8. **Comparative-effectiveness research and health care reform:** The inclusion of funding for research that compares one treatment with another—so-called comparative-effectiveness research—was one of the most controversial areas in the health care reform debate. Physicians fear that the results of comparative-effectiveness research will interfere with their ability to make decisions, political pundits see it as the first step in health care "rationing," and the pharmaceutical industry sees it as a means to decrease their profits. Stringent controls were placed on both the use of and funding for comparative-effectiveness research because of the lobbying efforts of many groups. In this chapter I will try to convince you that funding for comparative-effectiveness research is one of the most important parts of the health care reform legislation and provides one of

the greatest opportunities to improve care and decrease costs. I illustrate this point by describing several comparative-effectiveness research projects that had an impact on how patients with heart disease are treated and their cost of care, and I describe how my own care would have been far better informed by comparative-effectiveness studies. These illustrations will hopefully allay your fears about comparative-effectiveness research and convince you of the need to increase funding for this important research.

9. **Changing the way we practice medicine:** While the right and the left of the political spectrum have debated the merits of health care reform, the country's 150,000 doctors have found themselves in the middle. How will health care reform affect the way we practice medicine and the way we are reimbursed for our work? You will meet a group of primary care physicians who practice medicine in rural Louisiana. We will see how their practice will be positively influenced by key elements in the health care reform bill. These elements include funding for electronic health records and the development of new payment strategies that will reimburse physicians for nontraditional services. We will also see how some of the mandates of the new health care legislation and some of the proposed payment mechanisms and practice structures simply won't work in a rural environment that is over an hour away from a major full-service medical center. The story of this rural practice will also help to illustrate the need to tailor regulatory changes to different practice environments and how our health care delivery system cannot be a one-size-fits-all structure.

10. **Tort reform:** Tort reform has been a hot-button item in the debates over health care reform. Physicians have championed the need for reform, but there have been vocal admonitions against reform by Democrats and by their primary financial supporters—the trial lawyers of America. Our representatives in the House and in the Senate found it more expedient to ignore the issue of tort reform than to address it head-on. It is important to understand why tort reform is so important for doctors, the true costs of our current tort system, and the disparities in costs and manpower across states with and without tort reform. The discussion is illustrated with stories of doctors and patients who have firsthand experience with our current tort system. The important message from this chapter is that there are ways to make the system better so that doctors can be protected from capricious juries and that patients can receive appropriate compensation when they are harmed.

In the concluding part of the book, I describe what I believe are the key concepts that voters must focus on as states, the federal government, and the courts craft the health care reform legislation. We should view the health care reform act as the foundation and framing of a house. What it will look like once it is built and whether it will withstand the buffeting of time and weather are unclear. If the construction is overseen by an enlightened electorate, it is far more likely that the system will be strong enough to protect all Americans—the rich, the poor, and the aged. We should all remember that it was not by accident that the founders of this great nation placed "Life" before the calls for "Liberty" and "the pursuit of Happiness" in the Declaration of Independence.

Notes

1. *Kaiser Health Tracking Poll*: Kaiser Family Foundation, March 2010.
2. Blendon RJ, Benson JM. The American public and the next phase of the health care reform debate. *N Engl J Med.* Nov 19, 2009;361(21):e48.
3. *WHO Statistical Information System*: World Health Organization, September 2009.
4. *U.S. Health Care Costs: Background Brief*: Kaiser Family Foundation, 2010.
5. Johnson T. *Healthcare costs and U.S. competitiveness*: Council on Foreign Affairs.
6. *Accounting for the cost of US health care: A new look at why Americans spend more*: The McKinsey Global Institute, November 2008.
7. Kellermann AL, Lewin LS. The consequences of "no." *N Engl J Med.* Dec 17, 2009;361(25):2399–2401.
8. Hazardous health plans: Coverage gaps can leave you in big trouble. *Consumer Reports.* http://www.consumerreports.org/health/insurance/health-insurance/overview/health-insurance-ov.htm ed; 2009.
9. Polsky D, Grande D. The burden of health care costs for working families—Implications for reform. *N Engl J Med.* Jul 30, 2009;361(5):437–439.
10. Steinbrook R. Lobbying, campaign contributions, and health care reform. *N Engl J Med.* Dec 3 2009;361(23):e52.
11. Altman D. *The experts vs. the public on health reform*: Kaiser Family Foundation.
12. Fuchs VR. Cost shifting does not reduce the cost of health care. *JAMA.* Sep 2, 2009;302(9):999–1000.
13. Aaron HJ. The midterm elections—High stakes for health policy. *N Engl J Med.* Oct 28, 2010;363(18):1685–1687.

Chapter 1

Reforming the Private Insurance Industry

> At the heart of this debate is the question of whether we will continue to accept a health care system that works better for the insurance companies than it does for the American people. Because if this vote fails, the insurance industry will continue to run wild in America. They will continue to deny people coverage. They will continue to deny people care.
>
> **President Barack Obama, March 19, 2010**

> The real cure for what ails our health care system today is less government and more freedom.
>
> **Steve Forbes, "A New Birth of Freedom, Vision for America," March 30, 1999**

Susan G. knew from early childhood that she wanted to be a doctor. She stood out among her peers from her very first day as a medical resident. Her colleagues immediately looked to her as a leader of their group. Her confident yet gentle nature gained her the trust of her patients, and the nurses and staff physicians quickly saw that she was going to become an outstanding and caring physician.

One morning Susan awoke with severe pains in her chest and difficulty breathing. She immediately walked over to the emergency room where doctors performed an electrocardiogram and placed a small device around her index finger to measure the level of oxygen that was circulating in her blood stream. The electrocardiogram was normal—ruling out a heart attack; however, the level of oxygen in her blood was low, suggesting that something was significantly wrong with the function of her lungs—the organ that puts oxygen into the bloodstream. A CT scan was performed. It showed two masses in her lung—each the size of a quarter and enlargement of several lymph nodes.

A biopsy of the lymph node provided the diagnosis was adenocarcinoma of the lung—a form of lung cancer that is commonly found in smokers and older men and women but rarely in nonsmokers in their twenties. The cancer had spread from her lungs to the lymph nodes. Needless to say, Susan, her family, and the small group of friends and colleagues who knew the diagnosis were devastated by this news.

The traditional treatment for lung cancer includes radiation treatment combined with an aggressive form of chemotherapy—but the prognosis was grim. There was, however, a ray of hope. A group of leading experts in lung cancer in Boston had found that some young people who had the same form of cancer as Susan had specific mutations in the DNA of the cancer cells. DNA is the body's template for building proteins and tissues. The mutated DNA caused the production of a protein that was different from the normal protein in that it allowed or facilitated the ability of the cancer cells to multiply, to grow, and to spread to other parts of the body. In collaboration with the pharmaceutical industry, the lung cancer scientists had developed specific drugs to block the effects of these abnormal proteins—and these drugs had proved miraculously effective in early studies. The huge questions then became, could doctors identify a mutation in the DNA of Susan's cancer cells, was there a drug for people with that specific mutation, and would Susan's insurance cover the costs of her treatment?

Insurance policies that would cover the cost of hospital and medical expenses first appeared in the United States in the first half of the twentieth century. Hospitals began to provide services to individuals on a prepaid basis during the 1920s, a practice that led to the development of Blue Cross organizations. Today, over 200 million Americans have private health insurance policies, the majority paid for by their employers. A smaller number of people have individual health care policies. Individual health care policies have become unaffordable for most Americans and are not available for those with preexisting medical problems. The cost of employer-sponsored health care policies continues to rise: premiums have risen 114 percent over the last decade alone.[1]

Costs rose just over 7 percent in 2009 and another 9 percent in 2010—more than the increase in overall U.S. health care spending. In California, Anthem Health Insurance raised their rates a whopping 39 percent while other insurance companies have increased the costs of their policies between 50 and 75 percent.[2] These high costs are passed on to employers or to their employees. The increased costs for employers can result in a company's products being less competitive in the global marketplace. In this chapter, we will look at how the private insurance industry works, how the Patient Protection and Affordable Care Act will control some of the common abuses of the insurance industry, the limitations of the health reform legislation as it applies to the private insurance industry, and some recommendations for strengthening the legislation.

Private Insurance Industry in the United States

To ensure a profit, U.S. health insurers price the policies they sell to individuals based on their ability to predict the risk that a person will develop a costly medical condition. Since less than 20 percent of the population accounts for over 70 percent of health care costs and 5 percent of the population accounts for over half of all health care costs, insurance companies can make a profit if they eliminate a large portion of that 20 percent of the population from their insurance products.[3] They exclude high-risk patients by refusing to pay for care that is related to preexisting conditions, refusing to cover some high-risk people at all, and rescinding policies when people get sick. For group health policies, the costs simply escalate. These spiraling costs have led many employers to reduce benefits to employees, cap the amount paid for the care of a beneficiary in any year, decrease employee wages, or increase co-payments or cost sharing.[4] With the recession causing a glut of qualified applicants for a relatively few positions, some employers have been able to drop health care benefits altogether. A decrease in wages or an increase in co-payments can result in low-income families with health insurance having to choose between health insurance and other expenses such as housing, food, and education. Even middle-income families are adversely affected by the rising costs, and workers often make career choices based on the affordability of the health care benefits rather than what is best for their careers.[5]

Susan had to deal with her own insurance carrier's capricious policies. Her doctors had identified a group of experts who could possibly help her—but the insurance carrier would not pay for her to see the Boston doctors because they were out of network. Susan had selected an insurance product from the menu of benefits provided by her employer that was affordable for a medical resident with limited finances and large medical school debts—but the plan was affordable because it had limited benefits. Her policy mandated that she see a doctor who was part of a panel of approved providers—a so-called preferred provider network. Using a designated panel of doctors who had prospectively agreed to provide care at a predetermined price lowered costs for the insurance company—but for Susan, it precluded her from seeking the consultation of experts who might be able to help her. Susan's colleagues and family fortunately chipped in, and within days Susan was on a train to Boston.

Reforming the Private Insurance Industry

The Patient Protection and Affordable Care Act addresses the most egregious actions of the health insurance industry in its first ten pages.[6–8] It prohibits health insurance companies offering group or individual health insurance coverage from placing lifetime limits on dollars paid to an individual (2010), placing so-called unreasonable annual limits on spending (by 2014), rescinding coverage from an individual who develops a medical problem while they have insurance (2010), denying coverage to children with preexisting conditions (2010), and rejecting insurance coverage for an individual or a new member of a group policy because of a preexisting medical condition (by 2014). Private insurance companies are also forbidden from establishing rules that limit coverage eligibility for any full-time employee based on the salary of the employee or from instituting any eligibility rules that discriminate in favor of higher-wage employees—a group that has been found to have fewer medical problems. The health care reform act also expands the coverage an insurance carrier must provide for individual and families. A private health insurance company must extend benefits to dependent children up to the age of twenty-six and must provide full coverage for preventive services recommended by the United States Preventive Services Task Force including immunizations and preventive care and screenings (2010).

Susan's problems were not over. Her tumor had one of the mutations that the Boston doctors had been studying and they had a drug that had been developed that was targeted for people with lung cancer who had the same DNA mutation, but her insurance company would not pay for her routine care while she was enrolled in a clinical trial. It was absurd. The insurance company would pay for traditional treatment including radiation therapy, chemotherapy, and repeat CT scans to assess the effectiveness of the therapy at an estimated cost of $150,000. But they would not pay for routine care during the clinical trial—care that would only include CT scans at a cost of approximately $10,000. Fortunately, the clinical trial was able to cover almost all of the costs, and she was enrolled in the study. What is most important is that the health care reform legislation provides protection for individuals like Susan. An individual who is covered by a group or individual health plan can no longer be denied participation in a clinical trial as long as the study is a federally funded or is a non-federally funded study approved by the Food and Drug Administration that is evaluating the effectiveness of a new drug or device for the treatment of cancer or other life-threatening disease. The private insurance company is now obligated to pay for routine costs of care for the person in a clinical trial that are typically incurred by an individual with that disease who is not enrolled in a trial.

If Susan attempts to purchase her own insurance in the private market, she will not be afforded protection from denial because of her preexisting condition until 2014. In the short term she will be able to obtain insurance from a new high-risk pool designed to provide insurance for individuals who are at high risk of requiring expensive medical care or who have preexisting conditions that place them at high risk. U.S. citizens and legal immigrants who have a preexisting medical condition and who have been uninsured for at least six months will be eligible to enroll in the program. Premiums for the pool will be established for a standard population, and premiums may vary by age (no more than a fourfold increase for older Americans). Maximum cost sharing will be limited to $5,950 per individual and $22,900 per family. The health care reform act sets aside $5 billion to fund the pool.

In the future it will be far easier for people like Susan to understand what they are purchasing when they sign up for a health insurance plan. The bill mandates that private insurance companies use a standard summary of benefits that clearly explains to consumers the coverage they are receiving including exceptions, limitations on coverage, cost-sharing provisions, deductibles, coinsurance and co-payment obligations, the renewal ability, and continuation of coverage provisions so that the consumer can compare different products. Insurance companies must provide easily understood examples to illustrate common benefit scenarios including coverage for serious or chronic medical conditions and a contact number for the consumer to call with additional questions. They must make a Web address available where a copy of the actual policy can be reviewed. In addition, they are required to implement an effective appeals process that will make it easier for beneficiaries and their caregivers to resolve conflicts regarding payments and benefits.

The health care reform legislation also attempts to limit the escalating price of health care insurance premiums. First, an insurance carrier must submit to their state official and to the secretary of Health and Human Services for review any planned unreasonable increases in premiums prior to implementation of the increase. Second, the rates that an individual health insurance company sets for either the individual or small group market can only vary among individuals based on whether the insurance covers an individual or a family, the rating area in which the insured individual lives, the age of the person insured (rates can be up to three times higher for older adults), and whether the individual uses tobacco products (rates can increase by 50 percent for smokers). A state must report on trends in premium increases. They must institute penalties against health insurers that are unable to keep their costs in line. These penalties may include being excluded from state-run health insurance exchanges. Because most states are unprepared to monitor private insurance companies, the health care reform bill provides funding for grants to states to support efforts to review and approve premium increases

The increasing costs for group or individual insurance from private health care companies have been blamed on the fact that a substantial portion of health insurance premiums goes to pay for items other than direct patient care including administrative costs, high overheads, lucrative executive salaries, and profitable returns to investors. Indeed, the *Philadelphia Inquirer* reported in May 2010 that the CEO of New Jersey's largest health insurer received nearly $9 million in compensation in a year when the company laid off about 200 people.[9] Under the reform legislation, health plans will be required to report the proportion of premium dollars that are spent on actual care, defined as "clinical services, quality and other costs" (the medical loss ratio). They will have to provide rebates to consumers for the amount of the premium spent on "clinical services and quality and other costs" that is less than 85 percent of the premium for plans in the large group market and less than 80 percent for plans in the individual and small group markets. Health insurance companies will therefore be penalized when costs that are not directly linked to the cost of care for a beneficiary increase.

The health care reform legislation also seeks to decrease the extremely high administrative costs that are incurred by American health insurance companies as well as by providers. These high administrative costs are due to the fact that each health insurer has innumerable forms, claims, and denial management processes, different computer programs, and different rules for transactions. This lack of administrative consistency also increases costs for individuals and hospitals as physicians' offices and hospital accounts departments must spend numerous person-hours filling out the correct forms and sending and resending information through multiple different programs to receive payments. The secretary of HHS will develop operating rules for transactions and standardization for forms and data entry under the new legislation. Each health insurance plan will be required to certify that the data and information systems for the plan are in compliance with all standards and rules. Health insurers will be periodically audited, and if found to be out of compliance, they will face a penalty fee in the amount of $1 per enrollee. The importance of decreasing administrative costs is demonstrated by the fact that a failure to comply with administrative standards is one of the few elements in the health care reform bill that carries a monetary penalty.

Finally, the health care reform legislation mandates that all Americans have health insurance. At least half of the states are now questioning the constitutionality of this portion of the new law; however, it is fundamentally necessary for there to be universal coverage if there is to be any type of reform in the current health care insurance system. Historically U.S. health insurers priced the policies they sold to individuals based on their ability to predict the risk that a person would develop a costly medical condition—so-called risk rating. An insurance company could only make a profit if it was able to limit the number of high-risk individuals in its health insurance pool. Without some type of risk rating, people would be able to buy insurance only when they developed a risk for acquiring disease or actually became sick. If insurance companies only wrote policies for individuals who had a high risk of becoming ill or who were already sick, the dollars paid out for care would be high, and as a result the cost of a policy would be so exorbitant that consumers at low risk for disease would have to choose between purchasing an insurance policy with minimal coverage (which would be lower in price) or forgoing insurance altogether—a situation referred to in the health care marketplace as adverse selection. As more individuals declined to purchase insurance, the risk would be spread across fewer healthy people, and as a result, the premium costs for individuals with preexisting conditions would continue to rise. By mandating that all Americans must have at least a basic health care insurance policy by 2014, Congress has attempted to limit adverse selection and ensure that the cost of insurance is spread over low-risk young and healthy people as well as older and higher-risk people.

It is impossible to understand the Patient Protection and Affordable Care Act without understanding the concepts of mandatory insurance coverage and adverse selection.[10] Congress had only two viable options for increasing the number of Americans with health insurance: (1) mandating that every citizen purchase health insurance (recognizing that some individuals would require a subsidy) from the private insurance industry through state-monitored health care exchanges; or (2) providing free health insurance for everyone through the creation of a government-funded universal health insurance plan.[11] Providing free insurance was not deemed palatable because it would require new taxes and the displacement of the private industry. Instead of requiring mandatory insurance, Congress could have created a system that levied penalties on individuals who enrolled late (when they became sick) or created a system that automatically enrolled people but instituted a penalty for those who declined. Neither of these options was substantively different from the mandatory requirement for insurance and the creation of health care exchanges. The ironic fact is that most legislators—both Democrats and Republicans—favored the creation of health care exchanges. Political pundits now criticize the mandate—a criticism aimed largely at the voters and based more on party politics than doing what is best for the health care of the nation.

Flaws in the Patient Protection and Affordable Care Act

It appears at first blush that the health care reform legislation has effectively reformed the private insurance industry by banning their most egregious practices. But significant flaws remain. These flaws may result in an escalation of health care costs at the expense of the American public unless actions are taken to rectify them. Some of these flaws can be fixed by regulatory agencies as they craft the rules that will define many of the aspects of the health care legislation. Other gaps in the law may require new legislation. Let's look at these major flaws in the health care reform legislation and see how they will influence health care costs and quality over the next decade.

One thing that health care reform has not fixed is the fundamental economic structure on which the private industry is built—decreasing risk to increase rewards. Private insurance companies are built on the premise that all other factors being equal, an insurance company can turn a profit if they limit the number of people they insure who are at high risk for disease and costs and enhance the number of people who are low risk. As we have seen in the first part of this chapter, Congress has removed the mechanisms that insurance companies have traditionally used to eliminate high-risk individuals from obtaining or keeping their health insurance policies. So what do insurance companies do to balance their books? Their choices are limited! They can (1) decrease benefits, (2) pass costs directly to consumers or employers by increasing the cost of health insurance premiums, (3) pass costs on to consumers by increasing co-payments, deductibles, or coinsurance payments, (4) limit payments to doctors, hospitals, and other providers, or (5) lower dividend payments to investors and salary payments to their executives. Want to guess what they won't do?

The easiest way for an insurance company to increase revenues will be to institute reasonable increases in premium costs to levels that state and federal regulators will allow.[12] Here we run into the first major flaw found in the health care reform legislation. The health care reform act does not define reasonable increases in premium costs and provides no firm guidelines to the state agencies that will be faced with crafting an appropriate and fair definition. How the adjective reasonable is defined will have a major impact on health care costs and its affordability for American employers and employees. Recently, federal regulators have suggested that an increase of greater than 10 percent would incur federal scrutiny, and they have provided funds for states to oversee increases in premium costs.[13] However, this directive is a recommendation and not a mandate—and would not be sustainable in the present economic climate.

The enormous variability in regulatory authority across different states will also be an enormous impediment to controlling reasonable increases in rates. Even the twenty-eight states that have some authority to identify increases in insurance premium rates have very varying abilities to exert their authority, and many states have no authority to police rates whatsoever.[14] This results in an inconsistent insurance environment within the United States. Sara Rosenbaum, a professor of health law and policy at George Washington University, noted that "if insurers don't like the results of regulation in one state, they can pull up stakes and go elsewhere. That's why states often bend to the will of the industry."[14] If premium costs continue to escalate—even at single-digit rates—because states are unable to control them, it will be far more cost-effective for a low- or middle-income household to pay the fine for not having health insurance than it will be to purchase a health insurance policy, resulting in an adverse market in which individuals only buy health insurance when they become ill. Increasing premium costs will also affect employers as the cost for group insurance policies will also go up.

There is little agreement among economists as to whether the new health care legislation will rein in the aggressive practices of the insurance industry or whether the new laws will actually harm the industry. Some economists worry that the new health care law will lead to a wave of consolidation among health insurance companies. Wall Street analysts are actually predicting that while there will be a lot of losers among health insurance companies, some will be very big winners with a dramatic increase in mergers and acquisitions leading to a marked decrease in regional competition and a resulting rise in health insurance premiums.[15]

The health care reform legislation has also provided insurance companies with a window of opportunity for increasing rates because many of the rules have not yet taken effect. Judy Dugan, a research director of Consumer Watchdog in Santa Monica, California, said that "insurance companies appear to be making sure that when new federal rules for spending on healthcare kick in next year, they can keep their administrative bloat and profits intact."[16] A report by Healthwatch found that employer-sponsored family health care coverage in 2010 had increased 14 percent above the previous year's figures[17] A second survey found that workers were paying an average of 30 percent of the premium costs for family coverage and 19 percent of the premium costs for single coverage—a marked increase from the previous year.[18] With so many people out of work, employees have little leverage with employers. Transferring health care costs to employees is a mechanism to survive the recession for employers.

A study by the *Los Angeles Times* found that the cumulative effect of premium increases in early 2011 will effectively increase premiums from Blue Shield of California as high as 86.5 percent for thousands of individuals.[19] If California's Blue Shield's third planned premium increase in recent months is allowed, it will increase rates another 50 percent for 45,000 customers in the individual market, and 900 individuals will see their rates increase by 80 percent or more. Blue Shield countered that they were expecting to lose $20 million to $30 million on its individual policies this year—but that doesn't address the fact that they are making money on other policies and continue to pay their executives exorbitant salaries.

I received an e-mail from a Barbara L. in response to my op-ed piece in September 2009. Barbara was diagnosed with the same disease as Susan, but she did not have a genetic mutation in her cancer cells and required treatment with chemotherapy and radiation. Her plight points out another gap in the health care legislation. Her employer terminated her employment after her diagnosis because they feared that her costs would increase the company's health insurance premiums. Although health care reform legislation prevents health insurers from rescinding policies from individuals who become ill, it does not preclude employers from lowering their health care costs by terminating employees who develop medical conditions requiring significant expense or from terminating employees whom they see as being at high risk of developing significant medical problems.

The structure and funding of the high-risk insurance pool has led some health care economists to wonder whether it will work as expected.[20–22] As of June 2010, nineteen states declined federal dollars for the creation of a high-risk insurance pool—a federal fallback program will be needed to ensure that residents of these states have coverage. A second potential problem is cost—it is unclear that the current dollars allocated will be adequate to sustain the program. And what happens if the dollars run out or if states substitute the federal dollars they receive for state dollars that they already expend on health care? Over time, individuals who are not able to obtain health insurance from their employer or through an individual policy in the private sector and are not eligible for Medicare or Medicaid will be able to purchase health insurance from "exchanges." These will be discussed in a later chapter. Only time will tell how successful these various approaches will be for individuals in need of health care.[23]

Limiting benefits is another means by which health insurance companies can lower their costs. One common method of limiting benefits is known in the industry as buy-downs. These occur when an insurance company suggests to an employer or to an individual that increases in premiums can be mitigated or even eliminated by switching to a lower-cost policy. This lower-cost policy invariably has higher deductibles and/or greater limits on benefits. According to the Kaiser Family Foundation, the average deductible for family plans in the individual market increased from $2,760 in 2008 to $3,128 in 2009—a period of just one year. Not surprisingly, the same analysis showed that people buying health insurance on their own in the individual market from 2004 to 2007 paid 57 percent of their health care costs from their own pockets while people in the employer-sponsored plans averaged paying 30 percent of their health care costs out of their own pockets—still an incredibly high figure[24] A survey of employers found that even in the employer-sponsored health care market the percentage of people with very high deductibles increased from 16 percent in 2006 to 40 percent in 2009. Increasing deductibles in employer-sponsored policies will eventually make policies so skimpy that they won't provide meaningful coverage.[24] The health care reform bill mandates that every American must have insurance at the "bronze" level—a level at which the consumer is still responsible for 40 percent of their health care costs. In the case of an illness such as cancer or heart disease, that 40 percent might be both exorbitant and unaffordable. For the chronically ill, high deductibles may cause them to defer medical treatment to avoid burdening their family budgets.

For individuals who receive their health care coverage from their employers, the increase in premium costs will simply be passed down to the employees in either higher premiums or decreased benefits. A 2010 report by the PricewaterhouseCoopers Health Research Institute notes that an expected 9.5 percent growth in health care costs in 2010 and an expected 9 percent growth in costs in 2011 will result in employers increasing deductibles and requiring workers to spend more out-of-pocket at the point of care.[4] The report goes on to point out that the number of employers using coinsurance for physician visits has nearly doubled and one-third of all employers use coinsurance for brand-name drugs. In addition, the use of high-deductible plans rose from 6 percent in 2008 to 13 percent in 2010. The take-home message is that while the health care reform legislation may rein in unreasonable increases in health care premiums, the American worker will see few benefits in the near future as a result of health care reform as the cost of a premium will continue to escalate at a "reasonable" but unaffordable rate and those costs will be passed directly on to employees.

President Obama, in his address to a joint session of Congress in September 2009, made the following remark: "First, if you are among the hundreds of millions of Americans who already have health insurance through your job, or Medicare, or Medicaid, or the VA, nothing in this plan will require you or your employer to change the coverage or the doctor you have."[25] But an article by Ricardo Alonso-Zaldivar suggests otherwise. According to Alonso-Zaldivar, regulations found in the health care reform legislation mandating preventive care without co-payments, an appeals process for disputed claims that follow federal guidelines, and extended coverage to young adult children will increase costs.[26]

James Gelfand, health policy director for the U.S. Chamber of Commerce, said, "What we are getting here is a clear indication that most plans will have to change. From an employer's point of view that's a bad thing. These changes, whether or not they're good for consumers, are most certainly accompanied by a cost."[27] The ability of insurance companies to force employers to change plans will, like so much of the health care reform legislation, be predicated on new regulations and, in particular, on how the federal government defines "grandfathered" health plans. Plans that predate the health care law are exempt from many, but not all, of the new federal regulations. Thus, not only can their costs rise but their benefits can change as well. The question will be how much an employer can change the benefits of a health plan and still claim that it is grandfathered and exempt from new federal consumer protection. Only time—and the language of the regulations—will tell.

Another serious flaw in the health care reform legislation as it applies to the private insurance industry is that it fails to define the specific expenses that will be used to calculate whether a health insurance company utilizes 85 percent of its revenues on "clinical services, quality and other costs" or continues to utilize a greater percentage of its revenues on administrative costs, overhead, high salaries for its executives, and robust returns to investors. This is an important definition because insurers will have to pay rebates to beneficiaries if their overhead costs—anything not defined as "clinical services, quality or other costs"—is too high. It will be relatively easy to define "clinical services." The amount spent on "quality and other costs" is far more subjective.

In an article in the *New York Times* by Robert Pear, Alissa Fox, a senior vice president of the Blue Cross and Blue Shield Association, presented the health industry side of the story.[28] She noted that if the definition of quality and other costs is too narrow, "health plans will come under enormous pressure to cut back quality improvement activities including highly effective programs to reduce hospital infection rates." In the same article, Charles N. Kahn III, president of the Federation of American Hospitals, represented the view of most employers and hospitals. He fears "that the quality improvement category would become a catchall for a wide variety of expenses not directly related to patient care," thereby facilitating the ability of health insurers to limit their risk of having to pay rebates and maintain the salaries of their executives.

The battleground for setting the regulations that will determine what comes under the definition of "clinical services, quality or other costs" will actually be controlled by state regulators. Reed Abelson points out in an article in the *New York Times* that WellPoint, which operates Blue Cross plans in more than a dozen states, "wants to include the cost of verifying the credentials of doctors in its networks."[29] Other insurance companies argue that identifying fraud and even typical business expenses such as sales commissions for insurance agents should not be part of insurance premiums. Some insurance commissioners are being swayed by the industry's aggressive lobbying campaigns. Abelson points to a letter sent from the insurance commissioner for Florida that noted that a strict interpretation of the federal guidelines "could potentially disrupt the availability of private insurance, and do not take into account the integral role of health insurance agents." With billions of dollars at stake, Senator John D. Rockefeller wrote in a statement that the insurance companies were "working every angle of the implementation process to shirk their obligations under the new law."[29] Only strict enforcement of the "intent" of the health care reform legislation will mitigate these potential loopholes in the law. Even states that want to implement the many aspects of the health care reform law may have trouble doing so because insurance commissioners in almost half of the states do not even have the authority to enforce many of the consumer protection standards.[30]

Another unfortunate lapse in the health care reform legislation is that it allows insurance companies to set rates for premiums based on the "area" in which an applicant for health insurance lives.[31] This so-called community rating system takes into consideration the number of high-risk and the number of low-risk individuals in a given area to set the premium cost for insurance purchased in the private marketplace based on an actuarial analysis of the health care costs that the particular community will expend. Since everyone in the "area" has the same insurance costs, money is transferred from the fees paid by the standard- or average-risk people to support the increased health care costs of the high-risk people. This system might work in an affluent area where health care costs do not represent a substantial portion of a family's yearly income. In underserved areas, even modest amounts of cost shifting from high-risk individuals to low-risk individuals can make premiums unaffordable because low-risk individuals in underserved areas also have low incomes.[32] Underserved areas are further penalized in a community rating system because studies show that there are a larger number of high-risk individuals in poorer urban and rural areas and a lower use of disease prevention strategies. Shifting costs from poor high-risk individuals to poor low-risk people results in costs that are high in relation to the benefits that they will receive—a practice that is unsustainable. It would have been far fairer—but less politically acceptable—to mandate that insurance companies set rates that are equal everywhere as is done in most countries with universal health coverage.

Individuals and groups purchase their insurance from health insurance companies that are located within their state. Consumer groups and health policy analysts proposed that health care costs could be lowered if an individual could shop across state lines and find the cheapest policy. Some consumer groups have been enthusiastic about the fact that the Patient Protection and Affordable Care Act permits states to form Health Care Choice Compacts that allow insurers the ability to sell policies in any state participating in the compact, but this is shortsighted. The Health Care Choice Compacts will not encourage competition because insurance companies must agree to offer insurance products in other states. Competition would exist only if an individual could purchase insurance anywhere in the country and shop for the best price. There is in fact little competition among health insurance companies in any area of the country as evidenced by the fact that in well over half of all urban areas, a single insurance company covers over half of the population. The market dominance of single regional insurance companies has come in part from consolidation of smaller companies. The federal government has had little interest in applying antitrust laws to health insurance mergers as only two of 400 health insurance mergers have been challenged by the Department of Justice over the preceding decade. This is but one more example of the influence that the health care insurance industry has in Washington.

The health care reform bill imposes an excise tax on employer-sponsored health plans with aggregate values that are greater than $10,200 for individual coverage and $27,500 for family coverage. This so-called Cadillac tax will begin in 2018. The tax will be equal to 40 percent of the value of the plan that exceeds the threshold amounts and is imposed on the issuer of the health insurance policy.[33] A flat 40 percent tax on insurance costs above the defined thresholds provides extra revenue for the government and will deter employers and employees from purchasing insurance that is more than they might purchase in the absence of an excise tax; however, the excise tax has important drawbacks. There is little doubt that the cost of the excise tax will be passed down to employees enrolled in group health programs and to individuals due to higher insurance costs. The flat-rate excise tax will also be more onerous for individuals in the low- to middle-income bracket than for those in higher-income brackets. Congress could have undertaken two alternative approaches. It could have based the excise tax on the tax bracket of the individual purchasing the policy—an administratively more difficult but clearly fairer approach. Alternatively, Congress could have simply eliminated the tax-free treatment of employer-sponsored health insurance—the largest federal tax subsidy—something that many economists have been recommending for some time now. Neither of these alternatives was politically appealing.

Under the guidelines of the health care reform bill, the federal government will impose an annual fee on health insurance companies. These fees will raise $8 billion in 2014, $11.3 billion in 2015–2016, $13.9 billion in 2017, and $14.3 billion in 2018. For nonprofit insurers, only 50 percent of net premiums will be taken into account in calculating the fee. Exemptions will be granted for nonprofit plans that receive more than 80 percent of their income from government programs targeting low-income or elderly populations or people with disabilities and voluntary employees' beneficiary associations not established by an employer. The annual fee will raise substantial revenue for the government that can be shifted to support other government subsidies, but individual beneficiaries will undoubtedly cover the cost of these new fees.

A confounding part of the health care reform law is that many states are taking advantage of the opportunity to apply for waivers that would free them from some statutes of the law. Waivers are granted on the basis that compliance with a statute of the new law would cause an increase in premiums or a decrease in access to benefits. Robert Pear pointed out in an article in the *New York Times* that Maine won a three-year reprieve from the provision of the law that required insurers selling coverage to individuals and families to spend at least 80 percent of premium revenues on medical care.[34] The waiver was granted when the Obama administration found that the new standard would drive a large insurer out of the market, leaving thousands of individuals without insurance.

It is important to recognize that state governments will have to play a critical role in instituting and overseeing insurance market reform. The Department of Health and Human Services will provide grants to states to help them oversee health care reform; however, the states' ability or willingness to reform health care is questionable.[35] Many states have opposed implementation of health care reform or have filed lawsuits against the government claiming that parts of the health care reform bill are unconstitutional.[36]

Lobbying by the health care industry will be intense at the state level. Senator John D. Rockefeller IV noted that "the health insurance industry has shifted its focus from opposing health care reform to influencing how the new law will be implemented"—particularly at the state level.[37] In fact, a study by the National Institute on Money in State Politics found that enormous amounts of money have been given to state officials by the health care industry to influence their decisions.[38] Health care insurance companies and the pharmaceutical and device manufacturers spent $199 million on lobbying in California alone between 2004 and 2008, and the pharmaceutical industry spent an additional $80 million on a successful California-based advertising campaign to oppose a ballot initiative that would have lowered drug prices. It is far easier for lobbying groups representing the insurance industry to influence decisions by state legislatures than it is to influence Congress because state campaign finance laws and ethics rules are highly variable and are nonexistent in some states. Federal health care statutes will therefore meet rigorous obstacles in implementation at the state level.

Strengthening the Health Care Reform Legislation

Recognizing that the health care reform bill has flaws but is a work in progress, what rules and regulations regarding the health insurance industry must be clarified by the secretary of Health and Human Services or by the state and federal regulatory agencies that will oversee health care reform? I contend that there are a number of critical areas of the bill as it relates to private health insurers that must be clarified. The use of the adjective *reasonable* to characterize increases in premium costs must be narrowly defined. The Department of Health and Human Services has suggested that premiums should not increase more than 10 percent, but even that amount is excessive in a time of recession. Regulators must also look carefully at the area rating system to ensure that there is not bias and inequity in the creation of this designation. We must ensure that there is equity in our health care delivery system; otherwise we cannot claim that the system is reformed.

I also think that some aspects of the bill must be changed by additional legislative actions. The excise tax on Cadillac policies should be based on an individual's income and not taxed at a flat 40 percent rate—or alternatively eliminate the tax credits for health insurance. Health care costs could also be decreased if individuals were able to buy their health insurance from anywhere in the United States to have unequivocal competition in the marketplace. And state and federal legislatures must see to it that the private insurance companies are not able to continue to reward their investors and administrators by decreasing benefits for patients and reimbursements to doctors and hospitals.

Let's again look at Susan, whom we met in the beginning of this chapter. She will now be able to participate in a clinical trial and have her routine medical expenses covered, she will not be denied health insurance in the future because of her preexisting medical problem, and her current plan cannot be rescinded. In addition, her health care expenses cannot be capped. But the gaps in the reform bill raise significant questions. Will her premiums be affordable if she has to purchase her own insurance? Will her benefit package cover the exorbitant cost of chemotherapy if the experimental therapy fails? What will her out-of-pocket costs be and will they be affordable? What co-pays will she have to pay? And will the federal government be able to see to it that her insurance company pays for her to have an appropriate level of care—especially as new and increasingly more expensive drugs become available in the marketplace to treat her disease? The answer to most of these questions will only come with time and will depend in large part on how the various state and federal regulatory agencies interpret and modify the health reform legislation.

Notes

1. Schoen C. Nicholson, JL, Rustgi SD. *Paying the Price: How Health Insurance Premiums are Eating Up Middle Class Incomes*: The Commonwealth Fund Data; August 2009.
2. Helfand D. Anthem Blue Cross dramatically raising rates for Californians with individual health policies. *Los Angeles Times.* February 4, 2010.
3. Stanton M. *The High Concentration of U.S. Health Care Expenditures.* Research in Action, Issue #9: June 2006.
4. *Behind the Numbers: Medical Cost Trends 2011*: Health Research Institute. PWC, June 2010.
5. Holahan J, Garrett, B., Headen L, Lucas A. *Health Reform: The Cost of Failure.* May 21, 2009.
6. *Summary of New Health Reform Law*: Kaiser Family Foundation. March 26, 2010.
7. *Health Reform Implementation Timeline.* Kaiser Family Foundation, 2010.
8. Washington Post Staff, Landmark: The Inside Story of America's New Health Care Law and What it Means for All of Us. Public Affairs, New York, 2010.
9. Conaboy C. NJ Blue Cross execs defend pay hikes after layoffs. *The Philadelphia Inquirer.* June 14, 2010.
10. Cutler DM, Zeckhauser, RJ. Adverse selection in health insurance. *Frontiers in Health Policy Research.* June 1998; Garber AM ed. (MIT Press).
11. Oberlander J. Under Siege—The individual mandate for health insurance and its alternatives. *N Engl J Med.* Feb 16, 2011.
12. Helfand D. Blue Shield calls pending rate hikes reasonable. *Los Angeles Times.* March 1, 2011.
13. http://www.healthcare.gov/news/factsheets/ratereview02242011a.html. Nearly $200 Million Available to Help States Fight Health Insurance Premium Increases, Healthcare.gov, Posted February 24, 2011.
14. Mills A, Engelhard CL, Tereskerz PM. Truth and consequences—insurance-premium rate regulation and the ACA. *N Engl J Med.* Sep 2, 2010;363(10):899–901.
15. Big insurance, big medicine, review and outlook. *Wall Street Journal.* October 26, 2010.
16. Consumer groups want federal investigation of insurers' medical spending. *Los Angeles Times.* August 12, 2010.
17. Lillis M. *Insurance Costs for U.S. Workers have Surged this Year.* The Hills Healthcare Blog. http://thehill.com/blogs/healthwatch/corporate-news/116953-worker-health-costs-skyrocket-as-businesses-shift-burden-to-employees. Accessed September 2, 2010.
18. Hilzenrath D. Employers lifting health care costs to workers, survey shows. *Washington Post.* September 2, 2010.
19. Helfand D. Blue Shield's cumulative rate hikes could reach 86.5%. *Los Angeles Times.* March 12, 2001.
20. Carroll J. Interim federal high-risk groups may far exceed $5B allocation. *Manag Care.* Sep 2010;19(9):35–36.

21. Hall J, Moore J. *Realizing Health Reform's Potential: Pre-Existing Condition Insurance Plans Created by the Affordable Care Act of 2010*: Commonwealth Fund; October 2010.
22. Pollack HA. High-risk pools for the sick and uninsured under health reform: too little and thus too late. *J Gen Intern Med.* Jan 2011;26(1):91–94.
23. About the new pre-existing condition insurance plan, CMS Newsroom, July 29, 2010, www.healthcare.gov/news/factsheet/2010/07/preexistingconditioninsuranceplan.html.
24. Altman D. When premiums go up 39%. The Kaiser Family Foundation: www.kff.org/pullingittogether/031010.actma.cfa. Accessed March 10, 2010.
25. Obama B. Remarks by the President to a Joint Session of Congress on Health Care. Accessed September 9, 2009.
26. Alonso-Zaldivar R. Health overhaul to force changes in employer plans. *Yahoo News.* Accessed June 11.
27. Obama Breaks Promise on Healthcare Reform Coverage. http://www.newsmax.com/Newsfront/US-Health-Overhaul-Keeping/2010/06/11/id/361776. Accessed June 11, 2000.
28. Pear R. Health insurers lobbying to shape overhaul rules. *New York Times.* May 16, 2010.
29. Abelson R. For insurers, fight is now over the details. *New York Times.* July 23, 2010.
30. Pear R, Sack K. Some states are lacking in health law authority. *New York Times.* August 14, 2010.
31. Pauly MV. Avoiding side effects in implementing health insurance reform. *N Engl J Med.* February 25, 2010;362(8):671–673.
32. Reinhardt U. Is community rating in health insurance fair? *New York Times.* Jan 1, 2010.
33. Sessions S, Detsky, AS. The proposed excise tax on employee health insurance—good idea, or too clever by 40%. *JAMA.* November 25, 2009;302(20):2252–2253.
34. Pear R. Health law waivers draw kudos, and criticism. *New York Times.* March 19, 2011.
35. Jost TS. Implementation and Enforcement of Health Care Reform—Federal versus State Government. *nejm.org.* December 30, 2009;10.1056(10.1056/nejmp0911636).
36. Kirkpatrick DD. Health lobby takes fight to the states. *New York Times.* December 29, 2009.
37. Pear R. Health insurance companies try to shape rules. *New York Times.* May 15, 2010.
38. Bauer A. *Take $2 Million . . . and Call Me in the Session*: National Institute on Money in State Politics; December 15, 2009.

Chapter 2

How Will Health Care Reform Affect the Medicare and Medicaid Populations?

> Medicare will go deep into the red in less than a decade. But he [President Obama] and congressional Democrats are planning to raid, not aid, Medicare by cutting $500 billion from the program to fund his health-care experiment. The president also plans to cut hospital payments and Medicare Advantage, all of which will mean fewer treatment options for seniors.
>
> **Michael S. Steele, Protecting Our Seniors,**
> *Washington Post*, **August 24, 2009**

> When JFK and then Lyndon Johnson tried to pass Medicare, they said this was a government takeover of health care; they were going to get between you and your doctor—the same argument that's being made today.
>
> **President Barack Obama, town hall meeting, August 15, 2009**

In early March of 2010, I attended a dinner party. The host, a lawyer for one of the country's largest health care systems, complained about the fact that the new health care reform bill would have no "public option." A pediatrician who practices at an academic medical center was encouraged by the fact that the new legislation will ensure that the vast majority of children are covered by insurance, but he expressed his concerns that cuts in reimbursements for many adult services may have drastic consequences on the ability of our hospital to provide our current level of services. A former chef who now works in a small business worried whether his employer would continue to pay for his insurance or whether he would have to buy his own insurance through an insurance exchange—but he was happy that I can now keep my daughter on my policy until she is twenty-six and hopefully has a job. I asked, "Who here is happy with our current health care system?" An elderly couple at the table sheepishly raised their hands. "We have Medicare and a supplemental policy that I buy myself so everything gets paid for and we can see any doctors we want. And now Obama is going to fill the Medicare prescription drug 'doughnut hole' so the cost for our medicines will go down." They were very happy with a system that had raised controversy fifty years earlier when many thought it was the first step toward socialized medicine. The worry for all of the other young people around our dinner table was whether Medicare will last for another fifty years.

Medicare, the government-funded health insurance plan, covers 47 million Americans, making it the largest health insurer in the nation.[1] It was established by the Social Security Act of 1965 to provide affordable insurance for the elderly at a time when half of the elderly in the United States had no health insurance. President Lyndon B. Johnson enrolled the first Medicare beneficiary—former president Harry S. Truman—on July 30, 1965. Medicare was initially met with some skepticism as critics saw it as a first step toward socialized medicine. In 1964, George H. W. Bush described Medicare as "socialized medicine." Today Medicare has become an integral part of our society, although many people take it for granted and few understand its structure, its strengths, and its limitations. A speaker at a 2010 town hall meeting in Simpsonville, South Carolina, illustrated this best when he shouted, "Keep your government hands off my Medicare."[2]

Over the past decade the Medicare per-capita spending has increased annually by 6.8 percent—a rate that is slightly less than the 7.1 percent growth seen in the private insurance industry over the same time period. In 2010, Medicare will represent 12 percent of federal spending.[3] The cost of Medicare was estimated to increase to $1,038 billion in 2020 in the absence of reform according to the Congressional Budget Office.

In 1965, the median age in the United States was 28.4; today it is 36.6. Many of our elderly undergo expensive procedures that were not even available in 1965—coronary artery-bypass graft surgery, hip and knee replacements, and vascular procedures that use catheters and stents. The aging of the population raises concerns for Medicare because the ratio of workers paying Medicare taxes to retirees drawing benefits is shrinking, and at the same time, the price of health care services per person is increasing. Currently there are 3.9 workers paying taxes into Medicare for every older American receiving services. By 2030, as the baby boom generation retires, that number is projected to drop to 2.4 workers for each beneficiary.[4] Another challenge for Medicare is that the Hospital Insurance Trust Fund that finances Medicare payments for hospitalizations and the Medical Insurance Trust Fund that finances Medicare payments for outpatient services are expected to become insolvent by 2017.

Medicare has therefore become an important target for lowering health care costs through health care reform. In this chapter we'll look at Medicare and Medicaid as they exist today, how Medicare will change under the Patient Protection and Affordable Care Act, the laws that exist in the new health care law as it pertains to Medicare and Medicaid, and some recommendations about how the law needs to be modified.

About Medicare

Medicare is administered by the Centers for Medicare and Medicaid Services (CMS), a component of the Department of Health and Human Services (HHS). CMS can contract with private companies to act as intermediaries between the government and medical providers to process claims and payments, enroll physicians, and investigate fraud. Medicare is funded in part by payroll taxes. The underlying concept of its creation was that an individual could pay for insurance when young, well, and working, and the fees paid into Medicare would cover the individual when elderly and retired. The employee has tax withheld (1.45 percent) from each paycheck, and the employer pays a matching amount (1.45 percent) to the government on behalf of the employee. Individuals who are self-insured must pay the entire 2.9 percent tax themselves; however, half of the payment is deductible on their tax return. Some people will pay in more than they receive back, and others will get back more than they paid in. Many pundits incorrectly label Medicare as an entitlement program. An individual is only eligible to receive Medicare coverage if he or she has paid Medicare taxes for a minimum of ten years and has been a legal resident of the United States for at least five years. Individuals less than sixty-five years of age are eligible for Medicare if they are permanently disabled.

The Medicare population does not enjoy good health.[5] Sixteen percent of the Medicare population is under sixty-five and disabled, and 15 percent have multiple limitations, defined as two or more problems that limit their activities of daily living such as eating or bathing. Thirty percent of Medicare spending pays for care in the final year of a patient's life. Medicare patients also tend to be in the lower socioeconomic bracket—almost half have an income below 200 percent of the poverty level. The incidence of poverty increases with age and is more prevalent among women than men.

The Medicare program has four parts—A, B, C, and D. Part A pays hospital charges including doctors' fees, up to 100 days in a skilled nursing facility (the first twenty days are paid in full while the cost for the remaining eighty days is shared with the beneficiary), home health, and hospice care. Individuals who meet eligibility (forty months of employment) do not pay a premium. However, beneficiaries may pay a coinsurance for extended inpatient stays in a hospital ($275 per day for days 61–90 in 2010) or skilled nursing facility ($137.50 per day for days 21–100 in 2010). In 2009, Part A accounted for approximately 36 percent of Medicare spending. Medicare Part B pays for outpatient services including physician services, imaging studies, laboratory tests, vaccinations, medications for organ transplant recipients, medications that are administered by a physician during an office visit including chemotherapy, and preventive services including mammography and colonoscopy. Part B also pays for durable medical goods such as canes, walkers, wheelchairs, artificial limbs, and home oxygen. The health care reform legislation adds coverage without co-payments for an annual comprehensive wellness visit beginning in 2011. Part B is funded by general revenues and premiums. Beneficiaries with higher annual incomes (over $85,000 per individual, $170,000 per couple) pay a higher income-related premium ranging from $154.70 to $353.60. Because of the deductibles and coinsurance fees, one in five Medicare beneficiaries purchases supplemental coverage called a Medigap plan that is sold by private insurance companies.

Part C is health insurance that is provided by "Medicare Advantage" plans. These plans are managed by private health insurance companies who contract with CMS and who receive a fixed fee to cover the medical costs of each beneficiary. Medicare Advantage plans limit the providers that a beneficiary can see. Going outside of the "network" may require permission or an extra fee. Members may pay a monthly premium to receive additional benefits such as prescription drugs, dental care, or vision care. These additional premium payments increased 32 percent from 2009 to 2010. Individuals who are willing to stay "in network" receive extra benefits. Medicare payments to Medicare Advantage plans are approximately 14 percent higher than what the cost would have been if the beneficiary was enrolled in the traditional Medicare Part A or Part B.

Medicare Part D is open to individuals who enroll in a stand-alone Prescription Drug Plan or a Medicare Advantage plan with prescription drug coverage. The plans are administered by private insurance companies and do not cover all drugs. Part D is financed through general revenues, beneficiary premiums, and state payments for those eligible to receive drug coverage under state Medicaid programs prior to 2006. There is a "gap" or a "doughnut hole" in Medicare drug funding. Medicare subsidizes a beneficiary's drug costs when the individual is below the gap or above the gap but does not subsidize drugs costs that fall within the gap or doughnut hole. The health care reform legislation gradually fills in the doughnut hole with complete closure coming in 2020. Filling the doughnut hole would save the retired couple we met in the beginning of this chapter up to $3,610 in 2010.

Medicaid is a federal program designed to provide health care for low-income individuals.[6] Like Medicare, Medicaid was created in 1965 through Title XIX of the Social Security Act. Unlike Medicare, Medicaid is jointly funded by states. Each state provides up to half of the funding for Medicaid and actually administers its own Medicaid program. Eligibility rules for Medicaid coverage vary significantly from state to state. An important feature of Medicaid is that participation rates are relatively poor. A national average of 61.7 percent of eligible individuals are enrolled in Medicaid nationally with values ranging from just under 44 percent in Oklahoma to 88 percent in the District of Columbia.[7] In many states Medicaid is subcontracted to private health insurance companies. A child can be covered by Medicaid based on his or her individual status even if his/her parents are not covered. More than half of people in the United States who have AIDS receive Medicaid benefits and nearly half of all Medicaid beneficiaries are children.

In 2008, Medicaid provided services to approximately 49 million people at a cost to the federal government of $204 billion. This was a substantial increase over the 39.9 million enrollees in 2002. States are now spending approximately 17 percent of their funds on Medicaid. The laws of most states forbid them from incurring a deficit at the end of a year. The high costs of Medicaid, therefore, make it very difficult for states to create a balanced budget without markedly limiting Medicaid benefits or alternatively eliminating other important social programs or infrastructure expenditures. New regulations found in the Patient Protection and Affordable Care Act may make state finances increasingly more challenging as numbers of potential beneficiaries in a state increase at a time when many states are being forced to cut payments to hospitals, nursing homes, and doctors.

Medicaid should play an important role in health care reform. Medicaid's experience in providing insurance coverage for the poorest, sickest, and most disabled among us and its proven track record in providing ready access to care make it a logical and critical piece in strengthening the country's ability to provide care for a larger segment of the population. Diane Rowland, executive vice president of the Henry J. Kaiser Family Foundation, pointed out in testimony before the U.S. Senate Committee on Finance in May 2009 that "the comprehensive scope and limited cost-sharing of Medicaid is designed to address the complex health needs of the low income population, including the chronically ill and people with severe disabilities. When the health needs of its beneficiaries are taken into account, Medicaid is a low-cost program; both adult and child per capita spending are lower in Medicaid than under private insurance."[8] The Medicaid population also fares far better than the uninsured in every measure of access and quality of care and every state has an existing administrative structure that can be potentially expanded to cover an increased number of individuals.

How Does the Health Care Reform Legislation Change Medicare and Medicaid?

Medicare and Medicaid are the only parts of the massive health care industry that the federal government controls. Congress recognized that Medicare Advantage is simply not cost-effective and therefore included mandates in the new legislation that would lower its costs. It prohibits Medicare Advantage plans from imposing higher cost sharing for some Medicare-covered benefits than is required under the traditional fee-for-service program beginning in 2011. Medicare will further decrease payments to Medicare Advantage plans in 2011 by gradually moving the per-beneficiary payments closer to the per-beneficiary costs of Medicare fee-for-service. Rebates for Medicare Advantage plans will be reduced, and Medicare Advantage plans that can demonstrate that they provide a high quality of care will begin receiving bonus payments. In 2014 Medicare Advantage plans will be required to use at least 85 percent of their fees on the delivery of patient care; that is, their medical loss ratio can be no lower than 85 percent. Congress might have simply eliminated Medicare Advantage had it not been for the aggressive lobbying of the insurance industry.

The most important steps taken by the health care reform legislation are that it creates a group of pilot programs and demonstration projects that will test the ability of new health care delivery systems to lower costs while at the same time improving care for Medicare and Medicaid beneficiaries. These programs will be managed by the secretary of HHS and overseen in collaboration with a newly created Center for Medicare and Medicaid Innovation within the Center for Medicare and Medicaid Services (CMS).[9] They allow the CMS to experiment with new forms of provider-payment systems without disrupting hospitals and physicians. If a program proves successful, the secretary is authorized to expand the program to a larger Medicare population. Innovative pilot programs include the Independence at Home Program, the Medical Home, the Accountable Care Organization, and the Community Health Centers, and the use of the electronic health record.

Independence at Home Program

In 2012, the health care reform legislation provides funding for demonstration projects to assess the ability of an Independence at Home program The basic premise of this program is that people with two or more chronic diseases can have a higher quality of life and be treated at a lower cost in their homes than in nursing homes or in a hospital. The program will provide comprehensive and coordinated care across the entire spectrum of the individual's disease including hospitalizations, emergency room visits, and home care. The goal of the program is to reduce duplicative diagnostic and laboratory tests and the total cost of health care services while achieving higher patient and family satisfaction. A team consisting of a physician and a nurse practitioner will provide services for at least 200 chronically ill individuals over a one-year period. Spending targets will be prospectively determined on a per capita basis.

The strength of the program is that it can markedly improve patient satisfaction while at the same time keeping patients out of the hospital. The weakness of the Independence at Home program is that a practice must be large enough to have 200 patients with two or more chronic diseases and organized and wealthy enough to have a dedicated physician-extender. The participating practice must also have an integrated electronic health record and a willingness to take the risk that the payment might be significantly less than actual costs if the practice cares for a group of individuals who have a high acuity of illness or if social or environmental factors preclude the ability of the doctors and nurses in the practice to effectively provide care. An example would be a practice site located in an underserved urban area in which patients are unable to afford their medications. For example, I recently saw one of our patients with heart disease who came to our emergency room because of severe symptoms. She had not taken her medications in over a week because she was unable to pay for a refill of her prescription. The beneficiary of most of the cost savings will be the hospital and emergency room that usually provide a patient's care, but the costs of the program will be borne largely by the community-based practice.

Medical Homes

Medical Homes are designed to reduce hospitalizations and Medicare expenditures by coordinating the care of a Medicare beneficiary among the patient's primary care physician, nurses, and other support staff.[10] There is no single definition of *medical home*, but some fundamental components are shared by all definitions. An individual's personal physician provides timely contact when a problem arises followed by continuous and comprehensive care. The personal physician leads a team of nurses and advanced practice nurses who collectively take responsibility for the care of patients. The personal physician is responsible for coordinating care with specialists and other health care providers when appropriate across the entire spectrum of disease from prevention to end-of-life care. The health care team is also responsible for coordinating a patient's care with hospitals, home health agencies, nursing homes, family members, and community-based services such as social workers and occupational and physical therapists. The overarching goal is to ensure that patients get the appropriate level of care when and where they need it.

In 2007, the American Academy of Family Physicians, the American Academy of Pediatrics, the American College of Physicians, and the American Osteopathic Association published their Joint Principles of the Patient-Centered Medical Home.[11] They defined quality of care and patient safety as key elements of a patient home. The physician in the medical home is expected to use evidence-based medicine and decision-support tools to guide decision making, pursue continuous quality improvement, allow patients to actively participate in decision making, utilize information technology to optimize patient care, develop performance measures, undertake patient education, seek formal recognition as a medical home model, and facilitate the ability of patients and families to participate in quality improvement activities. Qualifying as a medical home is neither quick nor easy—individual practices must meet over fifty standards to qualify.[12]

Practices will receive fixed monthly payments (capitation) to cover the cost of coordinated care, and payments will reflect the projected costs for each patient based on a risk score. The risk score is calculated based on the patient's diagnosis and the comprehensiveness and sophistication of the practice's medical home program. These payments will cover new activities of the medical home such as e-mail access, telephone communications, and extended patient hours but must also compensate the physician for coordinating care with specialists, hospitals, and extended care facilities. Physicians should be able to share in savings that come about from incorporation of a medical home.[13]

Who wouldn't want to have care that is well coordinated, be able to see or at least communicate with a physician in a timely manner, receive educational materials about a disease, and receive care that is high quality and low cost? Unfortunately, there may be significant impediments to the creation of functioning medical homes. First, it is not designed for a small practice. A small practice doesn't have enough high-risk patients to make it cost-effective to hire a full-time care coordinator, nor does it have enough staff to have extended hours. A small practice may also have difficulties affording an electronic health record. Nearly half of the practices in the United States employ one to three doctors and less than 20 percent have 11 or more doctors in the practice. I believe that one important consequence of health care reform is that it will force doctors into larger group practices. It remains to be seen how this will affect medical care in the United States and in particular in rural areas.

A second problem with the medical home is that it is designed to care for the broader Medicare population—many of whom simply don't need a medical home.[14] The only patients who will benefit from a medical home are those with chronic disease and who are at high risk of needing a hospitalization in the subsequent year or two. A large percentage of the monthly payments to the medical home will be for patients who do not need the services while payments may be inadequate to support the care of the high-risk patients. Medical homes might also be more useful in urban and rural areas than in suburbia—but unfortunately it is the rural and urban practices that will have the most difficulty meeting the guidelines for a medical home because of financial barriers.

It is not surprising that the Congressional Budget Office did not expect cost savings from medical homes. Physicians have also questioned whether the medical home will provide adequate input from specialists at a time when specialists are playing an increasing role in patient care.[15, 16] Medical specialists have argued that patients with chronic medical conditions including congestive heart failure, diabetes, and asthma receive better care from specialists. Some specialists actually serve as the primary care physicians for their patients. There is a fear among specialists and their patients that the creation of medical homes will direct both patients and resources away from specialist care to support primary care. Health care economists speculate that costs of care will not change substantially with the development of medical homes because there is no incentive for specialists who remain in a fee-for-service reimbursement environment to collaborate with primary care physicians in lowering the costs of care.[17] Steven Schlossberg, chair of health policy for the American Urological Association, argued that "primary care will not always be the most cost efficient and effective provider for every condition and disease."[18] It is therefore imperative that analysis of the medical home demonstration projects assesses both quality of care and cost of care in comparison with traditional care delivered by a team of specialists and generalists.

Accountable Care Organizations

The Accountable Health Organization or Accountable Care Organization (AHO or ACO) is another approach to restructuring the Medicare health care delivery system to lower health care costs. An ACO is in its simplest form a group of doctors, nurses, hospitals, and other health care professionals who can presumably provide care at a lower cost and at a higher level of quality because they work together as part of a multidisciplinary team and therefore guard against redundancy and overutilization of tests and procedures. ACOs will not be piloted—groups of providers will be able to begin to function as an ACO in 2012 if they meet a panel of requirements that will be defined by HHS including the creation of a legal entity.[19, 20] By aligning incentives across the full continuum of care an ACO is complementary to the patient-centered medical home. In fact, some policy analysts believe that an ACO will not succeed without a strong alignment with high-quality primary care. Unlike the medical home, the ACO has the goal of integrating care across the entire spectrum of an individual's care including outpatient and inpatient care.

In some ways the ACO is the twenty-first century version of the integrated health maintenance organization (HMO). There are, however, significant differences. An HMO "locks in" or "enrolls" its beneficiaries—the members of an HMO can only receive care from hospitals and doctors that contract with the HMO. HMOs quickly lost favor among consumers because people didn't like to be locked-in to having to see a predefined doctor or to receive their care at a predefined hospital. ACOs by contrast do not enroll patients but instead enroll doctors. The cost of a patient's care is "attributed" to the ACO if the patient's primary care physician is part of the ACO, yet the patient can receive care from any doctor or any hospital. The primary premise of the ACO is that the cost of care will be decreased through careful integration across providers.

The ACO will initially have two methods by which savings can be shared between the government and providers. An ACO can elect to assume a smaller share of the potential financial gains that come from integration of care, but entail no risk of loss for two years and then transition in year 3 to accepting loss. Organizations that are willing to immediately take on risk can qualify for a higher proportion of shared savings from the start.[20] Savings occur if the cost of care attributable to an individual who receives their care through the ACO is below Medicare's predicted spending for that individual. If the costs of care are higher than the benchmark, the ACO does not receive any rewards and runs the risk of losing revenue depending on the structure of the ACO.

The ACO structure will work only if doctors and hospitals can clearly identify the costs of caring for each of their patients. This can be quite difficult. Take for instance an individual whose primary care physician is part of an ACO but who also sees a number of different specialists including a cardiologist and a gastroenterologist. If the cardiologist orders too many tests and procedures and the gastroenterologist prescribes a very expensive—but not particularly effective—medication, the total cost of care that would be attributable to the ACO would be high even if the primary care doctor provided both high-quality and low-cost care. I care for a large number of older patients who spend half their time in Florida. When they are in Florida they see a primary care doctor and a cardiologist who would not be part of my ACO. The care they receive in Florida, however, would be attributable to the ACO that I will be part of, yet I have no way of knowing whether the care they receive in Florida is appropriate or even cost-effective. It is unclear how Medicare will attribute the cost of such a patient's care or whether the sophisticated computer systems to track the cost and quality of care across many different providers and hospitals will be available in time.

"Hospitals are likely to dominate the ACO contracting process"[21] because of the enormous financial and operational complexities of an ACO, according to Jeff Goldsmith, president of Health Future. Most of the Medicare costs are hospital-based or hospital-related; only a hospital has the necessary capital to support legal and infrastructure costs, the ability to monitor quality and costs, the minimum number of fee-for-service beneficiaries, sophisticated technologies to link patients and their physicians, and the organizational structure and administrative wherewithal to successfully manage an ACO.[22] Hospitals would ideally allocate dollars across all of the physicians and other health care personnel who provided care for the patient. The individual could still receive fee-for-service payments. The dollars allocated by the hospital would serve as an incentive for doctors to provide care that was highly efficient rather than overutilizing procedures and imaging services. The guidelines for an ACO allow a hospital to develop a structure in which payments are partially or fully capitated rather than being paid as a fee-for-service, which may provide an intriguing opportunity to lower costs.

Hospitals, on the other hand, have an enormous impediment to effectively creating ACOs. With the exception of academic medical centers and highly integrated health delivery systems such as the Marshfield Clinic and the Mayo Clinic, most hospitals are staffed by a large number of independent physicians. Some of these independent physicians and physician groups provide high-quality and cost-effective care while others do not. It is unlikely that these hospitals will be able to cherry-pick the members of their staffs who provide cost-effective and high-quality care and would be ideal members of the ACO while excluding the members of their staff who overutilize tests and procedures, provide low quality of care, and would not be ideal members of an ACO. Even if legislative efforts at the state and federal level provide protection for hospitals, the financial consequences of excluding a group of physicians from the ACO might be problematic.

Hospitals that do not have a fully employed and integrated physician staff will also be unable to equitably allocate reimbursements across different groups of physicians who are participating in an ACO. Physicians in private practice can use the threat of moving their patients to another hospital to leverage favorable treatment from their hospital partner. The greater the margin associated with the service they provide, the greater their leverage. In fact, in an open staff model hospital it is unlikely that any form of capitation will be successful. Battle lines will immediately form to see who will take the biggest financial hit. It will undoubtedly be the physician group with the most leverage—and not the group that is doing the most work—that will receive the largest share of the capitation pie. Of course there is an alternative. The presence of ACOs may cause many private practice groups to become employed by a hospital or health system.

ACOs create a financial risk even for those health systems that are fully integrated. Scott Berkowitz and Edward Miller noted in a perspective in the *New England Journal of Medicine* that "if an AMC reduces charges by 10%, it may be eligible to receive 50% of the difference (i.e., 5%)—but that means its total Medicare payments would amount to 95% of its current reimbursement."[23] They point out that these potential losses could be mitigated by integrating care across the continuum of care, carefully allocating resources, effectively transitioning patients back to their community caregivers, and optimally utilizing bed capacity. Berkowitz and Miller, however, note that even within America's most highly ranked hospital, creating a working ACO is fraught with difficulty. The formation of an ACO requires the establishment of a costly health information technology platform so that providers can share information and data can be acted on quickly, the creation of collaborative teams across numerous independent departments, the need to create a rewards system that focuses on metrics that are not traditionally measured in an academic medical center, and a realignment of faculty goals at research-intensive medical schools.[24]

A recent analysis from a group at the VHA network of health care organizations found data that raise even more concerns about ACOs.[25] Using models derived from the Physician Group Practice demonstration of the Centers for Medicare and Medicaid Services, a structured health care delivery system that is very similar to an ACO, they predicted that ACOs will actually lose money in the first three years of their existence. They also posited that the high up-front investments needed to create an ACO, a return on investment time frame of greater than five years, and the inability of even large and experienced integrated physician group practices to rapidly recover their initial investment bode poorly for the widespread creation of ACOs. Indeed, the group noted that policy makers must recognize that substantial losses on the part of physician groups and hospitals that create the first group of ACOs could cause other groups to reject the ACO concept.[25]

ACOs also face complex legal challenges.[26] The original vision for an ACO was that a single hospital would ally administratively and economically with the medical staff within its service area and in so doing share in the economic gains that would come from reducing utilization. Hospitals and physician groups have seen larger opportunities from the development of ACOs, and it is these larger financial opportunities that have raised significant legal issues. The linkage of larger practice groups with each other and the alliance of hospitals that compete in the same geographic areas raise the potential for antitrust lawsuits—especially when some practices are left out of an ACO. However, if the antitrust laws are weakened, the ACO phenomenon may result in mergers, joint ventures, and alliances that result in the consolidation of the market into a single dominant provider. A dominant provider would have the leverage to obtain high reimbursements from private insurers independent of the quality of care they provide or the medical needs of the patients they care for, and any potential savings would be canceled out.[27]

Debate over the question of whether large regional networks are a new model for health care or "a blatant attempt to corner the market" are now ongoing.[27, 28] Thomas Greaney provides four steps that the Centers for Medicare and Medicaid Services and the Department of Health and Human Services must take to mitigate the possibility of anticompetitive behavior on the part of ACOs.[29] First, CMS should not certify ACOs that will impede competition in the private insurance market. This approach would preclude large hospitals from forming ACOs with competing hospitals in the same geographic locale. Second, CMS should ensure that ACOs provide public access to cost and quality information to improve competition among different ACOs. Third, CMS should preclude ACOs from limiting the ability of other ACOs to compete in the market. Finally, CMS and state regulators should have the power to prevent insurers from raising health insurance premiums because the cost of care has increased. I would add an additional requirement—CMS should allow ACOs to be regulated in such a way that they can have the freedom to change their design if the original structure turns out to be flawed.[30]

Extension Program Hub

Extension Program Hubs are an interesting and potentially important entity that will be evaluated using funding allocated by the health care reform bill.[31] A hub will include the state health department, the administrative unit responsible for the state Medicaid program, the state entity administering the Medicare program, and the departments of one or more health professional schools in the state that train primary care physicians. The hub may also include an association of hospitals, primary care research networks, professional medical societies, state primary care associations, state licensing boards, and other organizations that play a role in the delivery of health care. The goal of the extension agencies will be to assist primary care providers in implementing new care delivery systems such as the medical home or the ACO. Their design is based on the successful cooperative extension programs that have proved useful in providing practical information to agricultural producers, small business owners, and consumers in rural areas and farms across the country through linkages with offices located at land grant universities.

The extension program has a broad agenda that includes helping a practice to assess its quality of care, setting community priorities, strengthening the local primary care workforce, eliminating disparities in health care across different racial and ethnic groups, and developing tools with which to measure the impact of the program on the health of enrollees. The hubs must also develop a plan for financial self-sufficiency by garnering support from state, local, and private entities because funds will only be available for an initial period of six years.

Community Health Centers

The health care reform bill also provides funding for the expansion of existing health delivery systems. One important example is the appropriation of $125 billion for the expansion of Community Health Centers in the United States. Community health centers were launched in 1965 by the Office of Economic Opportunity as part of President Lyndon Johnson's War on Poverty.[32] Funding for the centers was doubled under the administration of President George W. Bush to increase the number of centers. The American Recovery and Reinvestment Act of 2009 provided additional funding—a one-time appropriation of $2 billion. Today, approximately 1,200 grantees operate more than 8,000 sites that serve 20 million people, 5 percent of the current U.S. population. Community health centers are supported by federal, state, county, and city grants as well as fees for services rendered to insured patients and a sliding "pay-as-you-can" scale for the uninsured. They provide primary medical care, dental care, behavioral services, and social services to a largely impoverished population who live in rural or urban areas. Like the medical home, the community health centers are committed to accessibility, affordability, high quality, and accountability and take a holistic view of medical care. They are particularly adept at reducing health disparities associated with poverty, race, and language through the availability of interpreters and transportation services.

Community health centers face unique challenges: high physician turnover; decreasing state and local aid; noncompetitive compensation packages for staff; difficulty in obtaining specialty referrals; and limited capital for infrastructure support including electronic health records. Fees paid to specialists rarely cover the cost of care. Perhaps the largest challenge is yet to come. It is estimated that community health centers will need to add 15,000 new primary care doctors to care for many of the 35 million Americans who will become insured over the next five years under the new health care reform legislation.[33] Many of the center physicians receive reimbursement of their medical student loans through participation in the National Health Services Corps. The health care reform legislation provides money to expand primary care training programs for residents, medical students, physician assistants, and dentists. It may not be possible to increase the number of primary care physicians necessary to serve the needs of community health centers without new appropriations for financing medical education and increasing the number of postgraduate training programs in the United States—a topic discussed in greater detail in Chapter 7.

Lowering Medicare and Medicaid Costs

The health care reform legislation takes a stick-and-carrot approach to lowering health care costs for Medicare and Medicaid beneficiaries. For example, the legislation will penalize hospitals if readmission rates for beneficiaries are higher than expected. This applied to patients with three diagnoses in 2010 and will expand to an additional number of diagnoses in fiscal year 2015. The health care reform bill also limits payments for tests of questionable value and for tests that provide lucrative payments for doctors who own their own testing equipment including bone densitometry and some advanced imaging services. The reform legislation provides grants to establish community health teams to support the patient-centered medical home, the creation of medication management services to provide multidisciplinary and interprofessional approaches to the treatment of chronic disease, the creation of regionalized comprehensive systems for rapid response to emergency, and trauma care including a transport communication system and emergency dispatch systems.

A major accomplishment of the Patient Protection and Affordable Care Act is that it takes the control of Medicaid eligibility away from the states and therefore ensures that eligibility criteria are consistent across the country. By 2014, every U.S. citizen and legal resident younger than sixty-five years of age will now be eligible for Medicaid if they have an income that is up to 133 percent of the federal poverty line—$14,404 for a single adult or $29,327 for a family of four in 2010. In addition, adults without dependent children—a group that most states have excluded from Medicaid coverage—will now be eligible to receive Medicaid. These new Medicaid regulations will cover almost half of the 32 million Americans expected to gain insurance as a result of the health care reform legislation. The federal government will also pay the states more to run the Children's Health Insurance Program (CHIP) although eligibility rules for CHIP will continue to be determined by the states.

In an article in the *Wall Street Journal*, Edward Miller, dean of the School of Medicine at Johns Hopkins, presented a cautionary tale about some of the unintended consequences of expanding Medicaid.[34] Hopkins hit above national benchmarks on all clinical quality measures for patients receiving dialysis, reduced costs for patients with complex medical needs, and achieved high patient satisfaction scores. Hopkins, however, lost substantial amounts of money—$57.2 million between 1997 and 2005—because the state of Maryland expanded Medicaid coverage did not cover all of the costs that the Medicaid program incurred. Losses were only stanched when the state was convinced to account for the severity of illness of the patient population in their reimbursement model and when Hopkins was able to invest heavily in primary care and sophisticated disease-management programs.

State Governments and Medicaid–Medicare Reform

Medicaid expansion comes at a time when most states are facing enormous fiscal shortfalls; therefore, some states are either unable or unwilling to support Medicaid. For example, in March 2011 the Commonwealth of Pennsylvania eliminated "Adultbasic," a barebones health insurance safety net that covered 40,764 residents who were not poor enough to receive Medicaid but who were not old enough to be eligible for Medicare. Pennsylvania governor Tom Corbett noted that expansion of Medicaid would add 750,000 Pennsylvanians to the state rolls and that "With the commonwealth facing a tremendous budget shortfall in the billions this year, we simply cannot afford the expansion of Medicaid."[35] A May 2010 report from the Kaiser Family Foundation estimated that expansion of Medicaid would cost Pennsylvania's taxpayers an extra $1 billion over six years beginning in 2014. Georgia governor Nathan Deal estimated that expansion of Medicaid in Georgia would add 650,000 new Georgians to the state's Medicaid rolls at a cost of roughly $2.5 billion over the next decade.[36]

Jan Brewer, governor of Arizona, proposed that 250,000 people be dropped from the state's Medicaid programs to deflate the increasing budget deficit in the state. Brewer discontinued Medicaid support for lung, heart, liver, and bone marrow transplants this past October—a move that was said to cause deaths in her state as patients whose life could have been saved by a transplant died. In New York, the legislature announced in March 2011 that it was considering the governor's proposal to cut $2.3 billion from the dollars Medicaid pays providers. In addition, New Jersey governor Chris Christie, faced with $1.3 billion in Medicaid debt, called for cuts of up to $500 million in Medicaid payments to providers.

It is the only way they can balance their budgets. It is not surprising that so many states have cut the number of Medicaid enrollees in the state, cut payments to doctors and hospitals, or decreased the services that they would pay for. What will states do in the years ahead if the economy does not rebound and continued debt impairs their ability to expand Medicaid roles?

It is not just state governments that are expressing their unwillingness to continue to fund Medicare and Medicaid. On April 5, 2011, House Republicans unveiled an even more troubling proposal to decrease the long-term costs of these two programs.[37] They proposed that Medicaid would be transformed into a block grant. States would receive a lump sum of federal money to care for low-income people and would be given more discretion over how the money was used. During a recession, the number of Medicaid-eligible individuals would rise, but the tax revenues of states would fall. This would leave the most vulnerable among us with less than optimal coverage at a time when health care was most needed. Block grants also eliminate the federal cost sharing that now ranges from 50 to 75 cents on the dollar.

House Republicans have also proposed that Medicare become privatized. Beneficiaries would receive a subsidy to spend on premiums for coverage from a private health plan rather than reimbursing doctors and hospitals directly for providing services for Medicare beneficiaries. Vouchers would presumably allow beneficiaries to shop for the most advantageous health insurance products; however, there is no evidence to suggest that this elderly and often infirm population would be able to effectively deal with insurance company red tape and the need to manage their own health care finances. Privatizing Medicare also obviates the greatest strength of Medicare—the ability to spread the risk over an enormous number of people through a single payer—and it is inconceivable that the private sector could provide Medicare coverage at a lower cost or with fewer administrative layers. There is little likelihood that the current Senate will agree to the changes proposed by House Republicans; it is nonetheless clear that the debate over the future of Medicare and Medicaid will become a pivotal issue in the 2012 elections.

Lowering Health Care Costs through Health Care Reform

A major focus of the Patient Protection and Affordable Care Act is the creation of new health care delivery systems including medical homes, accountable care organizations, and community health centers that will lower health care spending over the next decade. As I've described in this chapter, each of these delivery systems has flaws that may limit their ability to limit health care costs. I believe that federal regulatory bodies and the Department of Health and Human Services should focus greater efforts on reducing the need for hospitalizations among Medicare and Medicaid beneficiaries and reducing hospital readmission rates.

Patients with chronic disease and multiple hospitalizations make up 18 percent of all Medicare beneficiaries and account for 38 percent of all Medicare expenditures in the year after they meet eligibility criteria.[38] They will account for one-third of all Medicare expenditures over the next three years. Therefore, an intervention that decreases their rate of hospitalization could generate enormous savings for both Medicare and Medicaid.

Important lessons can be learned from new programs that have been created to keep patients with heart failure out of the hospital. Heart failure is the most common diagnosis at the time of discharge in the United States and accounts for over 1 million hospitalizations each year. This number is increasing exponentially because of the aging of the population and our ability to improve survival in patients with this disease. It is expected that by 2020 there will be over 15 million people in the United States who have heart failure—twice the number who had heart failure in the mid-1990s. Over 30 percent of heart failure patients are readmitted to the hospital within thirty days of discharge, yet "disease management" programs—especially those that utilize nurses or nurse practitioners—can effectively decrease the rate of hospitalization and limit 30-day readmission rates in patients with this chronic disease. The Patient Protection and Affordable Care Act unfortunately does not allocate funding for these types of programs, but the secretary of Health and Human Services should seek appropriate funding to correct this omission in the health care reform legislation.

There must also be a mechanism by which doctors can receive remuneration for developing disease management programs and for providing services for which there are presently no reimbursements. Doctors are too often penalized for not lowering readmission rates rather than being rewarded for developing new programs that are labor-intensive. It may not be cost-effective for a single practice to utilize a nurse or nurse practitioner to oversee a disease management program. We must develop mechanisms by which physicians can work through their local hospitals to improve patient care. This will require changes in both federal and state laws as physicians and hospitals will need to have some financial linkage. The Patient Protection and Affordable Care Act supports the creation of accountable care organizations that will potentially allow doctors, nurses, and hospitals to work together to lower health care costs—but their usefulness might be limited by the associated financial risk for hospitals and for doctors.

Demonstration projects and pilot programs that will evaluate the ability of new models of care delivery and new methods for physician and hospital reimbursement are important, but they must be looked at as research projects. We should not be surprised to find that some strategies that improve care might actually increase costs and that some delivery system reforms that lower costs may inhibit the delivery of high quality of care. Each demonstration project and pilot study will have to be carefully evaluated by individuals with a vast array of skills—from health economists to social scientists.

The Accountable Care Organization stands alone as the only program that is mandated to begin without thorough evaluation in demonstration projects. The fully integrated academic medical center should be the testing ground for these new programs. The fully integrated academic medical center has unique characteristics that provide a useful testing ground: a large group of employed physicians; an education and research mission that provides opportunities to pursue research in the science of care delivery; a focus on quality and not quantity of care; a long tradition of clinical excellence; and, in many cases, a linkage with a safety net hospital. The secretary of HHS would do well to test the theory of accountable care at these centers before attempting to establish a new care delivery system across the wide expanses of American medicine. The centers participating in these tests must, however, be protected from financial losses.

Political pundits consistently refer to Medicare as entitlement programs. This is disingenuous. Every employee pays into Medicare for their working lifetime. The fact that more funds are expended for the care of the elderly than are paid in by the young and healthy is a function of the aging of our population and the increasing costs of medical care. We should fix the problem by decreasing costs—not by eliminating the program. Medicaid, by contrast, is an entitlement—but every industrialized country in the world affords its citizens the right to receive health care. To do otherwise threatens the moral and social fabric of our country. We have an ethical obligation to expand Medicaid to provide health care for the many underserved individuals who are presently disenfranchised. Efforts to eliminate Medicare or Medicaid should be soundly defeated by a knowledgeable and compassionate electorate. We must, instead, focus on addressing some of the root causes of high Medicaid costs including a large population of uninsured, urban and rural poverty, unemployment, and disparities in access to care.

The only system reforms that will work at the end of the day will be those that improve quality of care while also lowering the cost of care. We will not be fulfilling our societal mission and in fact may be bringing harm to patients if we lower costs without carefully assessing the quality of care. New systems can be created that will improve the value of the care we provide—but finding them will take time and patience. We must also recognize that what works in a small rural community might not be effective in a large city and vice versa. It is unlikely that we will find a one-size-fits-all strategy of health care delivery. Our elected officials will be under great pressure to lower the costs of both Medicare and Medicaid regardless of the results of the demonstration projects and pilot programs. Those of us who vote will be responsible for ensuring that our public officials keep their priorities appropriately focused on improving quality of care first and lowering costs second and that they are not swayed by the lobbying efforts of the health insurance industry, manufacturers of drugs and devices, or even doctors and nurses. Many political analysts are focused on the 2012 election, but we must recognize that reforming our health care system will take decades and not just years.

Notes

1. *Medicare: A Primer 2010*: Henry Kaiser Family Foundation, 2010.
2. Brown R. Thank you, South Carolina. *New York Times.* December 20, 2009.
3. *U.S. Health Care Costs: Background Brief:* Kaiser Family Foundation. 2010.
4. http://www.go2healthplans.com/medicare.php.
5. *Medicare Now and in the Future*: Kaiser Family Foundation. October 2, 2008.
6. Rosenbaum S. Medicaid and national health care reform. *N Engl J Med.* November 19, 2009;361(21).
7. Sommers BD, Epstein AM. Medicaid expansion—the soft underbelly of health care reform? *N Engl J Med.* Nov 25, 2010;363(22):2085–2087.
8. Medicaid and Health Reform State of Diane Rowland, Sc.D. The Kaiser Commission on Medicaid and the Uninsured. Kaiser Family Foundation. May 5, 2009. http://www.kff.org/healthreform/upload/050509RowlandTestimony.pdf.
9. Mechanic R, Altman S. Medicare's opportunity to encourage innovation in health care delivery. *N Engl J Med.* Mar, 4 2010;362(9):772–774.
10. Rittenhouse DR, Shortell SM. The patient-centered medical home: will it stand the test of health reform? *JAMA.* May 20 2009;301(19):2038–2040.
11. Collaborative P-CPC. *Joint Principles of the Patient-Centered Medical Home.* February 2007.
12. O'Malley AS, Peikes D, Ginsburg PB. *Qualifying a Physician Practice as a Medical Home.* December 2008.
13. Hartzband P, Groopman J. Money and the changing culture of medicine. *N Engl J Med.* Jan 8, 2009;360(2):101–103.
14. Brown R. *Strategies for Reining in Medicare Spending through Delivery System Reforms: Assessing the Evidence and Opportunities*: Kaiser Family Foundation. September 2009.
15. Casalino LP, Rittenhouse DR, Gillies RR et al. Specialist physician practices as patient-centered medical homes. *N Engl J Med.* Apr 29;362(17):1555–1558.
16. Berenson RA. Is there room for specialists in the patient-centered medical home? *Chest.* Jan 2010;137(1):10–11.
17. Rittenhouse DR, Shortell SM, Fisher ES. Primary care and accountable care—Two essential elements of delivery-system reform. *N Engl J Med.* Dec 10, 2009;361(24):2301–2303.
18. Delivery reform: The roles of primary and specialty care in innovative new delivery models. *Senate Committee on Health, Education, Labor and Pensions (HELP)*: Testimony of Steven Schlossbert, MD; 2009.
19. Luft HS. Becoming accountable—Opportunities and obstacles for ACOs. *N Engl J Med.* Oct 7, 2010;363(15):1389–1391.
20. Berwick D. Launching Accountable Care Organizations—The proposed rule for the Medicare Shared Savings Program. *N Engl J Med.* March 31 2011;10.1056/NEJMp1103602(NEJM.org).
21. Goldsmith J. The Accountable Care Organization: Not Ready for Prime Time. *HealthAffairs blog.* August 17, 2009 (http://healthaffairs.org/blog/2009/08/17/the-accountable-care-organization-not-ready-for-prime-time).

22. Goldsmith J. Accountable Care Organizations: The case for flexible partnerships between health plans and providers. *Health Affairs.* 2011;30(1):32–40.
23. Berkowitz SA, Miller ED. Accountable care at academic medical centers—Lessons from Johns Hopkins. *N Engl J Med.* Feb 17, 2011;364(7):e12.
24. Kastor JA. Accountable care organizations at academic medical centers. *N Engl J Med.* Feb 17, 2011;364(7):e11.
25. Haywood TT, Kosel and Kosel, KC. The ACO model—A three-year financial loss? *N Engl J Med.* (10.1056/nejmp1100950, e27(1)).
26. Leibenluft RH, Luff and HS. *Health Reform and Market Competition: Opportunities and Challenges.* Arlington, VA. 2010.
27. MacGillis A. Are bigger health-care networks better or just creating a monopoly? *Washington Post.* August 16, 2010.
28. Conte A and Fabregas, L. Health system CEO fears monopoly, impact on care. *Pittsburgh Tribune-Review.* December 5, 2010.
29. Greaney TL. Accountable care organizations—The fork in the road. *N Engl J Med.* Jan 6, 2010;364(1):e1.
30. Lieberman SM, and Bertko, J. Building regulatory and operational flexibility into Accountable Care Organizations and "shared savings." *Health Affairs.* 2011;30(1):23–31.
31. Grumbach K, Mold JW. A health care cooperative extension service: transforming primary care and community health. *JAMA.* Jun 24, 2009;301(24):2589–2591.
32. What is a health center? US Department of Health and Human Services, HRSA, http://bphc.hrsa.gov/about.
33. Smith P. Health care reform reaches people in need through community health centers. *Pittsburgh Post Gazette.* April 7, 2010.
34. Miller E. Health Reform Could Harm Medicaid Patients. *wsj.com.* December 4, 2009 (http://online.wsj.com/article/SB10001424052748703994045574567).
35. Olson L. Corbett: Expanded Medicaid too costly for PA. *Pittsburgh Post-Gazette.* March 24, 2011.
36. Williams M. New health care law costing state, employees millions. *Atlanta Journal-Constitution.* March 23, 2011.
37. Pear R. GOP blueprint would remake health policy. *New York Times.* April 5, 2011.
38. Jacobson, G, Neuman, T, Damico, A, Medicare Spending and Use of Medical Services for Beneficiaries in Nursing Homes and Other Long-Term Care Facilities: A Potential for Achieving Medicare Savings and Improving the Quality of Care, The Henry J. Kaiser Family Foundation, Oct 2010. http://www.kff.org/medicare/upload/8109.pdf, http://www.cbo.gov/ftpdocs/63xx/doc6332/05-03-MediSpending.pdf.

Chapter 3

Can We Lower Health Care Costs by Eliminating Waste?

> Now, it's true that all of this will cost money—about $100 billion per year. But most of the cost comes from money that America's already spending in the health care system—it's just not all going to health care. Instead, too much money is going toward waste, or fraud, or unwarranted subsidies for insurance companies.
>
> **President Barack Obama, March 19, 2010**
>
> We are concerned that this dramatic expansion of government spending will create significant vulnerabilities. . . . Furthermore, we are concerned that the fraud and waste provisions in the new law fail to address these vulnerabilities.
>
> **Senator John McCain, April 15, 2010**

I saw a gentleman named Tom Sherman, an executive with a local company, for a second opinion several years ago. He had recently seen his general internist for his yearly physical examination. He played full-court basketball once a week but he complained that he had recently noticed that he was more short of breath when he ran the full length of the court and had some tightness in his chest. He had several risk factors for heart disease including a family history of heart disease and an elevated level of cholesterol in his blood. His internist, part of a large multispecialty group, was concerned about Tom's symptoms and suggested that he have a computed tomography (CT) scan of his coronary arteries, a sophisticated x-ray technology for imaging the arteries of the heart.

The CT scan showed an abnormality in two of the three arteries that supply the heart with blood; however, the CT scan could not determine whether the abnormalities were the cause of his symptoms since many people have abnormalities in their coronary arteries that are not significant enough to cause symptoms and require no treatment. His doctor then ordered another test called an exercise stress test. In a stress test a radioactive substance is injected into a person's vein while he or she is exercising. If the radioactive substance cannot be found in the heart after exercise, the abnormalities that were seen on the CT scan would be important. Tom's stress test was very abnormal. He had come to see me to figure out what to do next.

Tom had undergone two tests that suggested that he had an abnormality in his coronary arteries, but neither test could actually define where those abnormalities were and how serious they were. I recommended therefore that Tom undergo a cardiac catheterization and angiography—a procedure in which a catheter is placed into the opening of the coronary artery and dye is injected down the artery. The dye is imaged with an x-ray machine as it flows down the coronary artery. This is the only test that can definitively determine whether a coronary artery is significantly diseased. Tom had severe coronary artery disease—in fact, he had a significant narrowing in the major coronary artery. I recommended that Tom have bypass surgery because that is a treatment that is known to prolong survival in patients with a disease similar to Tom's. He had heart bypass surgery several days later and did quite well.

It would seem that Tom had an excellent outcome; however, as pointed out by Michael Lauer in an editorial in the *New England Journal of Medicine* about a very similar patient, the medical system had wronged Tom in two ways.[1] Consensus guidelines that define the appropriateness of various tests and procedures clearly document that a CT coronary angiogram is not appropriate for evaluating people who have symptoms and who have known risk factors. Tom, more importantly, was exposed to unnecessary radiation. The amount of radiation exposure he received resulted in a real risk of cancer—in particular, cancer of the lungs. Tom did well in terms of his coronary artery disease but clearly the system had failed him. He had undergone a procedure that wasted resources, increased our cost of health care, and provided no benefit for Tom. If we could decrease the types of wasteful procedures that Tom underwent, we could improve the quality of our health care and lower health care costs. As we will see, that is easier said than done!

President Obama and the congressional leadership have repeatedly noted that the spiraling increase in health care costs can only be halted by eliminating the large amount of waste in our health care system. This waste accounts for as much as $1 trillion of our health care costs. Wasteful expenditures include excessive administrative expenditures, unnecessary care, and fraud. Administrative costs account for 15 to 20 percent of total expenditures on health care—almost $500 billion annually—and are due to the fact that physician offices, hospitals, and patients must spend hours dealing with the complexities of multiple paper forms from the numerous sources of coverage and different insurance plans and the often obfuscating behavior of insurance company representatives who go to every length to delay or deny claims.[2] Unnecessary care is believed to be responsible for as much as 30 percent of health care spending—or up to $830 billion per year. Health care costs are also increased by fraud on the part of physicians or other providers who take advantage of the complexities of the system. A conservative estimate is that fraud will account for $75 billion this year. The rise in health care costs is also being driven by new technology and prescription drugs that invariably are more expensive than older technologies and older drugs but are not necessarily better than the older and less expensive treatments.

In this chapter we'll take a look at the causes of waste in our health care system, how the Patient Protection and Affordable Care Act will attempt to decrease waste, the impediments to eliminating waste that are inherent in our health care system, and some steps that still need to be taken to effectively control waste.

Medical Waste and Economic Waste

Victor Fuchs, a professor emeritus at Stanford and a Nobel laureate in economics, has defined health care waste.[3] He divides health care waste into two types: medical waste and economic waste. Medical waste is "any intervention that has no possible benefit for the patient or in which the potential risk to the patient is greater than potential benefit." The CT scan that was performed on Tom is the perfect example of medical waste. Tom did not benefit from having the CT scan—he should have simply had a stress test—and he was placed at risk because of the increase in radiation exposure.

Fuchs defines economic waste as "any intervention for which the value of expected benefit is less than expected costs." Economic waste is common for two reasons. First, physicians recommend treatments based on their having a value of expected benefits that is greater than their associated risks regardless of cost. And second, our health care system is predicated on a perverse fee-for-service structure that rewards physicians when they do more costly procedures or tests and penalizes them when they do fewer. In an article in the *New England Journal of Medicine*, Robert Levine, a physician from Norwalk Hospital in Connecticut, noted that "even if all physicians were highly ethical and ordered only tests and treatments they deemed truly important, it would take saints not to have their judgment skewed in favor of decisions that will provide them with financial rewards."[4]

Political pundits have pointed to physician avarice and greed as a primary cause of economic waste; however, in many cases doctors don't know what will work in a given patient and use probability to decide how a patient will be treated rather than codified guidelines. Medicine still involves as much art as science as doctors must often use their own personal experience and their judgment because studies that compare two different treatment options are not available to inform their decisions. For example, both endocrinologists and cardiologists intuitively believed that tight control of blood sugar levels would markedly decrease the risk of a person with diabetes developing the most common side effects of diabetes including cardiovascular disease, kidney disease, neurologic disease, and diseases of the eye. Patients with diabetes expend great expense in closely monitoring their blood sugar levels and modifying blood sugar levels with multiple drugs. The health care industry has developed expensive information technologies and equipment to link diabetic patients with their physicians or with highly skilled physician extenders including nurse practitioners and physician assistants. A recent large study, however, demonstrated that tight control of blood sugar levels did more harm than good.[5] Without studies that compare alternative strategies for treating different diseases, we are often left with only our personal experiences to inform our decisions.

Removing waste from a health care system sometimes causes ethical dilemmas. What is waste for society as a whole might be a lifesaving test or procedure for an individual patient. Health care economists have too often looked at the economic consequences of economic waste and not looked at it from the standpoint of whom to cover versus what to cover. Katherine Baicker and Amitabh Chandra from Harvard's School of Public Health and the John F. Kennedy School of Government pointed out that "in a world of scarce resources it will not be enough to eliminate waste: we will have to make active choices in our public insurance programs between increasing the number of people covered and increasing the generosity of that coverage."[6] If the coverage is more generous, fewer people can be covered if the health care budget remains unchanged.

Cost–Benefit Analysis

Businesses make their decisions about what to pay for and what not to pay for through cost-benefit analysis. This type of analysis is abhorred in the context of health care. An example of how cost-benefit analysis becomes difficult in real-world settings is the question of whether to screen young athletes prior to athletic competition. Each year nearly one hundred young athletes die suddenly during practices or athletic competition—many if not most of these being due to abnormalities in the electrical conduction system of the heart or to diseases of the heart muscle. Each of these deaths—occurring in an otherwise healthy athlete—is tragic. The standard evaluation of an athlete prior to participation in an organized sport in the United States has included only a history taken by a health care provider and a physical examination. Recent studies have shown that the addition of an electrocardiogram (ECG), a simple test that measures the electrical activity of the heart using sensors applied to the surface of the chest, can substantially enhance the ability of doctors to identify athletes who are at risk of sudden cardiac death.

For the past twenty-seven years, Italy has undertaken a mandatory national program that screens all competitive athletes with a medical history, physical examination, and twelve-lead ECG.[7,8] The Italian program is federally subsidized, is mandated for all athletes aged twelve to thirty-five, is anchored in Italian law, and has saved lives. Why wouldn't this system work in the United States? Barry Maron, a leading expert in athletes and sudden cardiac death from the University of Minnesota, posed five reasons why the Italian system would not work in the United States: (1) many would view a program limited to athletes to be exclusionary and discriminatory because many sudden deaths due to genetic heart disease occur in nonathletes; (2) sudden deaths are uncommon—occurring in only one in 220,000 participants; (3) false positive results would lead to additional expensive noninvasive testing and might promote inappropriate disqualification, unnecessary anxiety, and possibly chaos in a national program in the United States; (4) the initial annual cost of a national screening program would be about $2 billion; and (5) societal, cultural, and legal considerations may limit acceptance of mandatory screening as some athletes would want to participate despite the potential risk.[9] It is the yearly cost of $2 billion that will most likely ensure that this program is not instituted. But what is the cutoff where benefit and cost intersect favorably?

Health care economists have used a measure called the number of quality-adjusted life years (QALY) gained to distinguish different services based on their cost-effectiveness.[6] A cut point of $100,000 QALY gained is often used to separate services that are high cost from those that are low cost. For example, keeping a patient with end-stage kidney disease alive on a dialysis machine costs $60,000 per QALY gained. Other forms of treatment that cost less than $100,000 QALY gained include medical therapy for patients with HIV infections, liver transplantation for patients with end-stage liver disease, and the implantation of a cardioverter-defibrillator for patients at risk for sudden cardiac death—all treatments that will prolong life.[10] By contrast, coronary artery bypass grafting for patients with disease in a single vessel and moderate angina, exercise stress testing to look for coronary artery disease in a forty-year-old woman, or low-dose cholesterol-lowering therapy for a forty-year-old woman who doesn't smoke all have a cost per QALY gained of greater than $100,000 because none have been found to improve survival or decrease subsequent cardiovascular events. But eliminating high-cost procedures comes at an enormous price. The implantation of a left ventricular assist device—or artificial heart—in a patient with heart failure who is not a candidate for heart transplantation is associated with a cost per QALY gained of greater than $500,000; however, without the implantation of such a device the person would not survive. Former vice president Dick Cheney is a good example of someone whose life was spared by the implantation of a high-cost artificial heart.

Controlling Medical and Economic Waste

Economic and medical waste is difficult to control because they are so pervasive. The amount of potential waste is most clear when looking at the utilization of imaging procedures in the United States.[1] The United States has the world's highest per capita imaging rate. In fact, there were so many MRIs performed in one year that it equated to nearly one-third of the U.S. population having an MRI. Since 1992, the number of CT scans has quadrupled, and between 1993 and 2001, the number of radionuclide exercise stress tests increased by more than 6 percent per year.[11] These numbers cannot be attributable to excessive utilization in one town or in one region of the country, but span the entire spectrum of American medicine. We are a society that wants something done, and we want it done now. It is unacceptable for an American patient to have to wait a week and much less a month for an imaging study. We are not even able to wait days to see if the ache or pain gets better. Only a change in the national psyche will help stem the growing incidence of economic waste.

While medical waste is insidious due to our fee-for-service reimbursement payment strategies, some is reprehensible. I saw a patient not too long ago who had seen a cardiologist because she was experiencing heart palpitations—a rapid pounding in her chest. She came to see me for a second opinion. The cardiologist had recommended that she have an invasive procedure called an electrophysiology study to identify the cause of her symptoms. During the procedure the doctor would place catheters into her heart using a large vein and artery in her leg. The doctor would then measure the electrical activity of her heart. He told her that she would in all likelihood need a defibrillator—a type of pacemaker that shocks the heart when it detects a lethal irregularity in the heart rhythm. A defibrillator can cost upwards of $35,000. When I questioned the woman about her medical history and her symptoms and looked at her electrocardiogram, the cause of her palpitations was obvious. She didn't need an expensive and invasive study and certainly didn't need a defibrillator—she just needed to stop drinking six cups of caffeinated coffee each day. She stopped drinking caffeinated coffee, and her heart symptoms went away completely. I later found out that the cardiologist she had originally seen surgically implanted more defibrillators than anyone else in the country.

Medical Spending during the Last Days of Life

A substantial portion of health care costs is expended in the last months or days of a patient's life—some of which is wasteful spending.[12] One of my residents, a thoughtful and compassionate young woman, came to see me because she was concerned about the care that she was being asked to provide for one of her patients in the intensive care unit. The patient was sixty-four years old. She had been diagnosed with breast cancer five years ago and had undergone surgery, chemotherapy, and radiation to treat her disease. The tumor returned and had spread to her lungs and her brain. Her physician began another round of treatment with chemotherapy and radiation. She progressively lost the ability to breathe on her own, and she was brought to the intensive care unit. Her doctor was continuing to treat her with chemotherapy—not because it would increase her life, but because "that was what her family requested." My resident felt that she was needlessly prolonging this woman's life. The woman's family would not consider discontinuing therapy because they were convinced that the chemotherapy would "help them to get her home."

I suggested that the resident take the case to the hospital's ethics committee. The committee spoke with the patient's family and recommended that they obtain a palliative care consultation. The committee had no authority to do much else. The family refused to speak with the palliative care consultant, and the patient lived for two more months on a breathing machine with no letup in treatment. Would the family have continued therapy if they were paying the hospital bill?

This story is repeated daily at hospitals across the United States as patients and sometimes their doctors refuse to recognize when treatment is no longer warranted. Another glaring example of wasteful spending at the end of life was documented in a recent article in the *Annals of Internal Medicine*. A group from the Department of Geriatrics at Mount Sinai Hospital in New York studied patients who were admitted to hospice care because of end-stage disease that was associated with an expected life expectancy of less than six months.[13] They found that fewer than 10 percent of the hospices had a policy for how to care for patients who had an implantable cardioverter-defibrillator (ICD), the device that shocks the heart when it detects a lethal abnormality in the rhythm of the heart. Fewer than half of the patients had their defibrillators turned off once they entered the hospice facility, and over half reported a shock. The cost of care increased in this group of patients with terminal disease, but more importantly, their lives were extended and they experienced the painful shock of the defibrillator—an experience that patients describe as getting kicked in the chest by a horse.

Congress was not able to address the problem of end-of-life care because of the repercussions from Sarah Palin's claims about government-sponsored "death panels." The general public saw end-of-life care as one form of health care rationing—not as a compassionate form of medical care. An early version of the Patient Protection and Affordable Care Act provided funding for palliative care consultations for patients with end-stage disease. It provided payments to doctors who spent time with families advising them and counseling them regarding end-of-life issues and decisions, but unfortunately this part of the bill was deleted prior to the final draft. It seems incongruous that we spend so much money on care administered at the end of life, but we don't have the resources to provide expensive care to individuals who could actually benefit in terms of prolonged survival and decreased morbidity.

The state of New York passed a bill called the Palliative Care Information Act that requires a doctor to offer a patient information and counseling regarding palliative care and end-of-life options if a patient is diagnosed with a terminal illness.[14] Violations are punishable by fines and willful violations by a jail term of up to one year. The law has been criticized by both doctors and patient groups because its language is vague, it intrudes on the doctor-patient relationship, and end-of-life decisions are fraught with uncertainty for the doctor, the patient, and the patient's family. Few doctors have the necessary training in communication skills, emotional engagement, and cultural awareness to optimally approach these complex discussions with their patients. The New York legislators would have provided better service for their constituents if they had funded training programs in palliative care and provided opportunities for palliative care–trained professionals to bill for their consultations. Forcing doctors to address these complex issues through legislation may result in patient anger and cynicism. It will be interesting to measure the results of the New York legislation.

Patient Protection and Affordable Care Act and Waste

The Patient Protection and Affordable Care Act provides a large number of opportunities to utilize the fields of epidemiology, health services, sociology, psychology, human factors engineering, biostatistics, health economics, clinical research, and health informatics to improve the care and safety of the American public. Few of these initiatives will directly impact the types of waste that occur so frequently in American medicine. The only specific language in the bill that targets waste is that the secretary of HHS will decrease the amount of waste in drug delivery systems in extended care facilities by requiring prescription drug plans to utilize specific techniques for drug delivery that have been determined by the secretary in consultation with appropriate stakeholders to be effective. The bill also proposes to reduce waste, fraud, and abuse in public programs by allowing provider screening, enhanced oversight periods for new providers, and enrollment moratoria in areas identified as being at elevated risk of fraud and by requiring Medicare and Medicaid program providers and suppliers to establish compliance programs. The reform act funds the development of a database to capture and share data across federal and state programs regarding cases of fraud, to strengthen standards for community mental health centers, and to increase funding for antifraud activities. None of these steps will identify overutilization.

Placing the Burden of Cost Control on the Patient

Private insurers and the federal government have both tried to eliminate waste by focusing their efforts on the patient. They hypothesize that if a patient had a higher co-payment or a higher deductible, he or she would be less likely to seek medical attention for a problem that was a nuisance but was not severe or life threatening. Patients with a high co-payment and the new onset of back pain after strenuous exercise might rest their back, take anti-inflammatory agents, and limit their exertion for several days. Individuals with no co-payment and a low deductible might immediately try to see their physician and demand an MRI. Increasing co-payments and deductibles, while appealing, has not proven to improve health care or to limit costs because sick patients can't make informed decisions about what is wasteful and what requires treatment nor are they able to shop intelligently for the lowest priced medical care. Studies suggest that increasing co-payments worsens the overall health of the population and has no effect on lowering costs.[15–17]

A group from Brown University studied nearly one million people who were enrolled in Medicare plans that increased co-payments for outpatient care.[18] They compared enrollees in Medicare plans that had increased co-payments for their beneficiaries with a group of matched individuals who were enrolled in insurance plans in which co-payments had not changed. The group who had higher co-payments had significantly fewer visits to the doctor. They also had more hospitalizations and more days in the hospitals than the group in whom co-payments had not changed. This adverse outcome was particularly seen in people living in areas of lower income and education and among people who had hypertension, diabetes, or a history of a prior heart attack. Increasing co-payments or decreasing benefits can actually increase rather than decrease health care costs because people with higher co-payments only seek medical attention when they are very ill and require hospitalization and avoid seeing their doctor earlier in the course of their disease.

Placing Responsibility for Decreasing Waste on Hospitals

Another way that the health care reform bill will try to decrease waste will be to reduce Medicare payments to hospitals by specified percentages based on excess or preventable hospital readmissions and to reduce payment for certain hospital-acquired conditions by 1 percent. Reducing payments for hospital-acquired conditions is not new.[19] In 2006 a law was instituted that prohibited hospitals from billing Medicare patients at a higher rate when complications occurred that were reasonably preventable through the use of evidence-based guidelines. The initial group of complications covered by this law included foreign objects left in the body after surgery, damage to the lungs caused by the introduction of air into intravenous fluid lines, the administration of incompatible blood, falls and traumas, urinary tract infections in patients with urinary catheters, infections in the chest wall after coronary artery bypass grafting, bed sores, and infections of intravenous lines. In 2008, the Centers for Medicaid and Medicare Services encouraged state Medicaid programs to implement the same rulings and expanded the list to include poor control of blood sugar levels, clots in the veins of the legs or clots in the lung associated with knee or hip replacement, and certain infections in patients undergoing orthopedic surgical procedures or weight reduction surgery. Many experts complained that hospitals were being unfairly penalized because it was actually the doctors who were at fault. CMS announced in January 2009 that it would also cease all payments, including physician payments, in the case of three egregious surgical events: surgery on the wrong patient; performance of the wrong surgical procedure; and surgery on the wrong side of the body or on the wrong part of the body. These efforts are commendable, but it is unlikely that they will substantially influence medical or economic waste.

Unintended Consequences of Attempts to Eliminate Waste

What would appear to be a simple solution for decreasing health care waste can sometimes have unintended consequences. Sharon Inouye, a physician at Harvard Medical School, published an intriguing discussion about the unintended consequences of focusing on hospital falls—one of the eight selected hospital-acquired conditions that were targeted by the Center for Medicare and Medicaid Services (CMS).[20] Inouye points out how the CMS guidelines led to a resurgence in the use of physical restraints—the easiest means of decreasing falls since a restrained patient can't fall out of bed. Restraints, however, can cause immobility, functional loss, delirium, agitation, pressure sores, asphyxiation, and death. Manufacturers have developed newer means of preventing falls including chairs that are difficult to get out of, enclosed beds with a variety of alarms, and even sock alarms. All of these methods decrease mobility. Falls and trauma can be limited through a multidisciplinary program that involves the collaborative efforts of multiple caregivers, but these mechanisms unfortunately increase rather than decrease the costs of care.

Developing a Rational and National Strategy to Reduce Waste

One way to eliminate waste from our health care system is to restructure how physicians and hospitals are reimbursed. Some critics of health care reform have wondered why our legislators haven't simply eliminated the current fee-for-service payment system that seems to be a primary driver of increased costs. These critics invariably blame the lobbying efforts of the American Medical Association and other physician professional organizations for blocking Congress's ability to restructure the payment system. They miss the point. Everyone profits from the fee-for-service payment system: the companies that manufacture drugs and devices, the hospitals where patients receive their care, and the many parts of the large health care industry.[21] The only ones who don't profit are the many Americans who cannot afford the high price of health care—and unfortunately they are the only ones in the entire health care debate who don't employ expensive lobbyists.

So how do we eliminate waste from our health care system? I believe there are three targets. Physicians must first be compensated based on the value of the service they provide where value is defined as the health outcomes achieved per dollar spent—not on the volume of services they provide. Many of America's great health centers have proven that care is better and less costly when doctors are employed and are rewarded for the value of the care they provide—not by the number of procedures they perform or the number of tests they order.

One need only look at places like the Mayo Clinic, the Cleveland Clinic, the Marshfield Clinic, Intermountain Health, Johns Hopkins Hospital, and other superb multidisciplinary practices and hospitals in which physicians and nurses focus their efforts on the quality of care that is delivered. Michael Porter points out that "value should always be defined around the customer, and in a well-functioning health care system, the creation of value for patients should determine the rewards for all other actors in the system."[22] When achieving value becomes the core focus of a health care organization, the organization is able to support its costs as well as support the needs of patients; thus payers, providers, and suppliers all benefit. Revising the fee-for-service payment structure may not be applicable to all practices and especially for primary care practices in rural and underserved areas; therefore, health care reform will only be successful if there is a recognition that a one-size-fits-all approach will not work.

Porter also points out that "current cost-measurement approaches have also obscured value in health care and led to cost-containment efforts that are incremental, ineffective, and sometimes even counterproductive."[22] We are very good about measuring processes of care but have few metrics with which to measure quality of care. We also measure costs around individual departments of the hospital—pharmacy, physician services, nursing, physical therapy, housekeeping, transportation, and supplies—not around the patient. These costs are measured at a single time point in a patient's life—usually a hospitalization. We cannot fully understand the value of any treatment without measuring the total costs of care over the entire span of the disease (inpatient costs, outpatient costs, home health costs, rehabilitation costs, and pharmacy costs)—a need that is of particular importance for those with chronic disease. Rather than micromanaging physician practices and pursuing unnecessary and potentially dangerous cost containment strategies, we must learn to measure value and then reward providers for efficiently achieving good outcomes while at the same time penalizing those providers who deliver substandard and low-value care.

The second opportunity for eliminating waste will be to utilize practice guidelines developed by authoritative professional organizations such as the American Heart Association/American College of Cardiology and the American Cancer Society to guide patient care as well as physician reimbursement. People invariably fear a reimbursement system that doesn't reward doctors and hospitals for what they do. They worry that their doctors will be less responsive or do less than is necessary to avoid being penalized for having high costs in a system that is capitated. Utilizing practice guidelines to guide therapy and fees will be reassuring to patients because they will presume that what is being done for them has been blessed by higher authorities. Practice guidelines do not apply to everyone, and therefore there will be some patients who for one reason or another require an alternative form of treatment. Many practice guidelines are sullied by the obvious conflicts of interest of the writers or the sponsors; however, practice guidelines can prove beneficial when constructed in the appropriate fashion. The Institute of Medicine of the National Academy of Sciences has recently published standards for guidelines.

For those patients requiring an alternative form of therapy, there must be a workable system for arbitration. Under our current private health insurance system, physicians and patients often find that the insurance companies are unwilling to pay for care that is high in quality, appropriate for an individual patient, and necessary but it doesn't fit into a narrow pigeonhole defined by the insurance company. When physicians want to perform a study or a procedure that is not approved by the practice guidelines, they must be able to appeal to a "health care ombudsperson." The ombudsperson should be a physician with training in a specific area (for example, a cardiologist would always speak to a cardiologist about a particular patient). Ombudspersons should be selected like jurors in our legal system—a physician in any given geographic area will be selected at random to serve as an ombudsperson for no more than one or two weeks every other year. Ombudspersons would be graded on their performance, and those who do not receive passing grades would not be called upon in the future—a system not unlike the grading of referees in athletic competitions. Ombudspersons should be paid by the Department of HHS using a pool of dollars that is accrued from health care savings on a regional basis.

A system of reimbursement that is guided by practice guidelines would not have been feasible five years ago because it is heavily dependent on the ability of auditors to ascertain whether a particular patient's treatment is consistent with the mandates of practice guidelines. The Center for Medicare and Medicaid Services carries out audits of medical records today, but these are retrospective and time consuming and therefore have had little impact on utilization. The national priority for the development of electronic health records will make reviews of patient care far less challenging, but the introduction of electronic health records will be both difficult and costly.[23] Whether every case will be reviewed or just a portion of a physician's case file reviewed must still be determined. A demonstration project will be needed to better define the utility of this type of program. We must also become more efficient at moving consensus guidelines from academic centers to the physician who is practicing medicine in the community.

Let's return to Tom Sherman, whom we met in the beginning of this chapter. A review of his care would have shown that he presented to his primary care physician with symptoms consistent with a heart problem and that he had clear risk factors for having coronary artery disease. The CT scan he received would immediately jump out to the reviewer as a procedure that was not recommended by practice guidelines—and that was in fact not consistent with accepted practice. His private insurance carrier or Medicare would therefore not reimburse his doctors for the cost of the CT scan, and the ombudsperson would not support the doctor's appeal. I can assure you that once doctors recognized that they were going to incur costs and not receive reimbursement for procedures or tests that were not warranted, they would dramatically change their patterns of practice to ensure that they were complying with practice guidelines.

A final opportunity is to establish a commission modeled after the National Institute of Health and Clinical Excellence (NICE) that guides many of the policies of Britain's National Health Service.[24] NICE evaluates new technology and creates guidelines regarding the use of a wide range of drugs and devices. These guidelines are based on the evaluation of both the medical benefits and cost benefits of alternative treatment options.[25] Experts in the field populate a large number of committees that evaluate new drugs and devices, but there is also substantial input from individuals with a wide variety of expertise, including health policy analysts, health economists, sociologists, and patients. The evaluations are based on the results of clinical trials but also on information that comes from patients and clinicians. Each new technology is classified in one of four categories: recommended, optimized, only in research, and not recommended. The deliberations of the panel are public and transparent, and great care is taken to ensure that panel members have no conflicts of interest.

Decisions of the committees are distributed through a variety of mechanisms including podcasts, video casts, publications, and conferences. Communication teams work with the guideline committees to ensure that decisions are disseminated to the appropriate target audiences, provide tools to facilitate the incorporation of the guidelines into practice, demonstrate the costs or savings of new technologies at both the local and national levels, encourage input from physicians and patients, and evaluate the uptake of new guidelines. There is also a well-structured mechanism for appealing NICE decisions. The appeals committee consists of experts in the field, members of industry, patients, and the lay public. NICE provides an opportunity to decrease waste and lower health care costs by basing decisions regarding new therapies on the science of medicine and less on the art of medicine.

NICE is not without critics.[26] The most common complaint is that NICE uses arbitrary measures of cost-effectiveness rather than what is best for patients to evaluate new technology. Critics also contend that the decisions of NICE are political—considering value over outcomes. Indeed, some recommendations of NICE have been found to be ill conceived when studies are performed in large patient populations.[27] Other critics have raised concerns that NICE decisions unintentionally discriminate against the elderly and the mentally ill by only approving new and innovative technologies designed to treat younger patients and that NICE would be more effective if it looked at all treatment strategies for a particular medical problem rather than focusing on just new technologies. But no system of health care redesign is going to be accomplished without criticism, and it would seem that some form of guideline recommendations and oversight would be the most effective means of limiting waste in our health care system. NICE might not be the end point for the U.S. health care system, but we could learn a lot by closely evaluating its strengths and weaknesses, and we must remember that the UK, unlike the United States, has universal health care coverage.

The Patient Protection and Affordable Care Act did not adequately address the problem of health care waste; however, there will be numerous opportunities for the new institutes and programs established by the secretary of HHS to write rules and regulations that can control health care waste in the future. Those who craft the new regulations must do so in a transparent fashion, taking advantage of input from physicians, providers, patients, and the lay public. They must also learn from the institutions that have managed to provide value for patients across the entire spectrum of their disease. The task will not be easy, and progress will be slow, but in the end we will be able to develop a health care system that is more sustainable because it limits wasteful spending.

Notes

1. Lauer MS. Elements of danger—the case of medical imaging. *N Engl J Med.* Aug 27, 2009;361(9):841–843.
2. Davis K, Schoen C, Gutterman S, Shih T, Schoenbaum C, Weinbaum I. *Slowing the growth of U.S. health care expenditures.* The Commonwealth Fund. January 2007.
3. Fuchs VR. Eliminating "waste" in health care. *JAMA.* Dec 9, 2009;302(22): 2481–2482.
4. Levine RA. Fiscal responsibility and health care reform. *N Engl J Med.* Sep 10, 2009;361(11):e16.
5. Gerstein HC, Miller ME, Byington RP et al. Effects of intensive glucose lowering in type 2 diabetes. *N Engl J Med.* Jun 12, 2008;358(24):2545–2559.
6. Baicker K, Chandra A. Uncomfortable arithmetic—Whom to cover versus what to cover. *N Engl J Med.* Jan 14, 2010;362(2):95–97.
7. Corrado D, Pelliccia A, Bjornstad HH et al. Cardiovascular pre-participation screening of young competitive athletes for prevention of sudden death: proposal for a common European protocol. Consensus Statement of the Study Group of Sport Cardiology of the Working Group of Cardiac Rehabilitation and Exercise Physiology and the Working Group of Myocardial and Pericardial Diseases of the European Society of Cardiology. *Eur Heart J.* Mar 2005;26(5):516–524.
8. Baggish AL, Hutter AM, Jr., Wang F et al. Cardiovascular screening in college athletes with and without electrocardiography: A cross-sectional study. *Ann Intern Med.* Mar 2, 2010;152(5):269–275.
9. Maron BJ. National electrocardiography screening for competitive athletes: Feasible in the United States? *Ann Intern Med.* Mar 2, 2010;152(5):324–326.

10. Feldman AM, de Lissovoy G, Bristow MR et al. Cost effectiveness of cardiac resynchronization therapy in the Comparison of Medical Therapy, Pacing, and Defibrillation in Heart Failure (COMPANION) trial. *J Am Coll Cardiol.* Dec 20, 2005;46(12):2311–2321.
11. Lucas FL, DeLorenzo MA, Siewers AE et al. Temporal trends in the utilization of diagnostic testing and treatments for cardiovascular disease in the United States, 1993–2001. *Circulation.* Jan 24, 2006;113(3):374–379.
12. Drazen JM, Desai NR, Green P. Fighting on. *N Engl J Med.* Jan 29, 2009;360(5):444–445.
13. Goldstein N, Carlson M, Livote E et al. Brief communication: Management of implantable cardioverter-defibrillators in hospice: A nationwide survey. *Ann Intern Med.* Mar 2, 2010;152(5):296–299.
14. Astrow AB, Popp B. The Palliative Care Information Act in real life. *N Engl J Med.* May 19;364(20):1885–1887. September 1, 2011.
15. Newhouse JP, Manning WG, Morris CN et al. Some interim results from a controlled trial of cost sharing in health insurance. *N Engl J Med.* Dec 17, 1981;305(25):1501–1507.
16. Rice T, Matsuoka KY. The impact of cost-sharing on appropriate utilization and health status: a review of the literature on seniors. *Med Care Res Rev.* Dec 2004;61(4):415–452.
17. Chandra A, Gruber J, McKnight R. Patient cost-sharing and hospitalization offsets in the elderly. *Am Econ Rev.* Mar 1, 2010;100(1):193–213.
18. Trivedi AN, Moloo H, Mor V. Increased ambulatory care copayments and hospitalizations among the elderly. *N Engl J Med.* Jan 28, 2010;362(4):320–328.
19. Milstein A. Ending extra payment for "never events"—Stronger incentives for patients' safety. *N Engl J Med.* Jun 4, 2009;360(23):2388–2390.
20. Inouye SK, Brown CJ, Tinetti ME. Medicare nonpayment, hospital falls, and unintended consequences. *N Engl J Med.* Jun 4, 2009;360(23):2390–2393.
21. Hussey PS, Eibner C, Ridgely MS et al. Controlling U.S. health care spending—separating promising from unpromising approaches. *N Engl J Med.* Nov 26, 2009;361(22):2109–2111.
22. Porter ME. What is value in health care? *N Engl J Med.* December 23, 2010. 23;363(26):2477–2481.
23. Jha AK, DesRoches CM, Campbell EG et al. Use of electronic health records in U.S. hospitals. *N Engl J Med.* Apr 16, 2009;360(16):1628–1638.
24. National Institute for Health and Clinical Excellence Website. http://www.nice.org.uk/.
25. Kelly M, Morgan A, Ellis S et al. Evidence based public health: A review of the experience of the National Institute of Health and Clinical Excellence (NICE) of developing public health guidance in England. *Soc Sci Med.* September 2010;71(6):1056–1062.
26. Steinbrook R. Saying no isn't NICE—The travails of Britain's National Institute of Health and Clinical Excellence. *N Engl J Med.* Nov 6, 2008;359(19):1977–1981.
27. Agur W, Housami F, Drake M et al. Could the National Institute of Health and Clinical Excellence guidelines on urodynamics in urinary incontinence put some women at risk of a bad outcome from stress incontinence surgery? *BJU Int.* Mar 2009;103(5):635–639.

Chapter 4

Role of Disease Prevention in Health Care Reform

[Preventive] Services like these will go a long way in preventing chronic illnesses that consume over 75 percent of the health care spending in this country.

Michelle Obama, Washington Hospital, Washington, DC, July 14, 2010

Prevention gives you a better quality of life . . . but I have never seen any analysis that shows that in the long-run a society that uses a lot of prevention will have lower health care costs.

Uwe Reinhardt, Economist, Princeton University

Dr. Bonita Falkner is one of the leading experts in the world on hypertension and obesity in children and adolescents, and she has participated in crafting the consensus guidelines that help doctors understand, evaluate, and treat these two important problems.

Bonnie was born and reared on a farm in Glenwood, Minnesota. After graduating from medical school she came to Philadelphia in the mid-1970s to pursue her training in pediatrics. She wanted to specialize in pediatric nephrology—diseases of the kidney. The only training position available in Philadelphia for pediatric nephrology was filled; therefore, she obtained a position as a nephrology fellow in an adult training program at Hahnemann Medical College. During her fellowship she became interested in blood pressure in children.

Bonnie[1] describes what happened next:

> I started taking blood pressures in kids—it wasn't a standard procedure at the time. We didn't know what was normal and what was abnormal. Dr. Gotto Aresti, one of my mentors, connected me with an international group that was interested in blood pressure in children. We found that the blood pressure numbers that were used in adults simply didn't work for children—children would often show signs of damage in the kidneys and other organs affected by high blood pressure even at levels of blood pressure that were considered normal for adults.

These early observations led in 1977 to Bonnie's participation in a task force that created the first recommendations for how to measure and treat abnormalities in blood pressure in children and adolescents—a task force that she chaired in 2004. The publication of the pediatric blood pressure guidelines in 1977 did not have a dramatic effect on the treatment of children because many pediatricians were not comfortable with either measuring blood pressure or using drugs to treat abnormally high values in children.

In the late 1970s Bonnie began to visit schools, particularly those in underserved areas of Philadelphia, and city health clinics to measure blood pressure in children. She would often take medical students. They would talk to the children, measure their height and their weight, and take their blood pressure. A surprisingly high number of the children had high levels of blood pressure and many were obese. The visits were arranged with teachers and school nurses. "Today we probably couldn't do these studies," remarked Bonnie. "We would need all sorts of approvals from parents and school boards."

Bonnie and her team worked with the school nurses and teachers to educate the children about the needs to modify their diets. But as Bonnie points out: "Treating children with therapeutic lifestyle changes is extremely difficult. It doesn't work. We don't have an effective means to change their diets, and because the children in these underserved areas are economically disadvantaged, they can't simply buy fruits and vegetables and all of the foods that you want them to eat." Using medications to treat the high blood pressure was an option—but "many parents can't afford medications and until very recently there were no studies that pinpointed the best medicines to use in children," said Bonnie. She found it most intriguing that "kids with high blood pressure often had family members who as adults had significant elevations of their blood pressure." The problems were enormous and important but the solutions were not obvious or easy.

A major focus of the Patient Protection and Affordable Care Act is to facilitate the prevention of disease and to improve the wellness of the American population. Prevention can be defined as an intervention that lowers the risk of an individual becoming seriously ill by effectively treating risk factors such as high blood pressure or high cholesterol, screening to detect conditions before symptoms appear such as performing routine Pap smears, or preventing the development of disease through vaccination. Wellness is defined as any effort to modify an individual's lifestyle including changes in diet, physical activity, and smoking cessation. Senator Thomas Harkin (D-IA) noted that "in America today we don't have a health care system, we have a sick care system. We wait until people become obese, develop chronic disease, or become disabled—and then we spend untold hundreds of billions annually to try and make them better."[2] The data support his beliefs. Preventable causes of death such as physical inactivity, obesity, cigarette smoking, and the abuse of alcohol account for 90,000 deaths annually and nearly 40 percent of deaths each year in the United States. Heart disease, diabetes, and other chronic diseases account for 70 percent of all deaths in the United States and more than 75 percent of the cost of medical care, leading policy analysts to suggest that early recognition and treatment could lower health care costs.

The inclusion of efforts to promote disease prevention and to improve the wellness of the American public in the health care reform legislation is inherently good. We all aspire to having longer and healthier lives. The health care reform legislation's focus on prevention and wellness has raised controversy not because it is the wrong thing to do but because House and Senate leaders who crafted the legislation viewed it as a means of decreasing overall health care costs. Many health care economists disagree. Douglas W. Elmendorf, director of the Congressional Budget office, wrote: "Although different types of preventive care have different effects on spending, the evidence suggests that for most preventive services, expanded utilization leads to higher, not lower, medical spending overall."[3] The bill has also been criticized because it assumes that prevention and wellness can be legislated—an assumption that is likely not valid. In this chapter we'll look at the prevention and wellness programs that will be created and funded through the Patient Protection and Affordable Care Act, the economics of prevention and wellness, the enormous challenges that will be faced by our society in promoting prevention and wellness, and some ways in which health policy regulators can focus their efforts to effect the largest possible change in the nation's health.

Prevention and Wellness Programs in the Patient Protection and Affordable Care Act

Beginning in 2010 private health plans and Medicare were required to cover the entire costs (without co-payments or cost sharing) of a group of defined preventive services. Health insurance sponsored by large employers was not affected by the new requirements if it was in place prior to 2010 as they were grandfathered under the health-overhaul law. Lawmakers created this exception so President Obama could deliver on his promise that the law would not force wholesale changes in existing insurance plans. Premiums were expected to go up 1.5 percent on average for those plans that instituted prevention strategies and wellness programs as spending for the services would be spread broadly across the entire pool of insured people. Medicare will pay for its beneficiaries to have a single wellness visit each year with their primary care physician at which time their health risks will be evaluated and a personalized prevention plan will be established. Medicaid will institute a program for tobacco cessation by pregnant women, and some states will expand other prevention programs for Medicaid beneficiaries.

Disease prevention and population health will be overseen by a plethora of existing as well as new councils and task forces including a National Prevention, Health Promotion, and Public Health Council; an Advisory Group on Prevention, Health Promotion, and Integrative and Public Health; the Preventive Services Taskforce; the Advisory Committee on Immunization Practices; the Health Resources and Services Administration; and the Committee on Women's Health of the Department of Health and Human Services. The secretary of Health and Human Services (HHS) will create a national public-private partnership that will promote healthy lifestyles and raise public awareness of wellness. The Centers for Disease Control must implement a media campaign on health promotion and disease prevention as well as develop a website that individuals can use to create a personalized prevention plan.

The health care reform bill also provides grants to state and local governmental agencies to provide community-based preventive health services to reduce chronic disease rates and to develop a more robust prevention program. The bill provides resources for the development of programs to improve dental health and funding to establish an Epidemiology and Laboratory Capacity Grant Program to improve surveillance for infectious disease outbreaks in the community. The bill authorizes the secretary of HHS to contract with industry to purchase vaccines for adults, allows states to purchase vaccines at lower prices, and provides grants to states to immunize children and adults without charge. The bill appropriates funds to measure health disparities in the community, to evaluate employer-based health programs, and to support an Institute of Medicine-sponsored Conference on Pain. It establishes pilot programs to test the impact of providing high-risk populations in underserved areas with wellness plans and efforts to create community-based prevention and wellness programs that promote healthy lifestyles. The bill appropriates funds, albeit small, to develop projects aimed at decreasing the incidence of childhood obesity.

Section 2705 of the Patient Protection and Affordable Care Act—Legislating Wellness!

The Patient Protection and Affordable Care Act takes a lot of positive steps to improve the nation's health, but it also has flaws. One of its most serious flaws is section 2705. This section begins with a group of benign policies. It allows employers to pay for many preventive measures for their employees including membership in a fitness center, prenatal care and well baby visits, smoking cessation programs, and attendance at health education seminars. It allows employers to reward employees for taking part in these prevention or wellness programs. Individuals, however, will not be rewarded for simply taking part in a prevention program. The bill states that employers may provide a "premium discount, rebate or reward" based on "an individual satisfying a standard that is related to a health status factor." In other words, an employee who loses ten pounds, stops smoking, or can walk three miles will be rewarded but an employee who is unable to meet the "standard" will not.

The rewards for meeting the prevention standards are not small. The reward "shall not exceed thirty percent of the cost of employee-only coverage under the plan" and the reward can increase up to 50 percent of the cost of coverage if the secretary of the Department of Health and Human Services determines that it is "appropriate." A reward for one employee must result in an increase in costs for another since health care financing is a zero-sum game. The bill in fact condones an increase in costs for some employees by stating that a "reward" may be in the form of "the absence of a surcharge." The bill therefore allows a shift in the costs from employers to employees who do not satisfy the standards and from individual employees who satisfy the standards to those who do not.

In December 2009, 112 national organizations including the AFL-CIO, the AARP, the NAACP, and virtually every organization devoted to the cure and care of human disease including the American Heart Association and the American Cancer Society sent a letter to the members of Congress opposing the language in section 2705 of the Senate bill. The letter made cogent arguments against the bill, but these admonitions of the major societies had no effect on the final language of the bill, and as a result there remains the real possibility that individuals could see a marked increase in their health care costs because their waists are too thick or because they simply don't have time to join a gym or health club. Individual employees can receive a waiver if they have a medical condition that precludes them from participating in the wellness program—but the employer may "seek verification, such as a statement from an individual's physician, that a health status factor makes it unreasonably difficult or medically inadvisable for the individual to satisfy or attempt to satisfy the otherwise applicable standard." In this sense the health care reform law also breaches the basic ethics of confidentiality. Stephen Finan, senior director of policy for the American Cancer Society Cancer Action Network, made an interesting observation: "Employees might be required to disclose personal information they'd rather not share. We have a president who is struggling to quit smoking and apparently has relapses. If you smoke once a year, does that make you a smoker? If you don't tell your employer, could you be terminated from your insurance?"[4]

U.S. Preventive Services Task Force: Another Potential Flaw in the Patient Protection and Affordable Care Act

The U.S. Preventive Services Task Force is a panel of primary care physicians and public health experts who have used scientific evidence to identify and grade preventive services. The group has worked in relative obscurity for years, but now it will be in the forefront of health care reform. Its recommendations will have enormous financial implications because health insurers will be required to pay the full cost of services that the task force rates as either an A or a B. A rating of A is given to preventive measures that have a high certainty of substantial net benefit, and a B rating is given to measures that have a moderate certainty of substantial benefit. A wide range of preventive measures have received a grade of A or B and include abdominal aortic aneurysm screening for older men, breast cancer screening with mammography for women, colorectal cancer screening, cervical cancer screening for women, high blood pressure screening, and screening for lipid disorders in men and women who have risk factors for coronary artery disease.

Christopher Weaver pointed out that "the task force could become a political lightning rod. If it doesn't recommend a service, insurers might not pay for it, and advocates might argue the decision is a barrier to care. If the panel does back a service, it might increase patients' access, as well as create new business opportunities."[5] The committee has already come under fire. In November 2009 the task force recommended that women begin getting routine mammograms at fifty, rather than at forty. This decision—although it was probably correct—set off a firestorm.[6,7] Critics of the health care reform legislation viewed this decision as a first step in health care rationing while breast cancer advocates saw it as a decision that would harm women. General Electric, a major manufacturer of mammography equipment, joined the breast cancer societies in lobbying Congress. The firestorm was doused when Sen. Barbara A. Mikulski (D-MD) added an amendment to the Patient Protection and Affordable Care Act that explicitly mandated coverage for regular mammograms for women between forty and fifty. But mammography has not been the only issue.

Many health-related organizations have also raised concerns regarding the expanded role of the task force. The American Diabetes Association argued that the task force decisions regarding screening for diabetes were shortsighted, and the HIV Medicine Association claimed that the task force's failure to justify routine screening for HIV contributed to the fact that 20 percent of people with HIV don't know they are infected. The panel only revisits its recommendations every five years, raising the concern that many of its policies could be outdated.

I have a personal stake in the debate about the Preventive Services Task Force. I was surprised and disappointed by the fact that the task force does not recommend routine measurement of PSA, a biological marker for prostate cancer. This is a complex area, and there is great debate as to the usefulness of PSA in screening. The debate centers on the concern that randomized controlled trials have not demonstrated a mortality benefit of early detection of prostate cancer and that overdiagnosis could result in overtreatment. The committee failed to recognize the fact that most of the clinical trials measuring the effectiveness of a PSA in improving survival of men were highly flawed because a large number of men who were assigned to not have a PSA measured actually had a PSA measured because either they or their doctor felt it was important.[8] Indeed, the study of 162,243 men, European Randomized Study of Screening for Prostate Cancer, recently found that PSA testing reduced the rate of death from prostate cancer by 20 percent.[9,10]

Important lessons come from the debates over both mammography and screening for prostate cancer. Powerful lobbies can effectively change the mandates of the committee. The breast cancer lobby was able to override the committee's decision, whereas experts in prostate cancer—a far more silent disease—were unable to sway the decisions of the committee. A committee that only revises its policies every five years will make recommendations that will often be out-of-date before the recommendations are reevaluated. And finally, decisions on whether to screen an individual for a particular disease should be left to an individual and doctor after carefully discussing the risks and the benefits—not to a panel of so-called experts—unless there is substantive data supporting the usefulness or lack of usefulness of a particular test.

Prevention Doesn't Lower Health Care Costs— It Might Actually Increase Them!

Another major problem with the health care reform legislation is that the leadership in the House and Senate that crafted the legislation believed that if you can prevent people from getting sick, effectively predict those who will become sick, or identify disease early, you can lower overall health care costs. Mike Huckabee, the former Republican governor of Arkansas, said during the 2008 presidential race that a "focus on prevention would save countless lives, pain and suffering by the victims of chronic conditions and billions of dollars"[11] It's not that simple! The bipartisan Congressional Budget Office has failed to attribute any savings to increased efforts to prevent disease. Joe Antos, a former Congressional Budget Office analyst, noted that "preventive services often cost more than they save, you screen literally millions of people, sometimes at fairly high cost per screen. You'll pick up some true positives, people who really have the disease. You'll pick up some false positives."[12] A similar finding comes from Louise Russell, a research professor in the Institute for Health and a professor in the Department of Economics at Rutgers University in New Brunswick. She points out that "over the past four decades, hundreds of studies have shown that prevention usually adds to medical spending"—it doesn't decrease medical costs.[13]

Joshua Cohen and a group from the Center for the Evaluation of Value and Risk in Health, Institute for Clinical Research and Health Policy Studies at the Tufts New England Medical Center and from the Harvard School of Public Health reviewed nearly 600 studies that had appeared in the medical literature between 2000 and 2005 that evaluated prevention programs.[11] They divided the programs into those that assessed "prevention" options and those that measured the cost-effectiveness of "treatments." Some preventive measures saved money, but the "vast majority" did not. In fact, less than 20 percent of the preventive measures and a similar percentage of treatments decreased health care costs while nearly 80 percent of preventions and treatments increased costs. Reducing elevated blood pressures with medication, for example, reduces the incidence of heart disease and stroke and presumably decreases their attendant treatment costs. But as Louise Russell points out, "The accumulated costs of treating hypertension are nonetheless greater than the savings because many people, not all of whom would ever suffer heart disease or stroke, must take medications for many years."[13]

I am not suggesting that we shouldn't do everything in our power to prevent disease and keep people well. I agree with Sara Goodell and her colleagues who authored a report for the Robert Woods Johnson Foundation. They noted that preventive care measures that do not save money may still confer important health benefits and are worthwhile. "Like all other things we do to improve health, those things that are relatively low-cost are probably a good idea, and those that are expensive relative to what we gain should be looked at more closely."[14] I think that health policy experts must recognize that instituting the appropriate levels of prevention is difficult and costs money—it doesn't necessarily save money.

Addressing the Epidemic of Obesity— and Health Care Reform

The greatest problem for our nation's health today is the epidemic of obesity. The battle against obesity points out many of the difficulties we face in achieving disease prevention. Thirty-four percent of adults in the United States are considered overweight, and an additional 31 percent are obese. Obesity is responsible for between 6 and 10 percent of health expenditures in the United States, and the lifetime medical costs are enormous. Obesity increases the risk for coronary heart disease, type 2 diabetes, cancer, high blood pressure, high cholesterol, stroke, sleep disorders, arthritis, and gynecological problems according to the Centers for Disease Control and Prevention. The increasing rate of obesity in the United States has resulted in a total of 72.5 million obese Americans or 26 percent of the population.[15] Obesity is not just a problem of adults. Health statistics demonstrate that the prevalence of overweight children in the United States rose from 4 percent in 1963 to over 15 percent in 2000 when looking at children between the ages of six and eleven years. An even more disturbing finding was that there was also an increase in young overweight children (age two to five years) from 7 percent to over 10 percent over the same time period.[16]

There are many causes for the obesity epidemic. The advocacy group, Center for Science in the Public Interest, reported that more people eat meals away from home than ever before, U.S. children consume twice as many calories at restaurants as at home, and nearly everyone underestimates the calorie content of restaurant meals.[17] Half of restaurants provide calorie information but put it in places where it is unlikely to be seen. The health care reform legislation mandates that restaurant chains and vending machine operators post information about the caloric content in a prominent place so that it can be easily found. The mandate will be useful for individuals who count their calories and are health conscious; however, most health-conscious individuals don't eat at chain restaurants and don't use vending machines.

Complex Social and Economic Issues of the Obesity Epidemic

The Patient Protection and Affordable Care Act fails to recognize the complex sociologic, economic, and racial disparities that contribute to our nation's obesity epidemic. Obesity is a disease that disproportionately affects the underprivileged. One-third of children who enter Head Start, a public program that provides early childhood education for nearly one million low-income children, are overweight or obese.[18] Program directors report that lack of time, money, and knowledge on the part of parents are major impediments to controlling the weight of children. Cultural beliefs such as the supposition that heavier children are healthier also play a role in perpetuating obesity in the underserved populations.[18] The prevalence of obesity is also directly linked with urbanization.[19] Urbanization results in increased opportunities for eating and reduced opportunities for physical activity. A decrease in school gym programs, the increased use of computers and video games, and increased time watching television have also contributed to weight gain. Simply providing information about risk has little effect because information alone cannot overcome strong psychosocial, behavioral, and environmental barriers.

Bonnie Falkner has extensively studied the causes and treatments of obesity in urban populations and, in particular, in women.[20] She and her colleagues used funding from the National Institutes of Health and the Commonwealth of Pennsylvania to establish a Center for Excellence in Obesity. The goal of the Center is to reach out to underserved populations, focus on racial disparities, and create an intervention that can raise awareness among primary care physicians and help women to lose weight. The program was successful in improving awareness among the primary care providers in the area—measurements of height and weight and calculation of a standard index of obesity called the body-mass index or BMI became standard procedures in the participating practices. Physicians and nurses became increasingly aware of the scope of the problem. The impact on patients, however, was minimal at best. "Only a small percentage of eligible women agreed to participate, the drop-out rate was enormous and those who stayed and completed the study lost only a few pounds." "Education and outreach alone won't solve the problem," noted Falkner. "Measures that decrease the incidence of obesity in suburbia simply don't work in impoverished urban areas."

The women in the study described a strong cultural environment that impeded their ability to change their diet or activity levels. They "spoke about socio-cultural influences on food choices, such as taste and their preferences for traditional African-American foods including high-fat, high-salt foods and sweets and the strong connection between food and social affiliation." Women who were asked to enroll in the study had multiple impediments to their participation: they had family obligations and caretaking responsibilities; they lacked family support; it was difficult for them to find a safe place to exercise or a safe place to walk; and the foods that were recommended—fresh fruits and vegetables—were expensive and hard to find in their markets. The cost of buying new clothes was also an impediment to losing weight for women even when the cost of joining a weight management program was subsidized.

Reducing obesity in children is particularly challenging. Children are less active and more prone to eat foods that are high in sugar and fat. Some studies suggest that obesity might be imprinted at birth if infants are fed food that is high in fat and sugars, so educating nursing mothers and ensuring that they have the right foods for their children is of critical importance. In Philadelphia, the Urban Food and Fitness Alliance (PUFFA) has addressed policy and other factors that affect obesity and focuses on providing access to safe places to play and fresh fruits and vegetables in community centers and schools with a focus on the neighborhoods where Philadelphia's most vulnerable children reside, but the long-term success of these programs is unclear.

Individuals Must Often Support the Costs of Prevention

Another common problem in all areas of the country is high blood pressure. Controlling the blood pressure to limit its complications is just as challenging as having obese people lose weight. Most patients require more than one drug to control their blood pressure—a factor that markedly limits medication adherence.[21] The drugs must be taken regularly and thus may require accommodation of schedules. They are often costly and have side effects that can include fatigue, swelling in the legs, a dry cough, or lowered sexual function—depending on the particular combination of drugs. High blood pressure is also a silent disease—patients have no indication that their blood pressure is elevated, and they don't feel any different when their blood pressure is lowered. They often feel worse after starting medication because of the side effects. It is not surprising therefore that less than 30 percent of patients remain on an antihypertensive therapy after the second refill. Cost is a major factor in noncompliance. Residents of states that require prescription co-payments filled nearly 40 percent fewer prescriptions than their counterparts in non-co-pay states. Compliance is particularly poor in patients over the age of sixty-five.[22] Prevention programs must therefore encourage patients to keep taking their medications, reinforce their compliance through frequent blood pressure checks, and ensure that they have sufficient funds to continue to purchase their medications.

It is important to note that near universal Medicare coverage after age sixty-five has been associated with decreased racial and socioeconomic differences in health status and compliance with mammography recommendations.[23] Studies also show that Medicare recipients have increased use of health services and improved health outcomes when compared to younger but uninsured adults with cardiovascular disease or diabetes.[24] This data strongly suggest that the increase in the number of insured Americans that will come as a result of the health care reform legislation will improve some of the socioeconomic and racial disparities in health care by facilitating greater access to care as well as to prevention and wellness programs.[25]

Steps to Ensure Prevention and Wellness

What must the federal regulators and our state governments do to ensure that disease prevention and improved wellness actually effect improvements in the nation's health? Our legislative leaders must first face the reality that we will see no short-term cost reductions in health care as a result of any prevention or wellness programs. In fact, we should expect to see an increase in costs if the new programs are successful as more individuals will get screened and treated. It is estimated that if each person with diabetes underwent care that has been recommended by guideline committees—frequent eye examinations, studies to assess changes in kidney function, adequate control of blood sugar levels—the cost of care for patients with diabetes could increase threefold, but these increased costs would be associated with marked improvements in survival and quality of life.[26] There would be a similar decrease in the complications of high blood pressure if each person received the appropriate medications and actually continued to take their medications over time—but once again the total cost of care would increase substantially.

Doctors and physician-extenders including nurses, nurse practitioners, and physician's assistants must be reimbursed for carefully following patients with chronic diseases, and both public and private insurers must identify and support novel means of educating and following patients in at-risk populations. Congress must also recognize that many people at high risk for chronic disease will not have health insurance—those with chronic psychiatric disorders, the homeless, individuals who abuse alcohol and drugs, and the millions of uninsured illegal immigrants. These individuals account for the high cost of care in many urban hospitals across the country—especially at safety net hospitals. It is shortsighted and foolish to ignore this high-risk group. It is highly unlikely that these individuals will go to the local health club and exercise, but programs should be created at the federal and state level to screen the indigent for communicable diseases, provide healthy foods at food kitchens and shelters, and facilitate their ability to seek treatment for their addictions or chronic psychiatric problems.

The Department of Health and Human Services must focus a major amount of its resources on efforts to improve the wellness of the nation's children. Kenneth Thorpe, executive director of the national Partnership to Fight Chronic Disease and chair of the Department of Health Policy and Management at Emory University, wrote: "With younger and younger Americans suffering from overweight and obesity, the outlook is grim for finding a solution to stem rising health costs short of helping Americans transform their unhealthy behaviors."[27] We must focus on improving child health at the local, state, and federal levels by providing more nutritious foods, providing at least two daily meals to each child, increasing opportunities for physical activity during the school day and in after-school programs, providing safe athletic facilities in the community where children and young adults can congregate, and instituting curricula in the very early years of school focused on diet and nutrition. Many national organizations including the Institute of Medicine have focused on the health issues facing the nation's children. The funding appropriated by the Patient Protection and Affordable Care Act can actually effect changes if it is appropriately directed.

Many people unfortunately need intensive lifestyle modification and cannot accomplish it own their own. Programs such as the National Institutes of Health-sponsored Diabetes Prevention Program, which attempts to prevent or delay the onset of diabetes in high-risk individuals by intensive lifestyle modification programs or glucose-lowering drugs, have important effects on morbidity and mortality of diabetes but have been viewed as being too expensive for health plans or national programs. This is shortsighted, as without these aggressive and expensive programs it is unlikely that we will be able to put a dent in America's wellness quotient. Suburbanites who already belong to health clubs and country clubs will gain little from the mandates of the health care reform legislation. It is the population of our underserved and impoverished urban and rural areas that can best be helped by new initiatives funded by the Patient Protection and Affordable Care Act. The bill does not articulate a focus on the underserved, but hopefully this focus will evolve through the crafting and fine-tuning of the regulations by the secretary of HHS and the numerous task forces that will implement the mandates of the bill.

A major cause of obesity and high blood pressure is the high levels of salt and sugar that is in the foods that we all consume on a daily basis. The food industry includes information on the fat, salt, and carbohydrate concentrations of food, but it is inconceivable that kids read that before they reach for the box. The levels of sugar and salt in breakfast cereals—especially those that are aggressively marketed to children—are shockingly high. Federal regulators should work with the food industry to proactively remove salt and sugar from cereals and other foods that are popular with children. Programs that have involved governmental agencies and food companies have effectively lowered sugar and salt levels in foods in the United Kingdom, and there is no reason why similar steps could not be taken in the United States. The long-term cost effects on health and wellness of high levels of cereal and sugars are no different from the societal costs of cigarette smoking or alcohol, so, if necessary, federal regulators should tax foods that exceed minimal standards.

Bonnie Falkner shared an interesting story. Several weeks before I interviewed her she had taken her six-year-old grandson to his swim meet. She looked at all of the children in the meet. They came from a variety of suburban swim clubs. "It was striking to me that there were no obese kids," she noted. There was something very different about the lifestyle in suburban Philadelphia relative to children in the Philadelphia school system. Until federal and state authorities focus on mitigating those disparities, no amount of money or mandates will be able to prevent the epidemics of obesity and high blood pressure and their attendant costs to society and the economy.

Notes

1. Faukner, B. Personal communication. 2010.
2. Harkin T. http://harkin.senate.gov/press/release.cfm?i=232597 2010.
3. Elmendorf D. Letter to subcommittee on health, committee on energy and commerce, the House of Representatives. http://www.cbo.gov/ftpdocs/104xx/doc10492/08-07-Prevention_PSally.1.1.htm 2010.
4. Finan S. http://blogs.consumerreports.org/health/2009/12/health-care-reform-medical-underwriting-by-stealth.html. 2010.
5. Weaver C. Health lobbyists focus on a once-obscure group. *Washington Post.* July 15, 2010.
6. Truog RD. Screening mammography and the "r" word. *N Engl J Med.* Dec 24, 2009;361(26):2501-2503.
7. Partridge AH, Winer EP. On mammography—more agreement than disagreement. *N Engl J Med.* Dec 24, 2009;361(26):2499–2501.
8. Andriole GL, Crawford ED, Grubb RL, 3rd et al. Mortality results from a randomized prostate-cancer screening trial. *N Engl J Med.* Mar 26, 2009;360(13):1310–1319.
9. Schroder FH, Hugosson J, Roobol MJ et al. Screening and prostate-cancer mortality in a randomized European study. *N Engl J Med.* Mar 26, 2009;360(13):1320–1328.
10. Barry MJ. Screening for prostate cancer—The controversy that refuses to die. *N Engl J Med.* Mar 26, 2009;360(13):1351–1354.
11. Cohen JT, Neumann PJ, Weinstein MC. Does preventive care save money? Health economics and the presidential candidates. *N Engl J Med.* Feb 14, 2008;358(7):661–663.
12. Rovner J. Prevention efforts may not reduce health care costs. NPR. July 28, 2009 (http://www.npr.org/templates/story/story.php?storyId=111208400).
13. Russell LB. Preventing chronic disease: an important investment, but don't count on cost savings. *Health Aff* (Millwood). Jan–Feb 2009;28(1):42–45.
14. Goodell S, Cohen I, Neumann P. The Synthesis Project—New Insights from Research Results: Policy Brief No. 18. September 2009.
15. Grady D. Obesity rates keep rising, troubling health officials. *New York Times.* August 3, 2010.
16. Ogden C, Caroll, MD. NCHS Health E-Stat—Prevalence of Obesity among Children and Adolescents: United States, Trends 1963–1965 through 2007–2008 (http://www.cdc.gov/nchs/data/hestat/obesity_child_07_08/obesity_child_07_08.htm). Accessed June 4, 2010.
17. Wootan MG, Batada A, Marchlewicz E. Kids' Meals: Obesity on the Menu, Center for Science in the Public Interest, Aug 2008. http://www.cspinet.org/new/pdf/kidsmeals-report.pdf.

18. Hughes CC, Gooze RA, Finkelstein DM et al. Barriers to obesity prevention in Head Start. *Health Aff* (Millwood). Mar–Apr 2010;29(3):454–462.
19. Harpham T, Stephens C. Urbanization and health in developing countries. *World Health Stat Q.* 1991;44(2):62–69.
20. Cossrow N, Falkner B. Race/ethnic issues in obesity and obesity-related comorbidities. *J Clin Endocrinol Metab.* Jun 2004;89(6):2590–2594.
21. Gradman AH, Basile JN, Carter BL et al. Combination Therapy in Hypertension. *J Clin Hypertens* (Greenwich). Mar 2010;13(3):146–154.
22. Munger MA, Van Tassel BW, LaFleur J. Medication nonadherence: An unrecognized cardiovascular risk factor: Factors contributing to nonadherence with antihypertensive medication. *Medscape Today* (http://www.medscape.com/viewarticle/561319_2).
23. Decker S. Medicare and the health of women with breast cancer. *The Journal of Human Resources.* 2005;40(4):948–968.
24. McWilliams JM, Meara E, Zaslavsky AM et al. Differences in control of cardiovascular disease and diabetes by race, ethnicity, and education: U.S. trends from 1999 to 2006 and effects of Medicare coverage. *Ann Intern Med.* Apr 21, 2009;150(8):505–515.
25. Bernstein J, Chollet D, Peterson S. How does insurance coverage improve health outcomes? *Mathematica.* April 2010;1.
26. Beaulieu ND, Cutler DM, Ho KE, Horrigan D, Isham G. The business case for diabetes disease management at two managed care organizations: A case study of health partners and independent health association, The Commonwealth Fund, Field Report, April 2003, http://www.commonwealthfund.org/usr_doc/beaulieu_bcs_diabetesdiseasemangement_610.pdf.
27. Thorpe, K. The Obama Budget and Health Reform, Huffington Post Politics, 2/25/09, http://www.huffingtonpost.com/kenneth-thorpe/the-obama-budget-and-heal_b_169854.html.

Chapter 5

How Will Health Care Reform Affect the Medically Underserved and the Safety Net Hospitals That Care for Them?

> Despite federal stimulus support for state Medicaid programs, some cash-strapped states have cut Medicaid payments, and others are considering such cuts. As a result, many hospitals that treat large numbers of uninsured patients are struggling to survive.
>
> **Michael Spivey and Arthur L. Kellermann,**
> *New England Journal of Medicine*, **June 18, 2009**

It looks like a national plan will be modeled on Massachusetts and it's a disaster for poor people. The insurance offered doesn't cover everyone. It's filled with gaps like co-payments and deductibles.

Patients can't afford it, so they turn to the public sector and the public sector isn't there anymore.

Dr. Steffie Woolhandler, Harvard Medical School, September 8, 2009

The town of Braddock is located just east of Pittsburgh in Allegheny County. The town is famous for three significant events in the history of the United States. It was the site of the Battle of Monongahela, an early battle in the French and Indian War. The first of Andrew Carnegie's many public libraries was opened in Braddock in 1889. The event that had a far larger impact on both Braddock and western Pennsylvania, however, was the opening of Andrew Carnegie's first major steel mill, the Edgar Thomson Works, in the late 1800s. The thriving steel business led to an explosion in the population of the town due largely to its settlement by immigrants from Croatia, Slovenia, and Hungary. By the end of World War II, the town had grown to nearly 19,000 inhabitants.

Work in the Braddock steel mills at the turn of the twentieth century was difficult with long days, low pay, a high rate of accidents, and poor health care. The hours that each employee worked began to decrease as employers recognized that workers who had more rest had fewer accidents. Substantive changes in the health care for steelworkers came about as a result of the formation of strong labor unions in the 1930s. Employer-provided health care was an important benefit, and labor leaders began to negotiate for it in their contracts. By 1948, the National Labor Relations Board ruled that health benefits were a legitimate subject of collective bargaining, which encouraged the spread of health plans in the steel industry even after the end of the war. Hospitals that cared for union workers were able to grow and flourish.

Braddock Hospital opened its doors in June of 1906 with thirty beds. The insured population of Braddock grew, and so too did the hospital—more than doubling its size with a new 138-bed addition in 1973. The expansion of Braddock Hospital was ill timed. The collapse of the U.S. steel industry in the late 1970s and the early 1980s had a devastating impact on Braddock. The population decreased by 90 percent. The Edgar Thomson Mill shrank from 10,000 employees at the peak of Pennsylvania steel production to only 800 employees today. Over a third of the population of Braddock now lives below the poverty level. In 1996, when the University of Pittsburgh Medical Center (UPMC) bought Braddock Hospital, the loss of the steel industry and the impoverishment of the community were having a devastating effect on the hospital.

Mark Sevco is the vice president for operations of the UPMC Presbyterian/Shadyside Hospital, the flagship hospital of the large and highly successful

UPMC Health System in Pittsburgh, Pennsylvania. Mark has been an academic health center administrator for nearly twenty years. In 2004 he took on his most difficult assignment—president of Braddock Hospital. When Mark took over Braddock Hospital, it was losing over $6 million each year. A major cause of the economic distress of the hospital was a marked change in "payer mix." Mark found that 80 percent of the hospital's patients had either Medicare or Medicaid or no insurance at all—a significant change from the days of the steel industry when most of Braddock's patients had private insurance paid for by the steel companies. The levels of reimbursement for hospital care provided by Medicare and Medicaid made it difficult to support an infrastructure that had been built when the majority of patients had private insurance. The UPMC Health System had to subsidize the salaries of hospital-based physicians such as anesthesiologists, pathologists, and radiologists. Mark found it especially challenging to find surgeons, orthopedists, neurosurgeons, and ear, nose, and throat specialists to see patients in the Braddock emergency room because the reimbursements were too low to make it worth their while to drive from their offices or their homes in Pittsburgh to the hospital in Braddock. He could only provide those types of services when he paid the physicians a stipend for covering the emergency room.

"The first thing we did was to try and reduce our costs," Mark told me. "We introduced cost reduction initiatives including staff reductions, and we streamlined our management structure. We even contracted with the County to care for patients from the county jail, and we optimized our efficiency by instituting management systems for staffing the operating rooms and nursing positions, and we did everything we could to increase volume." These measures improved the finances of the hospital—but not to a level that was sustainable. "It was all about volume," Mark told me. "We simply couldn't attract enough patients with private insurance to cover the fixed costs we had for the operating rooms, the nursing staff, the physical plant, and 250 beds. Medicare and Medicaid weren't enough, and we were giving lots of free care." When the margin of the hospital remained at minus seven percent, the UPMC Health System was forced to close the hospital in January 2010.

The closure of the hospital in Braddock engendered enormous controversy.[1] The residents filed a complaint with the U.S. Justice Department claiming that the closure of the hospital violated the Civil Rights Act of 1964 because it adversely affected access to care for a community that was predominantly poor and black.[2] The suit did not stop the closure; however, the UPMC Health System agreed to expand its primary care offerings to Braddock residents for at least three years after the closure. The Health System also offered to provide transportation to health centers in nearby communities, yearly health screenings, and an ombudsman to help residents to access health care.

Hospital closures are happening across America—not because patients don't have health insurance but because they have skimpy insurance that doesn't cover their cost of care. In western Pennsylvania alone numerous hospitals serving impoverished areas have also closed: Brownsville Hospital, Aliquippa Hospital, Monsour Hospital, Jeanette Hospital, St. Francis Hospital, and Southside Hospital. The closure of Braddock Hospital after over one hundred years of service and the numerous other western Pennsylvania hospitals points to an important concern regarding the Patient Protection and Affordable Care Act: will safety net hospitals survive health care reform?

The Patient Protection and Affordable Care Act as it relates to safety net hospitals is built on two fundamental premises. The first premise is that a significant proportion of our country's uninsured will be able to purchase insurance from insurance exchanges. The insurance provided by the exchanges will theoretically be affordable for those with average income while those at the lower end of the economic spectrum will receive subsidies that will help them to purchase their insurance. The pool of patients who purchase insurance from the exchanges will be large—presumably mitigating the possibility that the exchanges will include a significant percentage of patients with chronic disease or preexisting conditions. The second fundamental premise of the health care reform legislation is that hospitals—and in particular, so-called safety net hospitals—will require less governmental support because the significant increase in the number of insured Americans will result in a marked increase in hospital revenues. Far fewer patients will ostensibly be seeking charity care, and far more patients will be paying customers. The health care reform bill therefore establishes a schedule for progressively decreasing support to safety net hospitals.

These two closely linked pillars of the health care reform bill sit on a very shaky foundation—there is no objective data to support the conjecture that the increased revenues from having more patients with insurance will balance out the cuts in fees paid to support charity care. The collapse of either pillar could result in individuals being unable to pay for their health care and could also result in a catastrophic failure of our country's system of safety net hospitals and physicians.

Health Care Safety Net

The health care safety net consists of a diverse collection of state, county, and city public hospitals and a group of private not-for-profit hospitals that care for a disproportionate number of underinsured or uninsured patients.[3] Today there are more than 1,000 community health centers across the country, but according to data gathered by the Kaiser Family Foundation, each community health center must care for approximately 16,300 patients. The community health centers are most commonly located in impoverished urban neighborhoods or in remote rural areas where there are few other health care providers and poor access to specialists.[4] Safety nets serve a population that has complex health and social needs and often provide far more than simple in-hospital care. The safety net hospitals often provide the only outpatient services in their communities and are often the site of the only trauma and burn centers in the area. Many safety net hospitals also serve as locations for both undergraduate and graduate medical education, and some are integrated with universities and their medical schools.

America's safety net has also extended to the suburbs as suburban poverty has increased over the past decade. A recent study by the Center for Studying Health System Change found that low-income people living in suburban areas face the same challenges in accessing medical providers as those in urban and rural areas.[5] They often rely on suburban hospital emergency departments for their care, but they also receive care from urban safety net hospitals and community health centers. The greater geographic dispersion of the suburban poor and attempts by suburban hospitals and doctors to redirect their care to urban safety net services compound their problems with access.

No fewer than 300 public hospitals have closed their doors in Los Angeles, Washington, St. Louis, Milwaukee, and other cities because of growing debt and diminishing revenues. In Atlanta, the 115-year-old Grady Memorial Hospital faced closure before it was bailed out with a $250 million gift from an Atlanta-based charitable organization.[6] One-third of Grady's patients have no insurance and another third have Medicaid, but Medicaid reimburses at a level that is below the cost of care at Grady. Grady has other important roles in the community. Its burn center serves over half of Georgia, it runs the only emergency ambulance service in Atlanta, it handles 850,000 outpatient visits a year, it is the only Level 1 trauma center in north Georgia, and it is one of the largest providers in the country for patients with AIDS, end-stage kidney disease, and sickle-cell disease. Grady has also served as a major teaching facility for Emory University and Morehouse School of Medicine. Its near closure serves to imprint the tenuous nature of America's medical safety net.

History of Safety Net Hospitals

The classic safety net hospital was the Johns Hopkins Hospital, built by the wealthy Baltimorean philanthropist for whom the hospital was named. Hopkins noted in his letter to the trustees of the hospital that "the indigent sick of this city and its environs, without regard to sex, age, or color, who may require surgical or medical treatment, and who can be received into the Hospital without peril to the other inmates, and the poor of this city and state, of all races, who are stricken down by any casualty, shall be received into the Hospital, without charge, for such periods of time and under such regulations as you may prescribe."[7] Hopkins also made the prescient observation that

> you will also provide for the reception of a limited number of patients who are able to make compensation for the room and attention they may require. The money received from such persons will enable you to appropriate a larger sum for the relief of the sufferings of that class which I direct you to admit free of charge; and you will thus be enabled to afford to strangers, and to those of your own people who have no friends or relations to care for them in sickness, and who are not objects of charity, the advantages of careful and skillful treatment.

This model of cost shifting from the rich to the poor would become commonplace in American medicine.

As care began to transition from homes to hospitals, private hospitals began to emerge across the country. Health care for the poor remained centered in many U.S. cities around municipal or state hospitals. Many of these municipal hospitals were affiliated with medical schools and thus provided a training site for medical students, residents, and postgraduate fellows. Physician-scientists at municipal hospitals also made discoveries that impacted the care of patients including the discovery of the cause and treatment of rickets and cholera at Baltimore City Hospital and the discovery of the clot buster streptokinase and the polio vaccine at Bellevue Hospital in New York.

By the late twentieth century hospitals had changed considerably from charitable institutions to businesses. This change came about in large part because of the increasing popularity of medical insurance after World War II and in particular the passage of the legislation that created Medicare and Medicaid in the 1960s. All of a sudden, hospitals could charge patients who previously could not pay for their care. In 1922 patient care revenues accounted for just over half of the total revenue of a general hospital, but by 1994 approximately 94 percent of hospital revenue was derived from services to patients.[8] This paradigm changed again at the beginning of the twenty-first century when total hospital expenses for general hospitals in the United States exceeded their patient revenues. Continued cuts in state Medicaid funding and decreasing reimbursements from Medicare and private insurance companies have now dramatically cut into the finances of most of the nation's hospitals with the largest impact being on safety net hospitals.

Disproportionate-Share Hospital Payments

Safety net hospitals still require subsidies because of their location in low-economic urban areas, the large proportion of charity care that they deliver, and inefficiencies in their delivery of care. Safety net hospitals have historically charged private payers more than suburban hospitals. They were then able to shift revenues they gained from caring for private patients to support the care of uninsured or underinsured patients. Some safety net hospitals received funding for patient care from county or state allocations. The bulk of the support has come from the federal government in the form of Medicaid payments to hospitals that are called disproportionate-share hospital (DSH) payments.[9] Additional payments come from Medicare and Medicaid for training residents and subspecialty fellows—direct graduate medical education payments and indirect medical education payments.

The DSH payments have not been without problems. Annual payments to the states are supposed to vary based on the amount of uncompensated care given in a particular state—but that has not been the case. Wyoming, a relatively poor rural state with few doctors and hospitals and a large number of uninsured individuals, receives only $100,000 per year in federal DSH payments while New York, a far wealthier state, receives $1.5 billion. The disparity between funding and need in different states appears even more dramatic if one looks at payments per person. The federal government pays Wyoming $0.55 per person and $3.13 per uninsured citizen whereas the government pays the state of New York $110.44 per capita and $632.09 per uninsured citizen. It can be argued that the cost of care is higher in New York than in Wyoming; however, the difference in cost of care is far less than the variation that exists in DSH funding.[10]

States are also given enormous leeway in how they make payments to hospitals. State politics therefore play a critical role in determining which hospitals receive DSH funds and how much they receive. Since the federal DSH subsidy to a state is now capped at 12 percent of a state's total Medicaid budget, political pressure that results in a hospital with little charity care receiving a large DSH payment means that a hospital with a high level of charity care but with less political clout will receive a far lower DSH payment than they deserve.

Despite its flaws, DSH funds are critical for the survival of safety net hospitals. Most safety net hospitals have negative margins even with DSH funds. A 2011 report from the National Association of Urban Hospitals found that operating margins of both rural and urban safety net hospitals are substantially lower than those of private hospitals—a fact that was confirmed by studies by the Agency for Healthcare Research and Quality.[11] Braddock Hospital is a perfect example of a safety net hospital that just couldn't survive with an operating margin that exceeded minus seven percent.

Safety Net Hospitals Falter When DSH Funds Are Redirected to Pay for Health Insurance

In 1994, Tennessee tried to redirect its DSH funds to expand Medicaid eligibility.[10] The basic concept that drove Tennessee to redirect funds to expand Medicaid was that if more people had insurance (Medicaid), hospitals would have less charity care and would need fewer DSH dollars. It didn't work in Tennessee. Within months, safety net hospitals were forced to limit or eliminate critical programs, forcing the state to reinstitute the DSH funding.

In Massachusetts, a state touted by health policy pundits as being the poster child for health care reform, reform has significantly harmed the state's safety net hospitals. The Boston Medical Center, one of the state's largest safety net hospitals, filed a lawsuit against the Commonwealth of Massachusetts claiming that the lowered Medicaid reimbursement rates had resulted in a $38 million deficit for the fiscal year ending in September 2009 and a projected $100 million deficit for the fiscal year ending in 2010.[12] The suit also charged that the state had used money that in the past had been allocated to support the care of the uninsured at Boston Medical Center to help pay the cost of insurance for the state's uninsured population. The cost of care at the Boston Medical Center did not differ from the other Boston teaching hospitals—only the number of patients with private insurance was lower than other hospitals. The Obama administration was forced to infuse $435 million to Massachusetts to keep Boston Medical Center open.

The calamitous effects of shifting dollars from hospital payments to provide insurance for individuals who were previously uninsured in Massachusetts are especially concerning when one recognizes that Massachusetts had one of the lowest numbers of uninsured citizens even before the implementation of health care reform.

Patient Protection and Affordable Care Act Threatens the Country's Safety Net

The Patient Protection and Affordable Care Act reduces national Medicaid DSH allotments by $0.5 billion in 2014, $0.6 billion in 2015, $0.6 billion in 2016, $1.8 billion in 2017, $5 billion in 2018, $5.6 billion in 2019, and $4 billion in 2020. The law requires the secretary of HHS to distribute the Medicaid DSH reductions in such a way that it imposes the largest reductions in states with the lowest percentage of uninsured and smaller reductions for states that receive a lower amount of DSH funding but have higher concentrations of uninsured individuals. The bill also reduces national Medicare DSH allotments by 75 percent and then raises the payments based on the percent of the population that is uninsured and the amount of uncompensated care that is provided. The Health

& Medicine Policy Research Group based in Chicago, Illinois, calculated the effects that health care reform would have on hospitals in Illinois.[13] Illinois received approximately $215 million in Medicaid DSH payments in 2009. This amount would decrease to $206 million in 2014 and to $139 million in 2020—at a time when the cost of health care will likely be significantly higher if we factor in only a cost of living increase.

In an article published in the June 18, 2009, issue of the *New England Journal of Medicine*, Michael Spivey and Arthur Kellermann noted that efforts by CMS and the Congressional Budget Office to eliminate or greatly alter the DSH program were "misguided."[10] They went on to point out that "with the number of uninsured Americans growing rapidly, cutting DSH funding would be foolish. Ending it could be disastrous."

The Patient Protection and Affordable Care Act creates other programs that will also threaten the financial stability of safety net hospitals. One such program is the plan to track spending on millions of Medicare beneficiaries and reward hospitals that spend less per beneficiary and penalize hospitals that spend more per beneficiary. Hospitals will also be accountable for the cost of care that is provided by doctors and other health care providers in the ninety days after a Medicare patient leaves the hospital, and hospitals will be penalized when patients are rehospitalized during that ninety-day time period. This initiative, called value-based purchasing, places safety net hospitals at great risk because these hospitals often care for sicker patients and those with chronic disease. The patients who are cared for at safety net hospitals often are unable to pay for medications and therefore have a higher rate of hospitalization. Take for instance patients who are hospitalized for a broken leg after a car accident. If they are unable to afford to fill the prescription for antibiotics that their doctor gives them when they leave the hospital, they have a much higher chance of developing an infection, which would require another hospitalization. Patients who are treated at safety net hospitals also lack the social support in their homes to facilitate their post-hospital care. Wealthy community hospitals might also try to avoid high-risk patients by sending them to the safety net hospitals.

Pay-for-Performance Can Also Threaten Safety Net Hospitals

Pay-for-performance is an increasingly popular approach to improving health care quality. Insurers reimburse hospitals and doctors based on their ability to meet predefined metrics in the care of their patients. A study by Jan Blustein and colleagues from the NYU Medical School, the Weill Cornell Medical College, and Harvard University points out how these programs could threaten the financial integrity of many safety net hospitals. The group looked at the performance of 2,705 U.S. hospitals in the care of patients who were hospitalized because they were having a heart attack or because they had developed congestive heart failure—two diseases seen commonly in U.S. acute care hospitals.[14] The group used process-of-care measures from the Hospital Quality Alliance—the same measures that will be used by Medicare analysts to adjudicate hospital and physician reimbursements—to assess the quality of care that was delivered. Hospitals that were located in areas with a low percentage of college graduates in the workforce or in areas with long-standing poverty performed worse on measures of quality than did hospitals that were located in a community with a higher quantity and quality of local economic and human resources. The take-home message of the study was that pay-for-performance programs would undoubtedly result in increasing socioeconomic inequity in health care financing and further threaten the economic structure of safety net hospitals.

Health Care Exchange

We will not be able to reform our current health system until we have devised a mechanism to provide health insurance for the 45 million Americans who have no health insurance. The Patient Protection and Affordable Care Act mandates that everyone must purchase health insurance or pay a yearly fine to reach this goal. The bill exempts those with financial hardship, Native Americans, and those whose religious beliefs preclude them from purchasing health insurance. The act seeks to fulfill the goal of providing insurance for the majority of Americans by creating health insurance exchanges.[15] The exchanges will facilitate the expansion of health insurance coverage, improve the quality of coverage, reduce costs, and potentially improve the quality of health care if they function as planned.

The creation of health care exchanges was an important element in almost every draft of the health care reform legislation and, as a result, raised little if any controversy during the congressional debates. The decree for mandatory insurance coverage has however, been one of the most controversial aspects of the new legislation after its passage and has resulted in nearly twenty-six lawsuits from states.

The health care exchanges, entities that sell insurance, will be operating by 2014. The exchanges must raise more money from the sale of health insurance policies than they pay out for medical care of the people their policies cover. They are in that sense identical to existing private health insurance companies. The exchanges will theoretically play several important roles in reforming our health care system: they will create competition between insurance plans, making them more affordable; they will provide insurance for a large number of

Americans, thereby creating an insurance risk pool that includes patients at both low risk and high risk of needing medical care; they will reduce administrative costs by simplifying the purchase of insurance; they will provide consumers with choice by making differences in packages and costs more transparent; they will be regulated and thus more fair in their treatment of beneficiaries; and finally, they will provide insurance for the poor through subsidies.

The exchanges will not be open to everyone. People who work at a company that has fewer than one hundred employees, work for a company that does not provide health insurance, are self-employed or unemployed, are retired but not eligible for Medicare, or operate a small business are the only ones who will be able to purchase insurance through an exchange. Exchanges that serve small businesses are referred to as the Small Business Health Options Program (SHOP). After 2017, medium and large businesses may also purchase insurance from the exchanges. Individuals who don't meet the criteria for buying insurance from an exchange but still want to purchase their own insurance can do so outside of the exchange at the same price since the health care reform bill requires insurers that offer plans on exchanges to charge the same premiums on comparable plans outside of the exchange.[16]

People who cannot afford health insurance will be able to obtain subsidies from the government to help cover the cost of premiums. Subsidies will be factored on a sliding scale that is based on need. A family of four with a total income of between $22,000 and $29,000 will pay a health care premium that is limited to between 2 percent and 3 percent of their income. A family of four that has a total income of between $66,000 and $88,000 a year will pay a health insurance premium that equals 9.5 percent of their total income.

The exchanges will be managed by the states or by nonprofit organizations that the states contract with. States can apply for federal money to help fund start-ups, and states can cooperate with each other to form multistate exchanges. The exchanges will not sell their own products. They will instead sell the products of health insurance companies. These products must meet certain federal requirements including providing a package of benefits that includes a set of predefined items and services, limits the amount of out-of-pocket expenses that individuals and families are charged each year, and offers plans from a standard menu that can be easily understood by customers and that makes it simple to compare competing plans. Insurance packages must be categorized as bronze, silver, gold, or platinum based on the percentage of their health care costs that the individual must pay (60, 70, 80, and 90 percent, respectively).

Insurance companies that fail to meet the federal standards will presumably be barred from selling their products through the exchanges. Brokers and agents will unfortunately still be allowed to sell insurance policies from the exchange so some excess costs still remain.

President Obama surprised Republicans and Democrats alike when he announced at the National Governors Association in February 2011 that he would support moving up the date when states can opt out of the law regarding health care exchanges from 2017 to 2014. States would have to show that they could come up with a better system to get a waiver, but the opportunity for flexibility was important for some states.[17] States must cover the same number of people but at a lower cost than in the exchanges. Opting out doesn't lift the responsibility that states have for expanding Medicaid coverage, a major financial hurdle for many states. It will be important to see whether states that opt out replace the exchanges with a form of health care coverage that takes advantage of unique opportunities in each state and whether that results in improved access to health care.

Some states have wanted to take a more aggressive approach to insuring optimal care for their residents and have taken advantage of the opportunity to opt out of the exchanges. In Oregon and in Vermont, for example, legislators are considering implementing a single-payer health care program for the state.[18, 19] The development of a single-payer system in Vermont was based on a legislature-funded study by the Harvard School of Public Health that evaluated potential systems that could create the largest savings while at the same time achieving universal coverage. The Vermont system will be a public-private partnership that is overseen by an independent board composed of payers, providers, and consumers. The board will be responsible for negotiating benefit packages and payment rates.[19]

Will the Exchanges Work?

A recent scholarly report evaluated the potential merits and limitations of health care exchanges. Written by Timothy S. Jost in December of 2009 for the Commonwealth Fund,[20] the report points out that the congressional staffers that created the health care reform act had an important decision to make—should the exchanges be established at the federal or at the state level? They chose the latter. Jost notes that insurance regulation has traditionally been left to the states and that a number of states have experience running exchanges. States could more readily experiment with different designs and respond more effectively to local concerns. But the fact that over half of the states have filed lawsuits to preclude the government from mandating that all state residents have health insurance bodes poorly for the hope that states will actually be able to create an exchange and effectively regulate insurers.

An exchange must control costs to be effective, and to control costs, states must facilitate the ability of their exchange to negotiate with insurers to bring down premiums and refuse to permit insurance companies that have unreasonably high costs from participating in the exchange. The exchanges must take a hard line with insurers to move them away from competition that is based on attracting the best risk and toward competition that is based on price and quality. States must also be able to adjust premium payments to health insurers retroactively to reward insurers who take on high-risk individuals by clawing back payments that were made to insurers who attracted only low-risk individuals. Successful exchanges could limit cost sharing, deductibles, and co-payments and permit insurers to offer only a limited range of policies so that potential customers could easily compare one insurance policy with another. To accomplish these tasks, state legislatures will have to stand up against the powerful health insurance lobbyists, a group that spent nearly $1 billion on lobbying to influence the structure of health care reform.

An exchange must also be large enough to avoid the Achilles' heel of any health insurer—adverse selection. If an exchange or any other health plan enrolls a large proportion of individuals who either have a preexisting condition or who are at high risk for developing chronic disease, the insurer will not be able to shift dollars that come from the premiums paid by healthy individuals to support the needs of individuals who are chronically or seriously ill. Congress took an important step to ensure that exchanges would be large enough to have a large enough number of participants so that there was a mixture of high-risk and low-risk patients (the risk pool): they mandated that all Americans must purchase health insurance or face a fine. If families find that it is cheaper to pay the fine than to buy the insurance, the exchanges will not be large enough to spread the risk and will not be financially sustainable.

Giving the states the authority to create and regulate exchanges also raises the question of how states will be able to afford another administrative cost-center at a time when many states and communities are struggling to support needed services such as police departments, fire departments, and schools as well as state-supported infrastructure such as roads and bridges. The *Atlanta Journal-Constitution* reported in its August 6, 2010, issue that Georgia governor Sony Perdue's office estimated that adding 700,000 Georgians to Medicaid rolls will add hundreds of millions of dollars to the state budget due to administrative and medical costs.[21] Any increase in costs at a time of economic peril in many states may obviate the ability of the states to carry out the process of creating exchanges.

Illegal immigrants will not have access to the exchanges or for that matter to any form of health insurance. It is also unlikely that individuals with chronic alcohol abuse or chronic psychiatric disease, intravenous drug abusers, or the homeless will sign up for the state exchanges. Yet these patients account for substantial hospital costs today, and hospitals will continue to have to cover their costs of care after the exchanges open in 2014. Marc Sevco pointed out that a significant number of our patients at Braddock Hospital had behavioral health problems and were in need of detoxification as well as treatment for chronic disease. I was proud of the fact that we provided ready access to medical services for these very impoverished people. But we never received any reimbursement for our services and without being able to shift costs from paying patients—it just wasn't sustainable. Safety net hospitals with a high proportion of illegal immigrants and homeless will be further challenged under health care reform.

Some States Are ahead of the Curve—Others behind It

Some states are taking a very proactive approach to health care reform and in particular to the creation of exchanges. The best example of this is California. Two bills were approved by the legislature and signed by the governor in 2010: AB 1602 and SB 900.[22] These bills established the California Health Benefit Exchange. The bills established an oversight board for the exchange that will include the secretary of the state's Health and Human Services Agency and four appointed members having expertise in the health care marketplace. The bill excludes anyone who is affiliated with a health plan, an insurer, hospitals, or clinics or physicians or nurses from being members of the board. The Exchange will fulfill the guidelines established by the federal legislation including setting the minimum requirements for health care packages, selecting the health insurers who can participate in the plan, requiring qualified individuals to purchase the plan, and establishing health care market reforms including making it illegal to rescind coverage from beneficiaries who develop disease or to deny coverage for individuals with existing disease.

For every state that is moving forward with the creation of the infrastructure needed to create health care exchanges, there is another state that has opted out. Some states have decided to opt out of the exchanges because they fear that they will lose substantial amounts of money on health care exchanges. One such example is Louisiana, which announced in March 2011 that it will return a $1 million federal grant it received to help set up the exchanges. Bruce Greenstein, health and hospitals secretary for the state of Louisiana, gave his reason for opting out of the exchanges. He said, "Envision an exchange, which, if we were to run it, has the governor's name on top of the letterhead. We know we would see a number of letters that would go out to businesses and families throughout the state announcing the increase in premiums."[23] States like Louisiana that opt out of creating their own exchanges will turn the responsibility over to the federal government. This might well be the best solution since the federal government has far more experience in running health care organizations—Medicare and Medicaid being two examples.

Health Care Reform in Massachusetts: A Template for Health Care Exchanges?

A second scholarly work to evaluate the concept of health care exchanges was a February 2009 study prepared by Drs. Rachel Nardin, David Himmelstein, and Steffie Woolhander from Harvard Medical School. This study evaluated the Massachusetts Health Reform Law that was passed in Massachusetts in 2006—the poster child for federal health care reform. The Massachusetts law expanded Medicaid coverage for the poor and made available a subsidized, Medicaid-like coverage for near poor residents of the state while also mandating that middle-income uninsured people either purchase health insurance or pay a fine. Fines were also levied on employers who did not offer insurance benefits.

Health care reform in Massachusetts didn't work as planned according to the report written by Drs. Nardin, Himmelstein, and Woolhandler. The health care reform in Massachusetts was more expensive than expected. The state had to drain money from safety net public hospitals and community clinics to support the high costs of near-universal coverage, both the newly insured and the previously insured have had substantial problems accessing doctors and care, reform failed to reduce the use of expensive, high-technology services, and cuts to safety net providers have threatened the viability of safety net emergency rooms. The reform bill paradoxically increased administrative costs by four to five percentage points.

The most egregious problem with reform in Massachusetts is that insurance for low- and middle-income families has now become unaffordable even when individuals purchased the skimpiest plans. Nardin and her colleagues point out that the cheapest plan available through the connector for a middle-income fifty-six-year-old who makes approximately $50,000 per year costs $4,872 annually. If beneficiaries become sick, they must pay an additional $2,000 deductible before the insurance kicks in and pay 20 percent of all of their medical bills up to a maximum of $3,000 annually. The total cost thus becomes $9,872—a number that excludes uncovered services such as physical therapy or some forms of home health care. Thus gaps in coverage including co-payments, deductibles, and uncovered services can also lead to bankruptcy even in those with health insurance. Nardin points out that "it is not surprising that many of the state's uninsured have declined such coverage."

Health care reform is even more burdensome for Massachusetts' low-income individuals. Residents earning less than 200 percent of the poverty level received their care free of charge from safety net facilities before reform passed. Access to care was excellent for low-income residents living close to a safety net facility, and the quality of care was often excellent particularly when received at a safety net hospital or clinic affiliated with one of the state's many fine academic medical centers. In contrast to the free care that patients received prior to instituting health care reform in Massachusetts, the new insurance policies require co-payments for office visits and prescriptions. As a result, poor state residents can no longer afford medical care despite the fact that they now have insurance. Many patients with chronic disease now avoid hospitalization until absolutely necessary. The flaws found in Massachusetts' health care reform laws that existed before federal health care reform have unfortunately been replicated in some parts of the Patient Protection and Affordable Care Act as it relates to the safety net.

How Can the Patient Protection and Affordable Care Act Be Modified to Protect the Safety Net?

Health policy experts Michael Spivey and Arthur Kellermann proposed four changes to the federal law that would allow continuing support for safety net hospitals through modifications of DSH funding.[10] They proposed that DSH funding should be restricted to physicians and hospitals that cared for uninsured patients. This would ensure that hospitals that were actually caring for the uninsured would be appropriately compensated for the free care they delivered. However, DSH funds must also be allocated to pay for the care of patients who have the bronze level of insurance that only covers 60 percent of the cost of a hospitalization and who cannot afford the 40 percent of the costs for which they are responsible.

Spivey and Kellermann also proposed that the ability of states to designate special classes of DSH providers should be eliminated. I would take this recommendation one step further: Funds for hospitals that have a disproportionate share of uninsured or underinsured patients should be paid directly from the federal government and bypass the state. The economic collapse of 2008 placed enormous financial constraints on state governments, and there is little doubt that a pool of money from the federal government is a tempting opportunity for state administrators and legislators to use for expenses other than health care. The only way that hospitals get their fair share of compensation for the delivery of free care is to have the dollars transferred directly from the federal treasury to the hospital. Spivey and Kellermann's third proposal is that hospitals that have an emergency department and participate in a state trauma program should receive additional DSH funding. In Massachusetts near-universal health care coverage resulted in a marked increase in the use of emergency rooms. This was due in part to the fact that Massachusetts did not have enough doctors to provide easy access for the great influx of newly insured patients. Without access to a primary care doctor, the newly insured patients sought medical care in the local emergency rooms. Neither emergency departments nor trauma programs are economically viable as stand-alone entities. I argue that targeted DSH funds should also be provided to hospitals with burn centers, dialysis programs, or regional emergency transportation services—all of which have high costs and low remunerations particularly when they serve lower-income neighborhoods.

Hospitals that support their region's plan for natural or man-made disasters should also receive supplemental funds according to Spivey and Kellermann. I agree that these hospitals incur costs that cannot be recouped from any of the payment strategies that are outlined in the health care reform legislation. I would argue that the federal government should also support a broad range of social services that provide an important medically related service to the community. The cafeteria at Braddock Hospital provided an important meeting place for the elderly of the community and also provided a cheap and reliable place where members of the community could seek shelter and food. DSH payments must also support the care of the indigent, individuals with chronic psychiatric problems or with alcohol or drug abuse, and all illegal immigrants. These patients were excluded from the Patient Protection and Affordable Care Act, but safety net hospitals incur substantial costs for providing for their care.

Perhaps the municipal hospital or safety net hospital is not an icon of the past but a model for the hospital of the future. Municipal hospitals could provide a no-frills, low-cost yet high-quality alternative to the typical private hospital. The municipal hospital of the future should focus on those areas of medicine most relevant to the care of the communities they serve while at the same time creating a regional center for high-quality care in defined areas. For example, a municipal safety net hospital could specialize in cardiovascular disease, cancer, trauma, reconstructive surgery, solid organ transplant, and end-stage kidney disease while avoiding areas such as cosmetic surgery, joint replacement surgery, and sports medicine. Municipal hospitals, by virtue of their alignment with a medical school, can also serve as exceptional training grounds for the next generation of physicians.

The modern municipal hospital, through affiliations with a medical school and university, could have a group of salaried physicians who could readily take advantage of "bundled" payments and who would receive incentives to provide high-quality care—not quantity of care. Municipal hospitals could also create innovative systems for linking the doctors in the hospital with the doctors in the community so that the care of an individual patient could be seamlessly transitioned from the hospital to the home. Programs for the in-home care of patients and close alliances with other social welfare organizations would also be practical. Medical students and residents would have the ability to see community medicine up close and to learn how medical care will be optimally provided in the future. This opportunity would hopefully inspire more doctors to pursue careers in primary care. The alliance between the municipal hospital, a medical school, and schools of nursing and pharmacy also provides the opportunity for students in all health care disciplines to learn together and work together in a multidisciplinary team approach to medical care. However, municipal hospitals will only be able to survive if they receive reimbursement for the care of the complex and underserved patients that at least meet the actual costs of their care.

It is unfortunate that the viability of the health care safety net is being undermined by some state governments. Rick Scott, the conservative governor of Florida, recently formed a commission to review whether government hospitals should continue to exist in Florida at all.[24] Scott once headed the largest for-profit hospital system in the country. He has targeted the Jackson Health System, a sprawling collection of hospitals and clinics in South Florida that cares for some of the state's most disadvantaged patients. The governor has held up payment of $35 million to Jackson that was approved by last year's legislature until the hospital shows a clear plan for long-term sustainability. Doctors at Jackson, meanwhile, struggle to take care of some of the state's most complex patients. Scott believes that there is no role for government-sponsored hospitals, yet he provides no workable solutions to how Florida will be able to care for the large burden of underserved patients in the South Florida area who receive their care at Jackson Memorial Hospital.

Assuming that most Americans would have insurance, the analysts who crafted the Patient Protection and Affordable Care Act eliminated much of the support for safety net hospitals. They also failed to recognize that even with insurance from the exchanges, many Americans will still be responsible for up to 40 percent of their health care costs. It will take substantive changes in the health care reform legislation to ensure that hospitals like Braddock Hospital and Boston Medical Center continue to serve the communities that depend on their survival.

Notes

1. Templeton D. Braddock feverish over hospital closure. *Pittsburgh Post Gazette.* October 20, 2009.

2. Bumstead B. UPMC Braddock Hospital closure may spark U.S. probe, Tribune-Review, Jan 15, 2010, http://www.pittsburghlive.com/x/pittsburghtrib/news/pittsburgh/s_662285.html.
3. Regenstein M, Hwang J. *Stresses to the Safety Net: The Public Hospital Perspective.* June 2005.
4. Hoffman C, Sered S. *Threadbare Holes in American's Health Care Safety Net.* The Kaiser Commission on Medicaid and the Uninsured. www.eff.org. August 2005.
5. Felland LL, Lauer J, Cunningham PJ. *Suburban Poverty and the Health Care Safety Net.* July 2009. Center for Study Health System Change. http://hschange.org/content/1074.
6. Dewan S, Sack K. A safety net hospital falls into financial crisis. *New York Times.* January 8, 2008.
7. Letter of Johns Hopkins to the Trustees, Snowden-Warfield, 2005, http://www.snowden-warfield.com/Stories/Letter-Johns-Hopkins-Trustees.htm.
8. Fishman LE, Bentley JD. The evolution of support for safety-net hospitals. *Health Aff (Millwood).* Jul–Aug 1997;16(4):30–47.
9. Coughlin TA, Liska D. *The Medicaid Disproportionate Share Hospital Payment Program: Background and Issues.* The Urban Institute. October 1997.
10. Spivey M, Kellermann AL. Rescuing the safety net. *N Engl J Med.* Jun 18 2009;360(25):2598–2601.
11. The Potential Impact of Affordable Care Act-Mandated Medicare DSH Cuts on Urban Safety-Net Hospitals, The National Association of Urban Hospitals, Jan 2011, http://www.nauh.org/docs/NAUH09%20study-fin%20challenges.pdf; http://www.ahrq.gov/data/hcup/factbk8/factbk8b.htm.
12. Goodnough A. Massachusetts in suit over cost of universal care. *New York Times.* July 15, 2009.
13. *Safety Net Hospitals.* May 2010.
14. Blustein J, Borden WB, Valentine M. Hospital performance, the local economy, and the local workforce: findings from a US National Longitudinal Study. *PLoS Med.* Jun;7(6):e1000297.
15. Aaron HJ, Reischauer RD. The war isn't over. *N Engl J Med.* Apr 2010, 8;362(14):1259–1261.
16. Kingsdale J. Health insurance exchanges—Key link in a better-value chain. *N Engl J Med.* Jun 10;362(23):2147–2150.
17. Demirjian K. President's opt-out stance may force health care law onto crowded docket. March 11, 2011.
18. Wong P. Doctor's bill's sponsor to speak about single-payer health plan. *Oregon Statesman Journal.* March 12, 2010.
19. Hsiao WC. State-based single-payer health care—A solution for the United States? *N Engl J Med.* Mar 31, 2011;364(13):1188–1190.
20. Jost T. Health Insurance Exchange in Health Care Reform: Legal and Policy Issues. http://www.commonwealthfund.org/Content/Bios/J/Jost-Timothy-Stoltzfus.aspx. December 2009.
21. Keefe B. Georgia, other states: Health mandates to devastate budgets. *Atlanta Journal Constitution.* August 6, 2010.

22. California's Health Benefit Exchange Legislation, Summaries of AB 1602 (Perez) and SB 900 (Alquist & Steinberg), ITUP, Aug 24, 2010. http://www.itup.org/Reports/Health%20Reform/ExchangebillsSummaries08242010FINAL.pdf.
23. Moller J. Louisiana to opt out of health insurance exchanges in federal law. *New Orleans Times-Picayune.* March 23, 2011.
24. Dorschner J. Scott announces board to study public hospitals. *Miami Herald.* March 23, 2011.

Chapter 6

How Can We Improve the Quality of Care in the United States?

> Now, a recent article in the *New Yorker*, for example, showed how McAllen, Texas, is spending twice as much as El Paso County—twice as much—not because people in McAllen, Texas, are sicker than they are in El Paso; not because they're getting better care or getting better outcomes. It's simply because they're using more treatments—treatments that, in some cases, they don't really need; treatments that, in some cases, can actually do people harm by raising the risk of infection or medical error.
>
> **President Barack Obama, Address to the American Medical Association, June 15, 2009**

A decade ago I saw a fifty-one-year-old patient named Mike G. who had come to my office for a second opinion. A year earlier his primary care doctor had ordered a routine exercise stress test for him because he was about to start an exercise program. He had no history of chest pain or any type of cardiac problem. The study had been equivocal, and Mike's physician had recommended that he have a cardiac catheterization and coronary angiography—a common procedure in which dye is injected into the arteries that supply the heart with blood. The cardiologist who performed the procedure told Mike that he had found a significant blockage in one of the arteries feeding the heart muscle with blood and recommended an angioplasty—using a balloon-tipped catheter to open the "clogged vessel." Mike agreed and the procedure was performed without complications.

Mike was well until three months later when he began to have a "squeezing" sensation in his chest when he exercised that went away when he stopped exercising. He called his doctor, who admitted him to the hospital where he underwent a second cardiac catheterization. The cardiologist told him that a blockage had "reoccurred" at the site of his earlier angioplasty—a process that at the time occurred in as many as 15 to 20 percent of patients who had a balloon angioplasty (stents have decreased this number appreciably). Once again the doctor used a balloon to open up Mike's coronary artery, and the following day he was discharged from the hospital. Three months later he again experienced chest pain when he exercised—but this time the pain did not go away when Mike stopped exercising. He was rushed to the hospital and immediately sent to the cardiac catheterization laboratory. Once again the cardiologist found a blockage at the same spot in the same coronary artery, and an emergency balloon angioplasty was performed. Mike was discharged several days later—but having lost confidence in his cardiologist, he came to see me for a second opinion.

There was little that we could do to help Mike's problem in terms of medicines or new procedures. I recommended that if the pain recurred, he should undergo coronary artery bypass grafting using a minimally invasive approach. When the pain recurred three months later, he underwent surgery and did quite well. He has had no subsequent problems. I was confused by the fact that Mike had not had chest pain prior to his first angioplasty procedure—but had significant pain each time the artery threatened to reclose. Something didn't fit. With Mike's permission, I asked the hospital where the original procedure had been performed to send me a copy of the films that recorded the images of the arteries in his heart and the initial procedure. Much to my surprise, the original study showed no abnormality. His doctor had performed the original procedure on a normal coronary artery and had, in fact, caused all of his subsequent problems!

In the fall of 1999, the Institute of Medicine released its report titled *To Err Is Human: Building a Safer Health Care System*.[1] The book was an instant best seller due in part to its observation that nearly 100,000 Americans died needlessly each year because of medical errors. The report attributed the errors to lapses in the care delivery systems found in American hospitals, not to the actions of individual physicians. In a second report, two years later, titled *Crossing the Quality Chasm: A New Health System for the 21st Century* the Institute of Medicine criticized the medical profession.[2] They pointed to the lack of continuity in the care of individual patients, the failure of doctors to effectively communicate with each other or with patients, the inability of doctors to use evidence-based guidelines to direct care, and the lack of accountability on the part of doctors toward their patients or to payers. The report called for the funding of projects to test new models for health care delivery and the identification of high-priority target conditions, but it did not suggest reforms in the structure of our health care delivery system that would improve the quality of care in the United States. The individuals who crafted the Patient Protection and Affordable Care Act have attempted in part to fill that void.

The story of Mike G. is one that resounds with many doctors as well as individuals who have been actively involved in developing health policy and health care reform. In a speech to the American Medical Association in 2009, President Obama pointed out that the problem with American health care is that we have "a system of incentives where the more tests and services are provided, the more money we pay."[3] He didn't come right out and say that doctors were corrupt—but he certainly implied it. The individuals who crafted the Patient Protection and Affordable Care Act were clearly guided by two fundamental beliefs regarding quality of care and the cost of care. The first was that the current fee-for-service reimbursement system for hospitals and doctors causes overutilization of tests and procedures that increase costs. They believed that there is thus an inverse relationship between cost and quality—and doing more for a patient is intrinsically bad care. This fundamental belief supports the concept that cost can be decreased and care improved by simply decreasing payments to doctors and hospitals that have high utilization of tests and procedures.

The second fundamental principle behind health care reform was that we can improve the delivery of care by measuring and publicly reporting the "quality" of care delivered by doctors and hospitals. Patients will then seek out high-quality doctors and hospitals, thereby lowering overall health care costs. In addition, payers can penalize those with low quality scores. In this chapter, we will look at these two fundamental premises of health care reform, discuss the steps that the Patient Protection and Affordable Care Act takes to improve health care quality, and describe how the bill should be modified to best meet its goals of improving the health of the American population.

The Cost–Quality Conundrum

Let's first look at the relationship between utilization, cost, and quality. The perception that we can insure quality in our health care system by simply eliminating overutilization comes from the stories of two obscure towns: Lebanon, New Hampshire, and McAllen, Texas. Lebanon, New Hampshire, is the home of the Dartmouth Institute for Health Policy and Clinical Practice. For over three decades an obscure group of researchers at Dartmouth College have collected data about how doctors and hospitals utilize health care services in the United States and published their results in a book titled the *Dartmouth Atlas* (the atlas is also available on the Web) and in scientific journals. Their data have come from Medicare databases and are most graphically displayed on a map of the United States. The map—a visual cue for health care reformers—colors the various regions in the country based on health care spending in the region. Beige indicated areas of lower spending while chocolate indicated areas of higher spending.

Peter Orzag, the White House budget director, used the maps in presentations during the health care debates, giving Congress and the public the idea that fixing spiraling Medicare costs would be easy—just pay doctors and hospitals in the dark brown zones (areas of overutilization) less.[4] The Dartmouth investigators took the concept one step further. They posited that not only do high-spending areas fail to provide better care, but they actually offer worse care. In testimony before Congress, the Dartmouth researchers tried to convince Congress that access to care and quality of care were worse in high-spending regions. They noted that "sending people with chronic diseases to higher-efficiency, lower-utilization hospitals for their care could result in lower spending, increased quality and [shorter] length of stay."[5]

The notion that "costlier care is often worse care" was reinforced in the minds of the public by an article by Atul Gawande titled "The Cost Conundrum: What a Texas Town Can Teach Us about Health Care" that was published in the *New Yorker* magazine in June 2009.[6] Gawande, a Harvard surgeon and author of several best-selling books about his experiences as a doctor, described his visit to McAllen, Texas—one of the most expensive health care markets in the country. Gawande referred to the findings of the Dartmouth group in noting that "the more money Medicare spent per person in a given state the lower that state's quality ranking tended to be." He also pointed out that "the four states with the highest levels of spending—Louisiana, Texas, California, and Florida—were near the bottom of the national rankings on the quality of patient care" and that patients in high-cost states were less likely to have a primary-care physician and to receive important preventive services.

Gawande contrasts McAllen and high-spending institutions such as the UCLA Medical Center in Los Angeles and NYU–Langhorne Medical Center in Manhattan with institutions like the Mayo Clinic, the Geisinger Health System in Danville, Pennsylvania, the Marshfield Clinic in Marshfield, Wisconsin, Intermountain Healthcare in Salt Lake City, and Kaiser Permanente in Northern California where doctors and hospital systems adopted measures to lower spending and improve patient care. He paints McAllen's physicians as greedy when he quotes a local cardiac surgeon describing McAllen as a "pig trough." The surgeon goes on to note that in McAllen "we took a wrong turn when doctors stopped being doctors and became businessmen." President Obama said almost the same thing in his remarks to the American Medical Association when he noted that our reimbursement system "is a model that has taken the pursuit of medicine from a profession—a calling—to a business."[3] With the *Dartmouth Atlas* in one arm and the *New Yorker* magazine under the other, the Obama administration had the ammunition it needed to forge ahead during the health care reform debates.

Despite the prevailing view of Democrats that the Dartmouth group is the poster child for health care reform, there has been vocal criticism from academicians and health care experts who are angered by the Dartmouth group's interpretation of their data and the way in which they have proselytized their findings. The level of controversy is reflected in two highly visible sets of publications. First, in its February 18, 2010, issue, the *New England Journal of Medicine* took the unprecedented step of publishing side-by-side articles.[7, 8] One article was written by Peter Bach, a physician and highly respected health care economist from Memorial Sloan-Kettering Cancer Center in New York. The companion article was written by Jonathan Skinner and Elliott Fisher, both of whom are from the *Dartmouth Atlas*.

The controversy also played out in a series of articles in the *New York Times*. In an article published in June 2010, two senior investigative reporters for the *Times*, Reed Abelson and Gardiner Harris, challenged the interpretation of the Dartmouth studies "that the hospitals and geographic regions with the highest medical spending are often the ones delivering the worst medical care."[4] The *Times* was unequivocal in its criticism of the Dartmouth findings. In their front-page article they noted that "there is little evidence to support the widely held view, shaped by the Dartmouth researchers, that the nation's best hospitals tend to be among the least expensive." They pointed out the flaws in the Dartmouth report and criticized Skinner and Fisher for berating critics for developing "a cottage industry in new studies trying to debunk our findings." When the Dartmouth researchers rebutted the article's claims on their website, the *Times* reporters responded with a second lengthy article in the June 16, 2010, issue of the paper.[9]

The *Dartmouth Atlas* and Health Care Reform

A thorough discussion of the Dartmouth research is outside the scope of this book; however, it is important for me to provide the reader with a fundamental understanding of the concerns that have been raised by health care economists and statisticians about the Dartmouth studies in view of the central role that both the studies and the investigators have played in the health care debates.

The *Dartmouth Atlas* analyzed all health care costs that were incurred by Medicare beneficiaries over the two years prior to their deaths. All costs were attributed to the hospital where they received most of their care and to the doctors at that hospital. Their methods assumed that the hospital controlled all of the health care costs. What are the flaws in the study? First, hospitals influence the acute care of a patient but may have little control of subsequent care in the outpatient setting or of subsequent hospitalizations. In fact, one-third of the Medicare beneficiaries included in the analysis had only been admitted to the designated hospital one time.

A second major flaw in the Dartmouth analysis is that it does not factor outcomes into the analysis—whether the patients survive their treatment or die. Cost and outcomes must be considered together. Take, for example, hospital A and hospital B. Hospital A admits five Medicare beneficiaries who are having a heart attack. They do not treat the five heart attack patients in an appropriate manner, and four of them die. Their spending would be low—because they didn't take advantage of all of the expensive procedures that could be used to effectively intervene in a patient with a heart attack—but their outcomes would be poor. Alternatively, hospital B keeps a cardiac catheterization laboratory open and a cardiologist on call 24/7. Four of the five patients admitted to hospital B survive because the hospital has all of the sophisticated technology and expensive medications necessary to intervene successfully—but the costs are high. The *Dartmouth Atlas* analysis would show hospital B as being more expensive and the area served by hospital B would appear dark brown on the Dartmouth map. Health care administrators would target hospital B for a reduction in reimbursement, and the collateral damage would be significant. With fewer dollars, hospital B would have to close its acute heart attack program, lowering the quality of care for heart attack patients but lowering health care costs.[4]

Another flaw in the *Dartmouth Atlas* analysis is that the focus is exclusively on patients who died—not on patients who survived.[10] The *Atlas* researchers argue that if all of the patients in the analysis died, it means that they all had a similar severity of disease. This argument is disingenuous. It ignores the fact that different hospitals take care of varying severity of illness. The death rate at a hospital that takes care of very sick patients should not be the same as the rate of death at a smaller community hospital that takes care of patients who are in relatively better health. In fact, the risk of death has been found to vary between 6 and 22 percent at different hospitals based on the severity of illness of the patients they treat. A patient who is very sick will also require greater resource use than a patient who is far less sick. If we don't account for the severity of the illness of a hospital's patients, hospitals that have low severity would look far more efficient than hospitals with high severity even if the efficiencies or outcomes of the hospitals were the same. Dollars that are consumed in the care of a patient who dies are therefore a poor substitute for costs of care for other patients in the same hospital or for the hospital as a whole.

The concerns about the interpretation of the *Dartmouth Atlas* by Democratic leadership are not simply based on empirical judgment. Research studies clearly support the concept that assessing utilization or cost without also measuring patient outcomes can provide misleading information. Two medical centers that were portrayed by the Dartmouth group as having excessive costs were Cedars-Sinai Medical Center in Los Angeles and New York University Medical Center. High-performing centers included the Mayo Clinic, the Cleveland Clinic, Intermountain Healthcare, and Geisinger Medical Center. Langberg and Black reported in a 2009 issue of the *New England Journal of Medicine* that the mortality rate among patients with heart failure was significantly worse than the national average for one of the high-performing hospitals while only two of the four high-performing hospitals reported lower than expected mortality in patients with heart failure.[11] All four of the high-performing group had only average success with pneumonia patients. By contrast, Cedars-Sinai and NYU—low-performing health centers according to the Dartmouth group—had mortality rates for all three conditions that were substantially better than the national average while rates for readmission were consistent with national averages. A study at six California teaching hospitals found similar results.[12] The six-month mortality for patients with heart failure was significantly lower at higher-cost hospitals than at lower-cost hospitals. Abelson and Harris, in their *New York Times* article, described a Wisconsin hospital that ranked fourth on the Dartmouth list of low-spending/high-efficiency hospitals but was sixty-seventh out of sixty-eight Wisconsin hospitals when mortality rates were measured. And, the *Dartmouth Atlas* ranks New Jersey dead last because of high Medicare costs, but federal health officials rank New Jersey second only to Vermont in terms of quality of care.[4]

It is clear that there are regional variations in the intensity of hospital and physician services regardless of the side of the debate you happen to be on. A recent study by the Dartmouth group looked at Medicare claims data from 1999 through 2006. They then divided regions into five groups according to the intensity of care. There was over a 50 percent difference between utilization in the highest group and the lowest group.[13] When a group from the Urban Institute in Washington DC adjusted the data to account for the severity of illness in the different groups, the difference in spending between the highest and lowest group was reduced to 33 percent.[14] How much variation should there be between the care given in different areas of the country? The constant yet uneven flow of new technology and drugs (most of which are more expensive than older treatments), the ever-changing scientific literature, and the almost constant revisions in practice guidelines make it almost impossible to avoid variation in patient care. New technology gets to Haynesville, Louisiana, far slower than it does to the Mayo Clinic or to Johns Hopkins. The question then becomes how much variation is acceptable—and more importantly, how much represents overuse and how much represents good medical practice? No one has yet answered these questions.

Measuring Quality of Care

There are also flaws in the second fundamental principle that guided the congressional staffers who crafted the health care reform legislation—that we can improve the delivery of care by measuring and publicly reporting the quality of care delivered by doctors and hospitals. We routinely measure various parameters that reflect how hospitals take care of patients, but these are measures referred to as process of care and are rarely measures of quality of care. What is the difference? Let's look again at Mike G. When he was admitted to the hospital for his initial cardiac catheterization, a series of events took place to ensure his safety. He was given a wrist tag with his name, a nurse made sure that the laboratory values that were obtained prior to his procedure were within the normal range, the nurse checked to make sure he was not allergic to any medications, and he signed a consent form. After the procedure he was given prescriptions for medicines that would help keep his artery open and that would lower his cholesterol. All of these were process measures.[15] The most important quality measure—did he need the procedure in the first place—was not evaluated. His doctor would have scored high on process measures but would have failed any measure of quality.

Quality measures are far more difficult to ascertain than process measures. The American College of Cardiology and the American Heart Association have focused their efforts on improving the quality of care for patients with heart disease for over fifty years. They have published practice guidelines that provide doctors with clear and concise recommendations about how to treat patients with a variety of heart problems.[16] In the age of rapid communication, the guidelines are constantly updated as new information becomes available from clinical studies, and physicians are often informed about guideline changes through social networks and the Web. The guidelines regarding the evaluation and care of patients with coronary artery disease note that the procedure Mike G. had is a "demanding, technically complex procedure" and that "the potential exists for substantial variations in quality among both operators and institutions."[17] The guidelines recommend that all procedures performed at a hospital be reviewed by a group of experts who can judge all of the facets of the procedure from start to finish. A review of the care provided by Mike G.'s cardiologist by a committee of his peers would have shown that he had received an unnecessary procedure. This type of review is unfortunately performed at very few hospitals in the country due to the complex political, financial, and legal issues that can arise when peers review each other's performance. The Patient Protection and Affordable Care Act would have been far more effective in improving the quality of care in the United States if it had enforced the need for hospitals to perform these types of quality reviews.

Measuring Quality of Care: The Health Care Reform Legislation

The concern about confusing process with quality is far more than an academic exercise because the Patient Protection and Affordable Care Act funds the development of a Physician-Compare website that will provide information on physicians enrolled in the Medicare program. The report card will be based on quality and measures of patient satisfaction. Patients will actually receive financial incentives for receiving their care from physicians who score well on their report cards. Private insurance companies and some employers are also beginning to direct beneficiaries to a small panel of high-quality and low-cost physicians to decrease their costs by as much as 15 percent.[18] If employees go to a doctor who is excluded from the plan, they must pay the entire bill out of their own pockets. Insurers are betting that the lower costs of plans that identify a very small panel of doctors will attract a substantial number of enrollees at a time when affordability is paramount while at the same time lowering their own health care costs. These efforts to direct patients to so-called high-quality physicians are unlikely to prove helpful because studies have been unable to find a relationship between public disclosure of report card evaluations and patient outcomes.

Another problem with our existing measures of so-called quality of care is that many of the measures are very attainable by most hospitals. Something simple like giving an aspirin to a patient who comes to the emergency room with chest pain or giving a beta-blocker to a patient who has been hospitalized after a heart attack is easy for most hospitals to accomplish. Only significant outliers are picked up. In a group of large employers who came together in 1998 to identify how they could work together to influence health care quality and affordability, Lea Binder, the CEO of the Leapfrog, noted, "The problem with the CMS [Center for Medicare and Medicaid Services] data is that most hospitals look average, which isn't what employers want. What they want is to compare hospitals."[19] It is unfortunate that no one is willing to provide the kind of quality measures that would really be useful in identifying high-quality doctors and hospitals, and therefore we are stuck with poor measures of comparison.

Patients should be concerned about both the public reporting of quality metrics and the efforts of both CMS and private insurers to use these metrics to direct patients to presumably high-quality providers.[20] If the metrics that are used to measure a doctor's or a hospital's quality of care are flawed, a health insurer may direct an individual to a physician or hospital that does not deliver the kind of care an individual wants or expects. An unintended consequence of public reporting is that physicians and hospitals may avoid seeing patients or even refuse to see patients who are chronically ill or have extensive disease in an attempt to improve their quality scores. Physicians may also limit their utilization of expensive technology or drugs or discount patient preferences and their own clinical judgment to score well on their report card.[20] Ironically, most patients don't pay attention to public reporting and go to doctors that they hear about through friends.[21] Many patients care more about access, cost, having a choice of physicians, and physician qualifications than they do about measures of quality of care.[22]

Pay-for-Performance

The health care reform bill also funds demonstration projects to test the use of pay-for-performance reimbursement strategies for doctors. The rationale for these pilot studies is that doctors will provide better care if they receive incentives to do so, but there is little evidence that they will actually lower costs or improve care.[23] In a report published in 2006, a group from Houston reviewed all of the existing studies on the relationship between pay-for-performance programs and the quality of health care and found mixed results.[24] Some studies showed a positive effect on access to care while others showed a negative effect—particularly for patients with significant disease.

Pay-for-performance programs can also have unintended consequences for medical care. A report in *Health Affairs* detailed a study of some 35,000 doctors in California who care for 6.2 million patients.[25] The doctors revealed that they drop noncompliant patients and refuse to treat people with complicated illnesses since their outcomes would make the doctor's statistics look bad. Researchers from the Brigham and Women's Hospital—one of Harvard's hospitals—found very similar results.[26] They found that cardiologists deny lifesaving procedures on very sick patients out of fear that they would receive a low grade for the care they delivered because the outcome in very sick patients was often poor. Another confounding problem with pay-for-performance programs is that relatively few primary care practices and even many subspecialty practices are large enough to reliably measure differences in common measures of quality.

Electronic Health Record

The congressional staff that crafted the health care reform legislation also made the assumption that the electronic health record will help to improve quality of care and lower health care costs. The bill states that doctors who fail to report on quality measures using the electronic health record by 2015 will be penalized. This mandate implies that all doctors will have access to an electronic health record by 2015—something that is highly unlikely. It also assumes that the electronic health record can be used to access quality metrics—right now most systems can't. Every existing electronic health record is created around billing codes—they do not provide an opportunity to readily input information that would be useful in judging the quality of care.[27] The congressional staffers who crafted the health care reform legislation also made the assumption that the electronic health record could improve the quality of care by reminding doctors that they needed to order a particular test or procedure and by helping the doctor to interpret complex data about a given patient. They unfortunately failed to pay attention to an exhaustive review of one hundred clinical studies that found that when doctors used the computer to make decisions about how to care for a patient, the doctors usually made better decisions than the computer.[28]

Value-Based Purchasing

It is not just physicians who will be judged by report cards. The health care reform legislation also directs the secretary of Health and Human Services to establish a "value-based" purchasing demonstration program that will reward hospitals for providing high-quality care. Our ability to judge the quality of a hospital is no better than our ability to evaluate doctors. A good example of the metrics used to evaluate the quality of care that hospitals provide are those that measure the care provided for patients with congestive heart failure. There are five quality indicators that have been established for the care of a patient with heart failure: Was the patient's weight recorded each day? Did the doctor evaluate heart function? Did the patient receive a drug called an angiotensin converting enzyme inhibitor (ACE) inhibitor? Was the patient counseled about smoking cessation? And was the patient given clear instructions at discharge? While all of these items are important, they are measures of process and not of quality of care. In fact, a study led by a group of UCLA researchers showed that when hospitals worked to ensure that these process measures were met, the outcome of the patients as measured by their long-term survival did not change.[29]

Substantive Steps Taken by the Patient Protection and Affordable Care Act

I would be disingenuous if I didn't point out that the Patient Protection and Affordable Care Act does take a number of substantive steps to improve the quality of care for individuals who are insured by federal insurance programs. Hospitals will be penalized if they have high rates of hospital-acquired infections or surgical errors. Beginning in 2014 long-term care hospitals, inpatient rehabilitation hospitals, and hospices will also be required to submit data on specific quality measures and inpatient cancer hospitals will be required to establish quality-reporting programs by 2014. Another group that has been largely overlooked in terms of quality reporting is skilled nursing facilities, home health agencies, and ambulatory surgical centers. This group will also be required to report quality measures and payments will be predicated on meeting defined quality metrics. The health care reform legislation also provides important safeguards for the elderly—in particular those who are cared for in nursing homes and similar facilities.

The Patient Protection and Affordable Care Act directs the secretary of HHS to establish a National Strategy for Quality Improvement in Health Care Services, Patient Health Outcomes, and Population Health. The secretary is charged with impaneling a multidisciplinary group of experts who will identify opportunities to create new quality measures and to identify existing quality measures that need updating, improvement, or modifications. The Department of Health and Human Services will then fund grants to organizations to implement the recommendations put forward by the group. Information gleaned from this work will be disseminated to the public through websites. Hopefully this group will recognize the need to develop more accurate and appropriate measures of quality that will allow us to move away from simply measuring processes.

The Patient Protection and Affordable Care legislation also appropriates money for the Center for Quality Improvement and Patient Safety of the Agency for Healthcare Research and Quality to develop and evaluate tools to improve the adoption of clinical research and best practice guidelines in the community. This is an important component of the health care reform legislation. Each year hundreds of medical journals report the results of large clinical trials that can inform doctors on how best to care for their patients. Professional societies publish thousands of new practice guidelines and updates each year. The translation of this mass of data from clinical trials and practice guidelines to actual changes in practice in the community is exceedingly slow. Doctors are overwhelmed by their daily workloads and have little time to peruse the many journals that publish new studies or to carefully read lengthy practice guidelines. Novel methods to bring new knowledge to the community practice are sorely needed.

The writers of the Patient Protection and Affordable Care Act correctly recognized that the best care for patients with chronic or complex disease is provided by a team of doctors and nurses who collaborate in the care of the patient. The bill provides funding for the establishment of community-based interdisciplinary teams composed of specialists, occupational and physical therapists, nurses, and primary care physicians. It also provides funding for grants that will allow hospitals or physician practices to incorporate pharmacists into the multidisciplinary care team to ensure that patients with chronic disease receive the most effective medications while being cognizant of costs and the potential use of generic drugs.

It is clear that the Patient Protection and Affordable Care Act was influenced by the personal interests of individual members of Congress, the congressional staff who wrote the bill, or influential donors because the bill targets funding for a group of medical problems that are underrepresented in the general population—what we might call "health care pork." The bill, for example, provides funding for grants to support research in pediatric emergency medical care systems, creation of pediatric emergency medicine programs, creation of national centers of excellence in the evaluation of depression, development of a national coordinating center for depression, development of a disease management program for depressive disorders, expansion of infrastructure to track the epidemiology of congenital heart disease, organization of information into a national congenital heart disease surveillance system, and expansion of research and related activities on congenital heart disease. The bill also appropriates funding for a young women's breast health education and awareness program, a national education campaign to increase young women's knowledge regarding breast health and breast cancer, an education campaign among physicians and other health professionals to increase awareness of breast health of young women, methods for early detection of breast cancer in young women, and prevention research on breast cancer in younger women. It is unfortunate that the bill didn't focus on diseases that are far more common and for which there is a great need such as heart failure, lung cancer, prostate cancer, and end-stage kidney disease.

The health care reform legislation does augment efforts at public health by providing grants to improve public access defibrillation programs, to study new treatments for breast cancer, to create a national diabetes prevention program targeted at adults at high risk for diabetes, and to enable states to award grants for the improvement of trauma services and for early detection of diseases caused by environmental exposures. The authors of the bill also recognized that the care of the American public could be markedly enhanced by helping people to participate in making important decisions about their care—particularly when there are a group of choices with various risks and outcomes. The bill therefore provides funding for the development, implementation, and evaluation of shared decision-making aids and tools and the creation of Shared Decision-Making Resource Centers. The bill seeks to improve the ability of patients to work their way through the complexities of a health care system by providing grants for patient navigators and by creating easy-to-understand summaries of drug risks and benefits.

The public has lost trust in their physicians because of numerous articles in the lay press detailing incidences in which doctors use devices or drugs because they have a monetary relationship with the manufacturer. The Patient Protection and Affordable Care bill attempts to limit doctors' conflicts of interest by prohibiting physicians from building and owning hospitals. It also mandates that drug companies, device companies, and medical supply manufacturers report payments and gifts that are made to an individual physician or to a teaching hospital. Drug and device companies must also disclose the names of doctors who have equity or another form of ownership in their company however, the regulatory agency had recently weakened this mandate by limiting public disclosure. The new law also limits the ability of a physician to refer patients only to testing facilities that they own and requires public disclosure of rebates or discounts that pharmaceutical companies provide to hospitals that use their drugs. These mandates are important and should improve health care quality while lowering costs.

The bill also appropriates awards to support the development of community-based collaborative care networks focused on low-income populations and for the establishment of offices of minority health within the Department of Health and Human Services and the National Institutes of Health. Perhaps most importantly, the bill requires the secretary of HHS, acting through the director of the National Institutes of Health, to implement the Cure Acceleration Network, a mechanism to accelerate the development of high-need cures.

What Additional Steps Should Congress Take to Ensure Quality of Care?

What must our elected officials do over the months and years ahead to see to it that the health care reform bill meets its goal of protecting patients and improving quality? Officials must first create new quality metrics and ensure their value by testing them in clinical trials. We must also dispel the myth that there is a direct link between cost and quality. There is no reason to assume that hospitals with higher costs and utilization are "bad" hospitals. This can only be shown with the proper types of analyses that assess patient outcomes and not processes and that adjust data for the severity of an individual's disease. Any efforts to direct patients to a panel of providers or to selected hospitals must be done with great caution and must be based exclusively on the quality of care that the panel provides and not just on cost. The primary goal of health care reform must be to improve the value of health care—not just to lower cost.

A major oversight of the health care reform legislation was that the individuals who wrote the Patient Protection and Affordable Care Act paid a great deal of attention to what they believed was a relationship between quality and cost but ignored the irrefutable link between quality and volume. The volume of a specific procedure that is performed by an individual doctor or hospital is the one metric that has repeatedly been linked to quality care. A radiologist should read at least 1,000 mammograms each year and perhaps over 2,500 per year to be competent. Hospitals that perform over seventy carotid endarterectomies (a procedure in which plaque is removed from the carotid artery to decrease the risk of stroke) each year have a mortality rate that is nearly half of that found in hospitals that perform fewer than forty of these procedures a year. Surgeons who perform at least forty radical prostatectomies each year have a better incidence of cancer control with a lower risk of incontinence and impotence than surgeons who have a lower volume—a metric that I paid particular attention to in choosing my own surgeon. In fact, for virtually every procedure that is performed by a physician in his or her office or in a hospital, clinical studies have unequivocally demonstrated a relationship between volume and quality.

The Leapfrog Group, a consortium of major U.S. Fortune 500 companies and other large private and public groups that spend billions each year on health care for their millions of employees and retirees, was formed to develop principles by which its members could guide their purchase of health care based on measurements of quality and patient safety.[30] The Leapfrog Group has recognized the direct relationship between quality and volume. A good example of their work is seen in their evaluation of programs that perform coronary artery bypass grafting (CABG) procedures. Hospitals that perform CABG must adhere to process measures and have a low mortality rate—but most importantly they must meet volume criteria (450 or more procedures per year).

So why is the word *volume* not found in the Patient Protection and Affordable Care Act? The answer is politics. Many if not most suburban communities in America have their own community hospitals. They view their community hospitals with a great sense of pride. The more programs the community hospital supports, the more proud the community can be. In states without certificate of need requirements, laws that mandate that hospitals providing a particular procedure meet volume requirements, each community wants its own prostate cancer center, its own open-heart surgery program, and its own acute care emergency room. Just look at the Philadelphia region. Fewer than half of the hospitals in the metropolitan region that support open-heart surgery programs have a volume that meets the Leapfrog guidelines and nearly a third have volumes that are less than half those prescribed by the Leapfrog Group. In some cases, these low-volume hospitals have higher than expected mortality; however, any congressional representatives who would vote to exclude their own community hospitals from receiving Medicare or Medicaid payments are unlikely to be reelected.

State politics play a key role in supporting these low-volume, low-quality programs. Until the federal government addresses the issue of hospital and physician volume, federal regulators will not be able to adequately improve quality. Since hospitals that do more of any given procedure have a lower cost for that procedure than hospitals that do fewer of those procedures, the overall health care costs could also be substantially decreased by instituting payment reforms that eliminate low-volume providers. CMS could institute these types of controls without having to worry about local politics—eliminating Medicare coverage to low-volume providers would solve the problem.

High-quality and trustworthy practice guidelines can help direct how a doctor delivers care, can be used to measure quality of care, and can serve as a core for improving health care quality. Creating guidelines is time consuming and expensive and can suffer from shortcomings in development if not done correctly. The U.S. Congress, through the Medicare Improvements for Patients and Providers Act of 2008, asked the Institute of Medicine (IOM) to study the best methods for developing clinical practice guidelines. The IOM identified eight criteria that marked high-quality guidelines.[31] They should be based on a systematic review of the evidence; be developed by a knowledgeable, multidisciplinary panel of experts; provide a clear explanation of the logical relationships between alternative care options and health outcomes; provide ratings of both the quality of evidence and the strength of recommendations; and be reconsidered and revised when important new evidence arises. A second IOM committee developed similar standards for creating "Systematic Reviews"—a review of the evidence that supports the benefits or harm of drugs, devices, or other services used to treat a single disease or medical problem.[32] These two authoritative reports should serve as the platform for medical societies to undertake the creation of useful guidelines and systematic reviews. This process must be adequately funded by the secretary of CMS through grants and contracts as part of the department's charge to improve the overall quality of health care in the United States.

Our escalating health care costs could clearly be tempered by developing a system of care that rewards quality. Michael Porter points out that when we improve quality and decrease cost, we provide value in our health care delivery system.[33] The Patient Protection and Affordable Care Act is a good start in rewarding doctors and hospitals based on the quality of care they provide. We must continue to bend the cost curve by developing metrics that actually measure quality and not simply processes of care, creating practice guidelines to guide medical therapy, developing new ways to transfer information from clinical trials to the practicing physician, and instituting legislation that rewards centers that have high volumes and high quality and penalizes centers that have low quality because of low volume. Achieving these lofty goals will be not be easy and it will not occur overnight—it will be a daunting challenge.[34]

Notes

1. Kohn LT, Corrigan I, Donaldson MS eds., Committee on Quality of Health Care in America. *To Err Is Human: Building a Safer Health System*. Washington, DC: National Academy Press; 1999.
2. Committee on Quality of Health Care in America, ed. *Crossing the Quality Chasm: A New Health System for the 21st Century*. Washington, DC: National Academy Press. Institute of Medicine, ed.
3. Obama B. Remarks by the President to the Annual Conference of the American Medical Association 2009.
4. Abelson R, Harris G. Critics question study cited in health debate. *New York Times*. June 2, 2010.
5. Understanding of the Efficiency and Effectiveness of the Health Care System, The Dartmouth Atlas of Health Care, 2011. http://www.dartmouthatlas.org/tools/faq/hospital.aspx.
6. Gawande A. The Cost Conundrum—What a Texas town can teach us about health care. *The New Yorker*. http://www.newyorker.com/reporting/2009/06/01 ed; 2009.
7. Bach PB. A map to bad policy—Hospital efficiency measures in the Dartmouth Atlas. *N Engl J Med*. Feb 18;362(7):569–573; discussion p. 574.
8. Skinner J, Staiger D, Fisher ES. Looking back, moving forward. *N Engl J Med*. Feb 18;362(7):569–574; discussion p. 574.
9. Dartmouth Atlas of Health. June 18, 2010 (http://economix.blogs.nytimes.com/tag/dartmouth-atlas-of-health/).
10. Abelson R. Weighing medical costs of end of life care. *New York Times*. December 22, 2009.
11. Langberg ML, Black JT. Dead souls—Comparing Dartmouth Atlas benchmarks with CMS outcomes data. *N Engl J Med*. Nov 26, 2009;361(22):e109.
12. Ong MK, Mangione CM, Romano PS et al. Looking forward, looking back: Assessing variations in hospital resource use and outcomes for elderly patients with heart failure. *Circ Cardiovasc Qual Outcomes*. Nov 2009;2(6):548–557.
13. Skinner J, Fisher ES. Reflections on Geographic Variations in U.S. Health Care, The Dartmouth Institute for Health Policy and Clinical Practice, March 31, 2010 (updated May 12, 2010). http://www.dartmouthatlas.org/downloads/press/Skinner_Fisher_DA_05_10.pdf.
14. Zuckerman S, Waidmann T, Berenson R et al. Clarifying sources of geographic differences in Medicare spending. *N Engl J Med*. Jul 1, 2010;363(1):54–62.

15. Fraker TD, Fihnm SD writing on behalf of the 2002 Chronic Stable Angina Writing Comm, Chronic Angina Focused Update: 2007 Chronic Angina Focused Update of the ACC/AHA 2002 Guidelines for the Management of Patients with Chronic Stable Angina, *J Am Coll Cardiol*, 2007, 50: 2264–2274. http://content.onlinejacc.org/cgi/content/full/50/23/2264.
16. ACCF/AHA Task Force on Practice Guidelines, ACCF/AHA Clinical Practice Guidelines, The American College of Cardiology: Statements and Clinical Practice Guidelines, http://content.onlinejacc.org/misc/guidelines.dtl.
17. Kushner FG, Hand M, Smith SC Jr, King SB 3rd, Anderson JL, Antman EM, Bailey SR, Bates ER, Blankenship JC, Casey DE Jr, Green LA, Hochman JS, Jacobs AK, Krumholz HM, Morrison DA, Ornato JP, Pearle DL, Peterson ED, Sloan MA, Whitlow PL, Williams DO, 2009 focused updates: ACC/AHA guidelines for the management of patients with ST-elevation myocardial infarction (updating the 2004 guideline and 2007 focused update) and ACC/AHA/SCAI guidelines on percutaneous coronary intervention (updating the 2005 guideline and 2007 focused update) a report of the American College of Cardiology Foundation/American Heart Association Task Force on Practice Guidelines, *J Am Coll Cardiol*, 2009 Dec 1: 54(23):2205–41. http://content.onlinejacc.org/cgi/content/full/j.jacc.2009.10.015.
18. Abelson R. Insurers push plans that limit choice of doctors. *New York Times*. July 18, 2010.
19. Sternberg S, DeBarros A. Hospital death rates unveiled for first-time comparison. *USA Today*. August 21, 2008.
20. Werner RM, Asch DA. The unintended consequences of publicly reporting quality information. *JAMA*. Mar 9, 2005;293(10):1239–1244.
21. Fung CH, Lim YW, Mattke S et al. Systematic review: The evidence that publishing patient care performance data improves quality of care. *Ann Intern Med*. Jan 15, 2008;148(2):111–123.
22. Hibbard JH. What can we say about the impact of public reporting? Inconsistent execution yields variable results. *Ann Intern Med*. Jan 15, 2008;148(2):160–161.
23. Glickman SW, Ou FS, DeLong ER et al. Pay for performance, quality of care, and outcomes in acute myocardial infarction. *JAMA*. Jun 6, 2007;297(21):2373–2380.
24. Petersen LA, Woodard LD, Urech T et al. Does pay-for-performance improve the quality of health care? *Ann Intern Med*. Aug 15, 2006;145(4):265–272.
25. Damberg CL, Raube K, Teleki SS, dela Cruz E, Taking Stocke of Pay-for-Performance: A Candid Assessment from the Front Lines, Health Aff, March/Apr 2009, 28(2), 517–525. nline.wsj.com/.../SB123914878625199185.html.
26. Resnic FS, Welt FG. The public health hazards of risk avoidance associated with public reporting of risk-adjusted outcomes in coronary intervention. *J Am Coll Cardiol*. Mar 10, 2009;53(10):825–830.
27. Haig S. Wrong Prescription. *Time*. March 26, 2009 (http://www.time.com/time/magazine/article/0,9171,1887841,00.html).
28. Garg AX, Adhikari NK, McDonald H et al. Effects of computerized clinical decision support systems on practitioner performance and patient outcomes: A systematic review. *JAMA*. Mar 9, 2005;293(10):1223–1238.

29. Fonarow GC, Peterson ED. Heart failure performance measures and outcomes: Real or illusory gains. *JAMA*. Aug 19, 2009;302(7):792–794.
30. Evidence-Based Hospital Referral, the Leapfrog Group. http://www.leapfroggroup.org/media/file/FactSheet_EBHR.pdf. Accessed March 21, 2011.
31. *Clinical Practice Guidelines We Can Trust*: Institute of Medicine. March 23, 2011.
32. Finding What Works in Health Care: Standards for Systematic Reviews, Institute of Medicine, March 23, 2011. *Systematic Reviews*: Institute of Medicine.
33. Porter ME. A strategy for health care reform—Toward a value-based system. *N Engl J Med*. Jul 9, 2009;361(2):109–112.
34. Lee TH. Putting the value framework to work. *N Engl J Med*. Dec 23, 2010;363(26):2481–2483.

Chapter 7

Will There Be Enough Doctors to Care for 35 Million New Patients?

> Our nation currently faces a shortage of physicians expected to worsen as the number of people over age 65 (who use more than twice the health care of younger adults) doubles. Even with significant changes to the health-care delivery system and improved prevention, the United States will face a shortage of more than 125,000 physicians in the next 15 years—a daunting problem considering that we only train about 27,000 new doctors a year.
>
> **Darrell G. Kirch, President, the Association of American Medical Colleges, *Wall Street Journal*, January 4, 2010**
>
> And we need to rethink the cost of a medical education, and do more to reward medical students who choose a career as a primary care physician—who choose to work in underserved areas instead of the more lucrative paths.
>
> **President Barack Obama, Address to the American Medical Association, September 15, 2009**

Tamara Fisicaro is a young woman who went from high school to the Cleveland-San Jose Ballet Company. Eventually she turned to medicine. This change was not surprising because medicine was in her genes. Her father and three siblings are all doctors. After completing her residency in internal medicine she spent an additional year as a chief medical resident—teaching students and guiding younger residents. She is married to a physician, and they have two children. Tamara works in a six-physician primary care practice in southern New Jersey—ten miles from Center City Philadelphia. She works three days a week and uses the other days to "catch up" on nonpatient work and "overflow."

Tamara and her colleagues work in an office that includes two nurse practitioners and two physician assistants. The physician-extenders provide acute care, short-term follow-up, and care for patients with chronic diseases including high blood pressure and diabetes. The practice includes a practice manager and numerous support staff that provide secretarial support, keep the records organized, handle all billing issues, and obtain precertification for procedures and referrals. Tamara receives a salary for her work but is eligible to receive a bonus. The office is open until 9:00 p.m. most nights and has Saturday hours until 1:00 p.m. The doctors provide only outpatient care—patients requiring hospitalization are cared for in the hospital by a doctor who just works in the hospital (a hospitalist) or by a specialist. The practice does not have an economic relationship with any single hospital—patients are sent wherever the doctors believe they will get the best care. Patients with minor problems are often sent to the local community hospital while patients with major medical needs are often sent to quaternary teaching hospitals in Philadelphia. The practice is part of a centralized corporation of thirty practices that negotiate together for contracts with insurance companies and with vendors for supplies. The larger group is multidisciplinary and includes pediatrics, endocrinology, urology, and ear, nose, and throat.

Tamara's practice is paper free—everything is done on the computer. She describes the electronic health record in one word—"fantastic." She uses the electronic health record to write prescriptions and to provide a problem list on each patient, and the practice uses it for quality reviews. A nurse enters the patient's allergies and vital signs, and an office staff scans documents into the medical record that arrive on paper including laboratory results. Drop-down screens remind her to order tests or procedures when appropriate. The electronic record enables the practice to link with the thirty partnering practices and also facilitates the ability of the practice to carry out clinical research.

Tamara doesn't see health care reform as a threat but rather as an opportunity for many of her patients to receive better care. Her practice is a window into Middle America. She notes that the majority of her patients "hold jobs that do not provide health insurance benefits." They are independent contractors, electricians, carpenters, mechanics, plumbers, builders, and shopkeepers. They range in age from the late twenties to the early forties and pay for their visits to the doctor out of their own pockets. Tamara also sees an opportunity for "getting paid for things that we don't now get paid for as well as providing my patients with better and earlier access to care." The largest obstacle Tamara has faced is getting mental health care for her patients. "Most psychiatrists don't take insurance, and even when they do, it is hard to find a psychiatrist who is able to see new patients," she notes.

Tamara Fisicaro is the new American doctor: young, female, smart, well-trained, committed to quality care, comfortable with a computerized society, and focused on primary care. Her practice is well positioned for many of the new health care innovations including accountable care organizations and medical homes. The problem this country faces—reform or no reform—is that there just aren't enough Tamara Fisicaros to go around! The United States has a critical health care workforce crisis today—and it will move to a catastrophic situation when 34 million Americans gain insurance coverage in 2014. Orin Hatch, senator from Utah, said, "The work force crisis is reaching crisis proportions."[1] Just look at Massachusetts. When the number of people with insurance increased, over half of all internists and 40 percent of family and general practitioners stopped accepting new patients.[2] There simply weren't enough doctors to go around. In this chapter we'll look at the crisis, how the Patient Protection and Affordable Care Act has failed to adequately address this critical problem, and what we must do to fix it.

The nation is short 16,663 primary care physicians (family physicians, general internists, pediatricians, and obstetricians and gynecologists) today, and that number will reach 140,000 by 2025 according to the American Academy of Family Physicians.[3] The current shortage of primary care physicians will be exacerbated by an increase in the number of people with health insurance including an expansion of the number of individuals covered by Medicaid if health care reform works. This will be particularly acute in states with restrictive Medicaid eligibility requirements, high rates of uninsured residents, and few primary care physicians—Oklahoma, Georgia, Texas, Louisiana, Arkansas, Nevada, North Carolina, and Kentucky.[4] The government's own figures show that 65 million people live in the 6,080 areas designated as having a shortage of primary care physicians. In Nevada, New Mexico, Montana, Utah, and Alaska the entire state is underserved. There is also a shortage across the country of cardiologists, oncologists, gastroenterologists, general surgeons, and cardiothoracic surgeons—specialists that are all in great need as our population ages.

The American Recovery and Reinvestment Act invested $300 million in 2009 in the National Health Service Corps, a group of primary care physicians who work in Health Professional Shortage Areas in return for two-year $100,000 federal scholarships or $50,000 in medical school loan repayments. These dollars will help to double the number of doctors in the program from 3,500 to 7,000—a drop in the bucket in the face of the over 4 million people the program already cares for. This gap could be closed if 4,000 medical students choose to pursue primary care medicine over each of the next ten years; however, only 1,200 students, fewer than 3 percent of each graduating class, choose a primary care career today. The number of students choosing primary care actually fell by half between 1997 and 2005. Those numbers are unlikely to change any time soon. This chapter looks at how the Patient Protection and Affordable Care Act addresses the workforce crisis, describes shortcuts that some states and municipalities are taking to increase the number of primary care physicians, and presents a prescription for how the federal government can best approach the impending workforce crisis.

How Does the Patient Protection and Affordable Care Act Address the Workforce Crisis?

What steps does the Patient Protection and Affordable Care Act take to solve the workforce crisis that this country faces? The new law increases Medicare reimbursements for evaluation and management services—the terms federal bureaucrats use for examining and talking to a patient. The bill allocates about $350 million in additional support for training programs in primary care. It also provides loan-forgiveness incentives to medical school graduates who practice primary care in underserved areas, and it requires state Medicaid programs to pay primary care physicians at least 100 percent of Medicare's rates for the same services in 2013 and 2014. What it doesn't do is provide the needed funding to increase the number of doctors or nurses that are trained each year, nor does it clarify the uncertainty that exists for physician compensation before 2013 and after 2014.[5]

The bill has a strong focus on physician-extenders: nurses, physician assistants, and nurse practitioners. Grants will be available for programs that produce physician assistants for careers in primary care, and the bill appropriates money for loan debt forgiveness for nurses who go into teaching to ensure the training of more nurse practitioners. Appropriations are allocated to support a demonstration project that will evaluate the ability of nurse practitioners to provide all of the care for chronically ill patients with the care being delivered entirely in the people's homes. Medicare payments to nurse-midwives will increase from 65 percent of what a physician is paid for a service to 100 percent of the Medicare fee schedule. Increased Medicare reimbursements for midwives will have little immediate impact because Medicare beneficiaries are predominantly over the age of sixty-five (with the exception of younger disabled women). The law's ultimate goal may be to provide incentives for nurses to establish freestanding practices in which they offer a full range of primary care services.

Some policy analysts believe that at a time when there are too few doctors, nurse practitioners, physician assistants, and pharmacists can make up the difference and are far less costly. The average salary for a nurse practitioner ($82,000) or for a primary care physician's assistant ($85,000) is substantially less than the average salary of a family practitioner ($161,000) or a general internist ($154,000). In fact, nurses and nurse practitioners have lobbied for years to have their roles and duties expanded. Some states now allow pharmacists to diagnose and treat disease under the supervision of a physician. A report from the Institute of Medicine in 2010 suggested that nurses be given both the education and the authority to take on more medical responsibility that would remove some of the strains placed on doctors.[6] But the American Medical Association quickly criticized the report. They noted that "nurses are critical to the health care team, but there is no substitute for education and training. With a shortage of both nurses and physicians, increasing the responsibility of nurses is not the answer to the physician shortage."[7] There are unfortunately no data to support either side of what will certainly be a continuing debate as we struggle to care for an increasing number of people with a diminishing supply of physicians and nurses.

The average primary care doctor sees thirty-eight patients each day.[8] That's one patient every seven minutes in an eight-hour day.[3] Add in time to return calls, enter data into the electronic health record, seek approvals from insurance carriers for tests and procedures, and speak with consultants, and you have a very long day. Doctors certainly need help—but will patients be satisfied seeing a nurse practitioner instead of a doctor?

The health care reform legislation also calls for the creation of a National Health Care Workforce Commission that will serve as advisers to Congress, the White House, and state and local governments on ways to expand and prepare the nation's health care workforce. The members of the commission were selected by the Government Accounting Office. I believe strongly that there is a great need for a commission to study the workforce issue and, in fact, called for the creation of just such a commission.[9] I was quite surprised, however, by the composition of the committee. Only five of the fifteen members are doctors, and the chair of the committee is a professor of nursing. It is also disappointing and concerning that not a single member comes from the Association of American Medical Colleges or represents the nation's program directors—those individuals charged with overseeing the clinical education of medical students and postgraduate trainees at America's academic medical centers.

The 1997 Balanced Budget Act and the Health Care Workforce Crisis

A great irony of the health care debate is that Congress had an opportunity to fix the workforce crisis in health care reform legislation but failed to do so. Since the latter part of the twentieth century, medical school graduates spend an additional number of years (between three and eight years depending on specialty) to become board certified in a medical specialty: internal medicine, pediatrics, family medicine, obstetrics and gynecology, psychiatry, pathology, or surgery. Thomas Nasca, CEO of the American College of Graduate Medical Education, described our current medical school graduates as a "primordial mass that needs to be shaped into physicians during post graduate training."[10] Medical school graduates are referred to as "residents" during this training period. This terminology comes from the fact that prior to the middle of the twentieth century doctors in many postgraduate training programs were required to live in the hospital (they were sometimes called house staff). Medicare funds the majority of residency training positions in the United States. Hospitals receive Direct Medical Education (DME) payments from Medicare to cover the salaries and benefits of their residents. They also receive Indirect Medical Education (IME) payments. These payments are ostensibly made to the hospital to pay the cost associated with educating residents and are tied to admissions of Medicare patients. Resident salaries range between $35,000 and $45,000 plus benefits.

In 1997 the Balanced Budget Act capped the number of residents that Medicare would support at each hospital at levels that were funded as of 1996.[11] The first available training positions in the United States are allocated to graduates of American medical schools—the remaining positions are filled with graduates of foreign medical schools. If there is an increase in the number of U.S. medical school graduates in any given year, training programs simply decrease the number of foreign medical school graduates that are accepted into U.S. programs. The total number of doctors trained in the United States each year doesn't change even if the number of medical school graduates increases! A bill was introduced into Congress during the health care reform debates that would have increased the total number of training positions in the United States by 15,000 positions a year. This would have provided training positions for the increasing number of American-trained graduates while at the same time not affecting the number of foreign-trained medical graduates entering American residency positions. Congress failed to pass the legislation. The health care reform bill does allow the government to redistribute training slots that are not being used by one hospital to other hospitals—a Band-Aid on a gaping wound!

Congress should not shoulder all of the blame for our inability to fix the health care workforce debacle. Policy analysts have placed an enormous reliance on data accrued by the group of health policy experts from Dartmouth that showed that America's doctors were distributed more heavily in wealthy areas than in poor neighborhoods. The Dartmouth group believes that we could solve our workforce crisis if we simply redistributed doctors from areas of high cost and high utilization to areas of low cost and low utilization.[12] This concept has driven the health care debates on Capitol Hill, yet experts from every professional organization disagree with the Dartmouth conclusions. Richard Cooper, a professor of medicine at the Leonard Davis Institute of Health Economics at the University of Pennsylvania and a leading authority on health care workforce issues, noted that the current distribution of America's doctors across wealthy and poor neighborhoods "should not detract from efforts to ensure that the United States will have an adequate supply of physicians for the future."[13] Congress, unfortunately, didn't listen to Dr. Cooper or other experts who continue to document a medical workforce crisis.

Changing Demographics of the Physician Workforce

Thirty years ago when I graduated from medical school, 6 percent of the students in my medical school class were women. Today, half or more of every graduating medical school class are women. Tamara Fisicaro is representative of many of these young women. They often have children during medical school or during their residency years and often pursue careers that allow them to have as much time as possible for child-rearing activities. Many women, like Tamara, work part time in primary care. Practice groups like Tamara's are particularly attractive because the doctors only care for outpatients and don't have to care for patients in the hospital. Many women are also attracted to the new specialty of hospital medicine. Hospitalists only care for patients who are in the hospital. They work very fixed hours without additional responsibilities such as call from home. Other specialties such as ophthalmology, dermatology, and radiology are also viewed as family friendly. No one has factored into the workforce calculations the fact that some women who are graduating from American medical schools will likely practice part time at least until their children are grown.

The search for family-friendly specialties is not limited to women—many men graduate from medical school and look for job opportunities that are lifestyle friendly. The lifestyle of the primary care physician who practices alone, sees thirty or more patients in the office six days a week, makes rounds in the hospital after office hours, and makes the occasional house call is no longer attractive to medical school graduates of either gender. U.S. medical students have as a result become increasingly more interested in non-primary care specialties. The shift in student interest is evidenced by the fact that the number of family medicine residents who graduated from U.S. allopathic medical schools fell from 8,232 in 1998–1999 to 4,848 in 2004–2005. Physicians today want to have as much free time as possible, and the concept of "shift work" is neither alien nor frowned upon. Established primary care physicians are also looking for lifestyle changes. They are leaving solo practice to join larger groups or to become employed by hospitals. In 1997 about 40 percent of doctors were in solo or two-doctor practices; by 2008, the number had fallen to 30 percent. More than 50 percent of practicing U.S. physicians are now employed by hospitals or integrated delivery systems.[14]

For some students, primary care is just not exciting enough. One student pointed out that "I love to use my hands and to see a quick result when I do something for a patient." He intends to become a cardiologist. The high technology that has entered much of medicine is very attractive to students. Today cardiologists can fix holes in the heart, open clogged arteries, and even replace leaky heart valves using catheters that are placed in large arteries. For others, it is all about economics. Medical school graduates have an average debt of approximately $160,000 from their medical education and an average debt of approximately $26,000 from their undergraduate education. These substantial levels of debt make a practice in primary care medicine problematic. In a free market society it is unlikely that anything short of strong financial incentives will entice students to pursue a career in primary care.

Workforce Crisis Is Not in Primary Care Alone

Another critical weakness of the Patient Protection and Affordable Care Act is that it focuses exclusively (albeit in a limited fashion) on the workforce crisis in primary care and completely ignores the parallel crisis in many other specialties in medicine. The decrease in the subspecialty workforce is due at least in part to the misguided admonition from health policy experts in the early 1990s that managed care and primary care would drive down the need for specialists. The policy analysts failed to recognize that the aging of the U.S. population, improved survival of people with a large number of diseases including heart disease and cancer, and the retirement of many baby-boomer doctors would lead to a marked shortage in specialty medicine. The number of general surgeons in the United States declined by nearly 26 percent between 1981 and 2005 while the population of the United States increased by almost 75 million. The need for surgeons is particularly critical in rural areas where the majority of surgeons are reaching retirement age.[15] The shortage in surgery, like the shortage in primary care, has been attributable to the fact that surgery is less lucrative than other specialties—new surgeons typically make about $165,000 their first or second year in practice, work long hours, face a postgraduate training program of six to eight years, and face a lifestyle that is not family friendly.

There are also significant workforce shortages in areas of medicine that are usually considered to be the most lucrative. There are 3,000 job openings for cardiologists that haven't been filled in both urban and rural areas and the problem is expected to get worse. Robert Bonow, a former president of the American Heart Association, noted that "there's going to be a shortfall, whether it's 16,000, 12,000 or 20,000—there's going to be a shortage [by 2050]."[16] A shortfall of cardiologists is especially worrisome in light of the fact that the population is aging and the baby boomers are rapidly reaching the age when they develop heart problems.[17] The United States also faces a shortage of 1,050 gastroenterologists by 2020 due in large part to an increasing need for cancer screening in an aging population.[18] Even the orthopedists are worried. Our aging population has an ever-increasing need for hip and knee replacements—a need that will require a 23 percent increase in orthopedic surgeons. Without an increase, "Waiting times for total joint replacement may increase to one to two years, to rival patient experiences in the United Kingdom."[19]

Lessons from Massachusetts

Lessons learned in Massachusetts should be a wake-up call for state legislators and the U.S. Congress. The fault lines in the health care workforce in the state were dramatically exposed when Massachusetts instituted near universal health care coverage. Senator Charles Grassley of Iowa noted that "in Massachusetts, health care reform efforts have increased the number of people covered, but there are reports that many people are now finding it difficult to find and get appointments with primary care providers." A survey of Massachusetts physicians supported these dire predictions as almost 40 percent of family practitioners and 56 percent of internists reported that they were not accepting new patients.[21]

How Have We Approached the Need to Increase the Number of Practicing Physicians in the United States?

Increasing the supply of America's physicians is being approached in a number of ways including increasing the size of existing medical school classes, creating new medical schools in affiliation with existing U.S. universities, expanding existing medical schools by developing new training opportunities at rural hospitals, and developing new freestanding medical schools without an affiliation with a university or a quaternary care hospital. Many of these efforts are designed and regulated at the municipal and state level because of the absence of national policies.

The simplest means of increasing the physician workforce will be to increase the number of students that are trained at each of today's existing medical schools. The Association of American Medical Colleges (AAMC) recommended that each medical school attempt to increase its class size by 30 percent. Unfortunately, this approach is limited by the existing infrastructure for both preclinical and clinical education at the majority of U.S. medical schools including the capacity of their physical plants. Several schools that had planned to expand their class size actually ended up decreasing the class size in response to the recent recession and decreases in funding from the National Institutes of Health and dividends from their trust portfolios.

Some states have created new medical schools with state funding. The first new allopathic medical school to be founded in twenty years was the Florida State University College of Medicine that opened in 2005. The new medical school was established using a unique blueprint established by the state legislature: clinical training would occur at community-based centers, a new curriculum would focus on the unique needs of Florida's elderly and minority populations, an admission process was designed to focus on identifying applicants from underrepresented populations, and the bill called for the development of a postbaccalaureate program to give applicants from target populations additional preparation before applying to medical school. The state of Florida allocated $50 million for facilities, $95 million for operating revenues, and a yearly allocation of $38 million. Other state legislatures have announced plans that target students who intend to work in primary care. These efforts provide the first two years of medical education at the main campus while providing clinical instruction in community hospitals that are at some distance from the main campus.[22]

Some new medical schools are taking very nontraditional approaches to medical education. The new medical school in Scranton, Pennsylvania, the Commonwealth School of Medicine, was created to attract students to northeastern Pennsylvania and to enhance the economy of Scranton. It has no affiliation with any of Pennsylvania's existing medical schools or research universities, utilizes a group of small community hospitals for its teaching programs, and is located in a region of the country that is losing rather than gaining population. It opened with a one-time subsidy from the state of $35 million—a sum that is less than one-tenth of the proposed legislative support for the new schools in Florida and other states.[23,24] When the Commonwealth of Pennsylvania cut funding to the school because of the state's 2011 budget crisis, the medical school was placed on probation by the national licensing board. The new medical school affiliated with Hofstra University and North Shore–Long Island Jewish Health System on Long Island, New York, will not have basic science departments, the departments that provide the foundation of the practice of medicine. "We are not going to create any of those departments [anatomy, physiology, pharmacology]. I want to link things so if we're learning anatomy and physiology of the heart, we let students get into the operating room and look at open heart surgery to see not the perfect world of the textbook but the real world," noted Lawrence G. Smith, dean of the new school.[25] The new Texas Tech School of Medicine in El Paso, Texas, will offer a medical degree in three years to students who are pursuing careers in family medicine. The program was developed to increase the number of students that pursue careers in family practice and to decrease the indebtedness of students by having them only pay for three years of education.[26]

The United States has increasingly depended on graduates of foreign medical schools to fill vacancies particularly in underserved urban and rural areas. Many of these foreign-trained physicians come from programs in the Caribbean Islands. The number of Caribbean schools quadrupled over the past decade while the number of American medical schools remained stagnant.[27–29] An increase in the number of U.S. citizens trained at for-profit Caribbean medical schools has raised considerable controversy. It is generally accepted that there are a minimum of twenty-nine Caribbean medical schools, but the exact number remains undefined. Only California makes site visits to the Caribbean schools to evaluate them for licensure purposes.[30] The students trained at the Caribbean schools receive their preclinical training in the islands. They receive their clinical training at community hospitals in the United States with no oversight from the Caribbean school much less from any U.S. governing body. Students graduating from Caribbean schools, like U.S.-trained students, must pass standardized U.S. board evaluations (USMLE) prior to being allowed to progress on to residency training; however, there is little documentation of the level of their clinical skills—something that the USMLE doesn't test.

In 2005, Senator Jeff Sessions, a Republican from Alabama, attempted unsuccessfully to cut off federal student loans to students at the Caribbean medical schools. Strong political pressure in many state legislatures has precluded the state's ability to regulate these offshore medical schools.[31] In August 2008 it was revealed that New York City's Health and Hospitals Corporation had signed a ten-year, $100 million contract with St. George's Medical School, a profit-making medical school in the Caribbean, to provide clinical training for their students in the city's public hospitals. This led to fears that there would not be enough training sites for the students currently enrolled in New York's allopathic medical schools and concerns that the New York medical community would be flooded with students of lesser caliber. St. George's admits 1,000 students each year compared with 160 at New York University School of Medicine. In addition, the real threat exists that Caribbean-trained physicians could over time outnumber the number of U.S.-trained physicians.

Danger around the Corner

The Medicare Payment Advisory Commission (MedPAC), a quasi-governmental advisory commission, has correctly recognized that American doctors would be far better prepared to provide medical care in the twenty-first century if they received education in areas that have not been traditionally taught in medical schools or hospitals doing postgraduate medical education: evidence-based practice, effective use of information technology, quality measurement and improvement, cost awareness, care coordination, leadership of interdisciplinary teams, and shared decision making.[33] Since including these new didactic subjects in a graduate medical education program would require substantial reorganization of the teaching program and significant new costs, MedPAC believed that Congress would need leverage to enforce the new policies. They therefore recommended that Congress withhold one-third of all GME payments—more than $3.5 billion per year—and reimburse hospitals their share of the withheld payments only if they met a group of performance measures that will purportedly be developed by a not yet established advisory body. Glenn Hackbarth, a lawyer and chair of MedPAC, wrote that "all, some, or none of this amount could be paid out, depending on whether the advisory body successfully develops standards for increased accountability and on the extent to which GME programs meet those standards."[33] I do not believe that in the current fiscal environment we will ever see the funds once they are withheld; in fact, President Obama pointed to a decrease in GME funding as a cost-saving measure in his April 2011 talk to the nation.

MedPAC could have taken a far different approach to changing the curricula for medical education. They could have recommended that the Association of American Medical Colleges (AAMC) include information about health care policy, sociology, psychology, group dynamics, leadership, and decision making on the Medical College Admission Test, which would have leveraged undergraduate institutions to include the social sciences in their premedical programs; in addition, they could have recommended that the American Board of Internal Medicine include topics on health policy, evidence-based practice, and quality measurements and improvements as well as cost awareness on the medical board examinations—thereby moving didactic lectures on these topics into the medical school curriculum. MedPAC instead recommended taking punitive steps against America's teaching hospitals at a time when academic medical centers are already stressed by lower reimbursements and draconian cuts in NIH funding. Targeting GME dollars at a time when this country needs to spend more—not less—to increase the size of our physician workforce is simply capricious and shortsighted. It is likely that many teaching hospitals in underserved areas will be unable to withstand yet another blow to federal funding and some teaching programs will be forced to close.

What Should We Do to Increase the Size of the Health Care Workforce?

What must we now do to address the workforce crisis that faces the United States? First, and foremost, Congress must pass an amendment that would increase the number of postgraduate training slots by 15,000. It will be problematic for the country to train more doctors unless we create more training positions funded through Medicare or other federal sources. No hospital or medical school is able to afford to support even a few postgraduate positions at a time when hospital reimbursements are decreasing precipitously. Congress must also ignore the recommendations of MedPAC and not withhold one-third of the present GME dollars. GME dollars must not be used as a lever to direct trainees where or how they will practice—but rather to create the necessary infrastructure to train the best possible doctors. The medical school and postgraduate curriculum must be designed by doctors and not by Washington lawyers and policy wonks.

Congress must develop a national policy on the workforce and on the structure of new medical schools and not leave it to the vagaries of individual state legislators. Troyen A. Brennan, chief medical officer of the Aetna Health Insurance Company, noted, "I think the prudent approach would be to have the federal government undertake or sponsor a comprehensive study of the adequacy of the current physician workforce and projected future needs."[34] Daniel Rahn, president of the Medical College of Georgia, and Steven Wartman, president and CEO of the Association of Academic Health Centers, voiced similar sentiments. They noted that a "crucial factor precipitating the health-care-work-force crisis is a lack of comprehensive work-force planning on the parts of academe, government, and the health care professions."[35] The Commission established by the Patient Protection and Affordable Care act is one step, but the Commission will need a broader membership to be effective. It must include as members individuals with expertise in medical school education.

American medical schools also must shoulder responsibility for changing the demographics of medical students. They must make efforts to recruit students and teachers who have diverse backgrounds and who are more consistent with the increasing ethnic and racial heterogeneity that is present in the U.S. population. One approach is to target recruitment efforts toward students in middle schools and high schools across the country—not just toward college students. They should identify students who show the greatest potential for being able to uphold the standards of care and medical professionalism that are required to fulfill the societal mission of a physician and then mentor them through formalized programs that address all aspects of the premedical pathway so that they can excel in the classroom as well as on the standardized medical school admissions test.

We must also break our reliance on a premedical curriculum of chemistry, physics, and math and readjust the premedical coursework to place equal importance on the social sciences, psychology, health policy, bioethics, and molecular biology. Many students report that their career in medicine was derailed by inorganic or organic chemistry. This was validated by a longitudinal study of incoming Stanford University freshmen who indicated that they hoped to become physicians.[36] The principal reason for a student's loss of interest in continuing as a premed was a negative experience in organic or inorganic chemistry.[37] Calls to restructure the premedical curriculum are not new.[38] The Association of American Medical Colleges has finally heeded these calls and revised the Medical College Admission Test so that as of 2015, it will now include an assessment of students' critical analysis and reasoning skills, their understanding of the behavioral and social sciences, their knowledge of sociocultural determinants of health, and their capabilities in research methods and statistics. Undergraduate institutions will have to quickly adapt to these new changes.

The largest impediment to attracting students to primary care and indeed to medicine is the cost of an undergraduate and medical school education. These costs will drive the choices of college graduates and our medical school graduates until we can fix the problem. No matter how intrigued a student might be in pursuing a career in medicine, the harsh reality that they will finish medical school with a level of debt that averages $160,000 serves as a major impediment to pursuing a medical career. This financial reality is even harsher for those students who have an interest in pursuing a career in the less remunerative areas of medicine including practices in rural and underserved urban areas. The financial impediments are most onerous in families of lower socioeconomic backgrounds—thereby limiting the ability of many Hispanic and African-American applicants to pursue a medical degree. Despite the fact that many believe that the practice of medicine should be seen as a "calling" rather than as a chosen profession, that "call" can go unanswered by students who recognize that they will have to practice for many years before they can erode the substantial indebtedness that arises from their medical education. Medical education is free in Europe, and the salaries earned by residents and subspecialty fellows are also substantially higher than in the United States. With no debt and higher starting salaries, young European doctors are far more willing to pursue careers in primary care. A federal program or state program that reimburses students for the cost of their medical education if they work for ten years in a primary care practice would go a long way to solving many of the nation's workforce problems at a cost that would be quite reasonable. Free medical education in for all students would be an even more appealing solutions.

We need to make the practice of primary care medicine more attractive to our medical school graduates.[39] In particular, primary care practices need help with infrastructure and organization. Because most primary care physicians practice in small offices and clinics, they cannot afford the capital improvements that will be necessary to compete in the increasingly sophisticated medical care marketplace. They need access to information technology, creation of multidisciplinary teams including nurses and nurse practitioners to help them care for their patients, coordinated care with hospitals and specialists, and work schedules that are compatible with a reasonable lifestyle and adequate family time. Tamara Fisicaro's practice is a model for the future—but a model that is not yet common across the United States. There also must be increased reimbursements for the cognitive specialties—not just for primary care but also for doctors who care for patients with infectious diseases, rheumatologic diseases, and blood disorders. This will not be easy—a fact that is pointed out in an article in the *New York Times* that quoted Dr. Peter J. Mandell, a spokesman for the American Association of Orthopaedic Surgeons. He noted, "We (orthopedists) have no problem with financial incentives for primary care. We do have a problem with doing it in a budget-neutral way."[40]

The United States would also benefit by facilitating the ability of foreign-trained medical students to enter residency programs in the United States. A recent study found that foreign-born physicians who didn't graduate from a U.S. medical school but received their postgraduate training in the United States performed as well as U.S.-trained physicians when analyzing nearly a quarter of a million hospitalizations of patients with congestive heart failure or acute heart attacks. By contrast, U.S. citizens who trained abroad—largely at Caribbean medical schools—had higher patient death rates for these two diseases.[41] If these data can be confirmed in subsequent studies, it will provide important information regarding alternative opportunities to increase the size of our physician workforce. This is of particular importance since foreign medical graduates are more likely to pursue careers in rural and underserved areas. The federal government should also pass legislation that would require state regulatory agencies to visit and certify any foreign medical schools from which they accept students with a particular focus on the rapidly enlarging offshore medical schools.

Tamara Fisicaro is the prototype of today's physician. She is highly skilled and exquisitely trained in the fundamentals of caring for patients with a vast variety of human disease. After four years in college, four years in medical school, three years as a medical resident, and one year as a chief resident, she has spent nearly half of her life preparing herself for a career in medicine. She is committed to her community where she cares for patients and raises her family. Unlike earlier generations of primary care physicians, she is part of a large group, works part time, only cares for patients in the outpatient setting, takes full advantage of the skill sets of nurses and nurse practitioners, and is comfortable using a computer to record her thoughts, order tests, and review a patient's history. As we build the medical workforce of the future, we must recognize that medical students today have different expectations, concerns, and demographics than doctors had a generation ago.

Notes

1. Pear R. Shortage of Doctors an Obstacle to Obama Goals. *New York Times.* http://www.nytimes.com. April 27, 2009.
2. Specter of Doctor Shortage Looms over Obamacare. http://www.newsmax.com. March 28, 2010.
3. Sanchez C. Health law may worsen family doctor shortage. *Tennessean.* http://www.tennessean.com. April 11, 2010.
4. Ku L, Jones K, Shin P, Bruen B, Hayes KC. The States' Next Challenge—Securing Primary Care for Expanded Medicaid Populations, *N Engl J Med* 2011, Feb 10, 364: 493–495.
5. McHugh MD, Aiken LH, Cooper RA et al. The U.S. presidential election and health care workforce policy. *Policy Polit Nurs Pract.* Feb 2008;9(1):6–14.
6. *The Future of Nursing, Leading Change, Advancing Health.* The Institute of Medicine 2010.
7. Patchin R. AMA responds to IOM report on future of nursing (http://www.ama-assn.org/ama/pub/news/news/nursing-future-workforce.page). Accessed October 5, 2010.
8. Baron RJ. What's keeping us so busy in primary care? A snapshot from one practice. *N Engl J Med.* Apr 29;362(17):1632–1636.
9. Feldman AM. *Pursuing Excellence in Health Care: Preserving America's Academic Medical Centers.* Boca Raton: Taylor-Francis; 2009.
10. Nasca T. Medpac, ACGME, and the New Regulations: What's the Problem? Paper presented at Association of Professors of Medicine Winter Meeting. February 25, 2011; San Juan, PR.
11. Goldfarb S. The Coming Doctor Shortage. http://www.frumforum.com. September 2, 2009.
12. Fisher ES, Wennberg DE, Stukel TA et al. The implications of regional variations in Medicare spending. Part 1: the content, quality, and accessibility of care. *Ann Intern Med.* Feb 18, 2003;138(4):273–287.
13. Cooper RA. Regional variation and the affluence-poverty nexus. *JAMA.* Sep 9, 2009;302(10):1113–1114.
14. Kocher R, Sahni NR. Hospitals' Race to Employ Physicians—The Logic Behind a Money-Losing Proposition. *N Engl J Med—Health Policy and Reform.* March 30, 2011.
15. Doescher MP, Lynge D, Skillman SM. *The Crisis in Rural General Surgery*: Rural Health Research Center, University of Washington; April 2009.
16. Sheth S. A Closer Look at the Cardiology Workforce Shortage. http://www.healthecareers.com. November 2, 2010.
17. Bonow RO, Smith SC, Jr. Cardiovascular manpower: the looming crisis. *Circulation.* Feb 24, 2004;109(7):817–820.

18. Growing Shortage of Gastroenterologists to Affect Screening Capacity for #2 Cancer Killer. http://www.medicalnewstoday.com. January 8, 2009.
19. Iorio R, Robb WJ, Healy WL et al. Orthopaedic surgeon workforce and volume assessment for total hip and knee replacement in the United States: Preparing for an epidemic. *J Bone Joint Surg Am.* Jul 2008;90(7):1598–1605.
20. Iglehart JK. Reform and the health care workforce—Current capacity, future demand. *N Engl J Med.* Nov 5, 2009;361(19):e38.
21. *MMS Physician Workforce Study—2009.* Waltham: Massachusetts Medical Society September 14, 2009.
22. Sataline S, Wang SS. Medical schools can't keep up. *Wall Street Journal.* April 12, 2010;Health Industry.
23. http://www.census.gov/population/projections/res.tab2.xls.
24. Umbach T. *A Roadmap for Medical Renewal and Economic Development in Northeastern Pennsylvania.* July 2006.
25. Goldstein J. The Wall Street Journal HealthBlog. *Wall Street Journal.* April 4, 2008 (Http:blogs.wsj.com/health/2008/04/04/what-does-it-cost-to-start-a-medical-school-anyway/).
26. Mangam K. Texas Tech announces 3-year degree in family medicine. *The Chronicle of Higher Education.* March 25, 2010 (http://chronicle.com/article/Texas-Tech-Announces-3-year/64830/).
27. Cooper RA. It's time to address the problem of physician shortages: graduate medical education is the key. *Ann Surg.* Oct 2007;246(4):527–534.
28. Salsberg E, Grover A. Physician workforce shortages: implications and issues for academic health centers and policymakers. *Acad Med.* Sep 2006;81(9):782–787.
29. Roman M. There's a serious problem, but lack of clarity forestalls solutions *Modernhealthcare.com.* June 5, 2006.
30. Thomas CY, Hoein R, Yan J. *Assessing the export of nursing services as a diversification option for CARICOM* 2005.
31. Hartocollis A. New York hospitals create outcry in foreign deal. *New York Times.* August 5, 2008.
32. http://www.hst.org.za/pphc/Phila/pphcsub2.htm.
33. Hackbarth G, Boccuti C. Transforming graduate medical education to improve health care value. *N Engl J Med.* Feb 24;364(8):693–695.
34. Iglehart JK. Grassroots activism and the pursuit of an expanded physician supply. *N Engl J Med.* Apr 17, 2008;358(16):1741–1749.
35. Rahn D, Wartman SA. For the healthcare workforce, a critical prognosis. *The Chronicle of Higher Education.*2007;54(10):B14.
36. Barr DA, Gonzalez ME, Wanat SF. The leaky pipeline: Factors associated with early decline in interest in premedical studies among underrepresented minority undergraduate students. *Acad Med.* May 2008;83(5):503–511.
37. Lovecchio K, Dundes L. Premed survival: Understanding the culling process in premedical undergraduate education. *Acad Med.* Jul 2002;77(7):719–724.
38. Thomas L. Notes of a biology-watcher. How to fix the premedical curriculum. *N Engl J Med.* May 25, 1978;298(21):1180–1181.
39. Bodenheimer T, Grumbach K, Berenson RA. A lifeline for primary care. *N Engl J Med.* Jun 25, 2009;360(26):2693–2696.

40. Pear R. Shortage of Doctors an Obstacle to Obama Goals, Apr 26, 2009, http://www.nytimes.com/2009/04/27/health/policy/27care.html?_r=1&pagewanted=print.
41. Norcini JJ, Boulet JR, Dauphinee WD et al. Evaluating the quality of care provided by graduates of international medical schools. *Health Aff (Millwood)*.Aug 2010;29(8):1461–1468.

Chapter 8

Can Research Guide Us to Improved Care at Lower Costs?

Obama has promoted a program of "comparative effectiveness research" that he claims will be used only to study competing medical treatments. But this program could actually lead to government boards rationing treatments based on age.

Michael S. Steele, Protecting Our Seniors: GOP Principles for Health Care, *Washington Post,* **August 24, 2009**

The R-word is kind of an incendiary work I think in this country but if you just sort of forget about the word for a second and think about what we're really trying to do here, the premise is that if we have better information we'll have better decisions. There's a lot of things that we do in this country for which we have absolutely no evidence or very poor evidence.

Newell McElwee, Merck & Co., June 4, 2010

In April of 2002, I attended a meeting in Bethesda, Maryland, sponsored by the National Institutes of Health. The meeting was attended by doctors and scientists from across the United States as well as from Europe. The purpose of the meeting was to discuss a new strategy for treating patients with congestive heart failure, a disease of the muscle of the heart in which patients experience shortness of breath, swelling in their legs, and fatigue because the heart is unable to effectively pump blood to the body. The new treatment strategy was a surgical procedure that my American colleagues called "SAVER" (surgical anterior ventricular endocardial restoration) and my European colleagues called the "Dor" procedure. Dr. Vincent Dor, one of Europe's leading surgeons and the individual who first developed the procedure, was an attendee at the conference.

You can imagine what the failing heart looks like by comparing an orange with a grapefruit. The orange is the normal heart; the grapefruit is the failing heart. The theory behind the Dor or SAVER procedure was that the function of the heart could be improved by surgically reshaping the enlarged heart so that it would once again approximate the size of an orange. The information that was presented at the meeting was fascinating, and I left the meeting with great excitement because SAVER could provide a new treatment option for my many patients with heart failure. Each of us who attended the meeting also left with a rubber model of the structure of the normal heart.

Surgeons around the world began to perform an increasing number of SAVER procedures, particularly in patients who were undergoing coronary artery bypass graft surgery (CABG), to treat patients who had both an enlarged heart and blockages in their coronary arteries. Their interest in trying the technique was based on a group of studies showing that reconstruction of the heart not only decreased the size of the heart but also improved heart function.[1–3] The SAVER procedure was not without drawbacks. It increased the amount of time it took for the surgeon to complete the bypass operation and increased the cost of the surgery. Not all cardiac surgeons or cardiologists believed that the SAVER procedure actually worked because none of the studies had directly compared patients who had undergone CABG and SAVER with those who had undergone CABG alone.

Dr. Robert Jones was one of the heart surgeons who questioned the value of the SAVER procedure. Jones and his colleagues at Duke University undertook a study called STICH—Surgical Treatment for Ischemic Heart Failure. They randomly assigned 1,000 patients who had heart failure and were undergoing CABG for treatment of coronary artery disease to receive CABG alone or CABG with heart reconstruction (SAVER).[4] Some U.S. surgeons refused to participate in the study because they were convinced that SAVER worked; therefore, Dr. Jones and his colleague Dr. Eric Velazquez, a Duke cardiologist, traveled the world enlisting the aid of doctors at sites in Canada, Poland, and western Europe. It took four years to complete the enrollment into the study and another two years to complete the study. The results were presented in April 2009. The combination of surgical reconstruction of the heart and CABG reduced the size of the heart, but this anatomical change had no effect on patient survival or the need for subsequent hospitalization.[5] A new, innovative, and more costly surgical approach was no better than the standard technology.

Similar stories have been told throughout the history of medicine. Doctors, and in particular surgeons, use their imagination and their intellectual prowess to create new ways of tackling a medical problem. They must then convince their colleagues that a new procedure actually works. In the case of a surgical procedure, this is often done by performing the operation in a series of patients and reporting the outcome: Did more people survive the operation than would be expected? Did fewer people suffer side effects from the surgery? Other doctors then compare their own outcomes with the results reported with the new technique to see whether the new method is better or worse. If the new technique seems to be beneficial, surgeons can incorporate it into their own work. In some cases they read about the new technique and then try it themselves. Sometimes they visit the doctor who developed the new technique and actually watch it being performed.

New pharmaceuticals and medical devices are regulated by the Food and Drug Administration and must be evaluated in clinical trials before they are made available to patients. To get approval, the manufacturer must demonstrate the superiority of the new drug or device in a clinical trial in which a group of patients with a specific disease are randomly assigned to either the new treatment or to a placebo (or no treatment in the case of a device). New surgical techniques or new drugs or devices are rarely if ever compared with older techniques or treatments. Since new treatments are invariably more expensive than older treatments, the cost of health care continues to rise. However, as I illustrated in the story about the Dor procedure, new treatments are not necessarily better than older ones.

Studies that compare two alternative treatments for the same medical problem are now referred to as comparative-effectiveness research.[6] This term has found its way into the everyday vocabulary of the American public because of its exposure in the health care reform debates and the commentaries of many political pundits. Comparative-effectiveness studies can compare everything from new drugs or devices to reimbursement strategies or health delivery organizations. These studies can improve the care of patients by informing both doctors and their patients which treatments are best. It is intuitively reasonable that comparative-effectiveness studies should play a large role in helping public and private insurers decide what treatments to pay for and what treatments not to pay for while at the same time helping doctors to provide the best possible care for their patients. The attempts to include funding for comparative-effectiveness research in the health reform legislation has, however, been met with vocal, well-organized, and at times vitriolic opposition. In this chapter, we'll look at the controversy surrounding comparative-effectiveness research, how the Patient Protection and Affordable Care Act supports comparative-effectiveness research, and changes in the legislation that will be necessary to ensure that this important work can have a positive impact on the way we practice medicine.

Why Comparative–Effectiveness Research Has Become a Lightning Rod in the Health Care Debates

Opponents come from both sides of the political spectrum, yet they share the common view that comparative-effectiveness research is the first step in government-sanctioned health care rationing. In an op-ed in the *Washington Post*, columnist George Will noted that comparative-effectiveness research, "which would dramatically advance government control—and rationing—of health care, should be thoroughly debated, not stealthily created in the name of 'stimulus.'"[7] Many opponents fear that comparative-effectiveness studies can be used to justify withdrawal of expensive treatments from coverage if they do not demonstrate substantial benefits over less expensive therapies—a de facto form of rationing. Millions of people have also read or listened to statements by Lyndon LaRouche, who has described the council that will oversee comparative-effectiveness research as "the group which has been designated to prepare the list of which medical procedures will henceforth be permitted, and which will not"—a task that he describes as supporting "Nazi-era" rationing.[8]

Physicians have also raised fears about comparative-effectiveness research. Some doctors question whether it will threaten their autonomy and professionalism and therefore might not be in the best interest of patients. Others have also raised the specter of rationing. Tom Price, a physician and Republican congressman from Georgia, sent out an "alert" warning people that comparative-effectiveness research would create "a permanent government rationing board prescribing care instead of doctors and patients." He went on to say that "every policy and standard will be decided by this board and would be the law of the land for every doctor, drug company, hospital, and health insurance plan."[9] Physician organizations have also raised concerns that comparative-effectiveness research will not take into account individual patient differences and therefore may impede the development of therapies that are tailored to a particular patient's needs—so-called personalized medicine.[10]

The most interesting arguments against comparative-effectiveness research have come from pundits who warned the public of the potential for the government to combine comparative-effectiveness studies and electronic medical records in an Orwellian scheme to regulate health care. Radio talk-show host Rush Limbaugh warned his millions of listeners that once the stimulus bill "computerizes everybody's health records," a new federal bureaucracy "will monitor treatments to make sure your doctor is doing what the federal government deems appropriate."[11] Betsy McCaughey, a former lieutenant governor of New York, warned that the inclusion of both funding for comparative-effectiveness research and support for electronic medical records would "enable electronic monitoring of individual patient-care decisions by the federal government and punishment of clinicians who fail to comply with imminent rationing guidelines."[12] Far more rational—but certainly less vocal—have been the fears of the pharmaceutical companies that comparative-effectiveness studies could substantially eat into their profits if new proprietary drugs did not show a comparative benefit to far less expensive generic compounds.[13,14]

Patient Protection and Affordable Care Act and Comparative-Effectiveness Research

Congress recognized the importance of comparative-effectiveness research but was clearly influenced by the vocal opposition and the lobbying efforts of the pharmaceutical industry. Needing key votes to pass the health care legislation, they took a very conservative approach to incorporating comparative-effectiveness research into the bill. The act specifically precludes the secretary of Health and Human Services from denying coverage of items or services solely on the basis of comparative-effectiveness research. Congress also crafted the language of the bill to try to put to rest Sarah Palin's notion that "death panels" would decide who received care and who didn't. The bill specifically affords protection for the elderly and the disabled by mandating that the "Secretary [of HHS] shall not use evidence or findings from comparative clinical effectiveness research ... in determining coverage, reimbursement or incentive programs [under Title 18] in a manner that treats extending the life of an elderly, disabled or terminally ill individual as of lower value than extending the life of an individual who is younger, non-disabled or not terminally ill." It is also important to note that federal Medicare guidelines stipulate that a treatment option that has been shown to be effective cannot be withheld from a Medicare beneficiary regardless of cost.

The health reform act authorizes the establishment of a nonprofit corporation to be known as the Patient-Centered Outcomes Research Institute to oversee all federally sponsored comparative-effectiveness research—a further attempt to separate comparative-effectiveness research from health policy and health and human services administration. The nongovernment institute will identify national priorities for research, establish a research project agenda, and carry out the research project in collaboration with academic centers and government agencies. The bill explicitly forbids the institute from developing or using any measures that compare effectiveness with cost. All of the institute's activities will be overseen by an independent board of governors that will include health care consumers and patients as well as physicians and representatives from the health care industry. The public will be able to attend all meetings of the institute. I worry that the presence of industry representatives on the board of governors of the institute will result in an undue amount of corporate influence and that the institute will be just one more bureaucratic entity that will slow rather than speed the use of comparative-effectiveness research.

Potential Value of Comparative-Effectiveness Research

Comparative-effectiveness research is one of the most important parts of the health care reform act and the part of the bill that is most likely to effect a change in health care costs. This view is supported by a recent Commonwealth Fund report that noted that comparative effectiveness research promises the greatest short- and long-term savings of the top fifteen ways of bringing health care costs under control and that it is the most likely mechanism to reduce the out-of-pocket health care costs of U.S. households.[15] Many existing drugs and devices have never been subjected to the rigorous scrutiny of a clinical trial that compares them with existing therapies. This view of comparative-effectiveness research is shared by Gail Wilensky, an economist who served in the administration of President George H. W. Bush and was an advisor to Senator John McCain (R-AZ). She recently noted,

> It is just enormously frustrating to me that many interests, including quite a few physicians, do not recognize CER [comparative-effectiveness research] as a companion project to NIH's basic research that would help doctors and patients determine what are the most effective therapies for a particular condition or disease. And I am frustrated and disappointed by some of the Republican posturing too, which asserts that additional information provided through CER is a threat or a first step to rationing care. I believe that providing information about what works when and allowing that information to be used as part of a reimbursement decision is reasonable and sensible.[16]

From a personal perspective, my own care as a patient could have been greatly informed by comparative-effectiveness research. The first decision I needed to make after being diagnosed with prostate cancer was how to treat the cancer. I had four choices: (1) watch my cancer to see if it became more aggressive over time—something called "active surveillance,"[17] (2) destroy the cancer cells by placing small radioactive seeds into the walnut-sized prostate gland (brachytherapy), (3) destroy the cancer cells by shooting beams of radiation at the gland from outside the body (external beam radiation), or (4) surgically remove the gland. Not a single study had compared these four approaches, and as a result, I had to decide which approach to take without science to guide me—a difficult and frustrating experience.[18]

Even after deciding on surgery, I still had to make a difficult decision. For nearly thirty years, prostate surgery has been performed using an "open procedure" in which the surgeon makes an incision in the skin from just above the pubic bone to just below the belly button and directly removes the gland. Surgeons have more recently performed the operation using a robot to guide instruments that are placed in the lower abdomen through five small holes. Robotic surgery has been extensively advertised and hyped, and hospitals have a compelling need to perform robotic surgery once they have invested millions of dollars in purchasing a robot and hiring a robotic surgeon. The surgeons who do the robotic surgery tout its benefits—yet few of them are trained in the traditional approach so comparisons are difficult. The glitzy advertisements featuring the robotic surgery on many hospital websites were not helpful because they were produced by the manufacturer of the robot. It was hard—if not impossible—to find unbiased and scientific information about which procedure was best.

I finally decided to have the traditional open procedure. My decision was informed by a study that appeared in the *Journal of the American Medical Association* just a month before my diagnosis.[19] A group from Harvard University found that while patients who had undergone robotic surgery had a shorter length of stay in the hospital and fewer respiratory and miscellaneous surgical complications, they had a higher incidence of incontinence and erectile dysfunction—the two major side effects associated with prostate surgery. In addition, there were questions about whether the cancer was as well controlled with robotic surgery as with the open procedure.

What neither of the articles said, but I knew to be true, was that robotic surgery was more expensive than the traditional surgery. In fact, all types of robotic surgery accounted for a 6 percent increase in the cost of individual surgical procedures between 2005 and 2007.[20] The number of robots sold in the United States increased by almost 75 percent between 2007 and 2009—robots cost between $1 million and $2.5 million. Manufacturers, however, don't make profits just on the sale of the robot—the consumables used in each operation are quite expensive. Only large-scale randomized trials of robot-assisted surgery versus traditional surgery will show whether the long-term outcomes of robot-assisted surgery are superior to those of conventional procedures. I learned from my own experiences that without comparative-effectiveness research to improve care and lower costs, patients must make difficult decisions that are often based more on hope than on reality.

Can Comparative-Effectiveness Research Lower Costs?

One question about comparative-effectiveness research is whether the results can be used administratively to effectively lower health care costs. Several states have attempted to do just that. One is the state of Washington.[21] Beginning in 2003, Washington State enacted a group of policies designed to use comparative-effectiveness research to reduce overuse and underuse of health care services. The policies were applied to payments made by Medicaid, the workers' compensation program, the state government employee benefit plan, and the corrections department and covered all health care costs. The centerpiece of the effort is the Health Technology Assessment program (HTA). This state government-sponsored program evaluates treatment and diagnostic options and uses the information to decide what they will and will not pay for. Decisions are made by the health technology clinical committee that is composed of practicing physicians.

In October 2009, the committee reported the results of its initial reviews in the *New England Journal of Medicine*.[22] Of the nine evaluations of new technologies, the committee supported payments for four of the new technologies but declined to support payments for five of the technologies. The committee only reviews technologies that have a high likelihood of overuse or underuse or those in which there were concerns regarding safety or cost-effectiveness. A good example of the value of their deliberations was their decision not to pay for weight-loss surgery in children less than eighteen years of age.

Decisions by the state's Health Technology assessment program have on occasion raised controversy, but overall the committee's decisions have been well received and the committee's structure has been seen as a possible model for other states. In March 2011, public opinion began to change. The committee had to make two controversial decisions: should the state continue to pay for spinal injections for pain and for continuous home glucose monitoring for children with diabetes?[23] The committee voted to restrict coverage of continuous glucose monitoring unless the child had a past episode of low blood sugar and to limit coverage for spinal injections to treat back pain.

Some health policy advocates have lauded Washington's efforts to bend the cost curve while others have found the actions of the committee disconcerting. I find solace in the fact that the decisions of the Washington committee are evidence-based and made by physicians—not health policy analysts.

Oregon is another state that has used comparative-effectiveness research to improve the quality and cost of health care.[24] In 1989 the state of Oregon created the Health Services Commission, a volunteer group of seven health professionals and four consumer representatives, to set priorities for funding decisions. The group used scientific evidence as well as opinions from experts and the lay public to develop a list of treatments and then listed them based on their priority. After developing the health care budget, the state legislature drew a line on the list—services above the line were included in all benefits packages while services below the line were not.

Oregon has used the priority list since 1994.[25] It was not surprising that the line was drawn at a higher point to reduce the number of covered services and the accompanying costs as health care costs grew. The Oregon plan has not been without its detractors. In the late 1990s the federal Health Care Financing Administration began denying Oregon's request to limit services. Opponents have questioned whether a program that works in a state with 4 million people would work in a larger state or in the country as a whole; however, it is still being used two decades after its development.

Comparative effectiveness studies can also be used to test the role of various health care delivery systems in improving the quality of health care and lowering health care costs. The RAND Health Insurance Experiment, carried out more than three decades ago, is one of the best examples. The study randomly assigned families to one of five health insurance plans.[26] Four of the plans were fee-for-service but differed in their levels of cost sharing. The fifth plan was a health maintenance organization in which care was free. The results of the study demonstrated that increased cost sharing resulted in decreased health care use (and therefore costs) and that individuals with free care used about one-third more care than those in the cost-sharing plans. The group that received free care was no healthier on average than those individuals who were covered by a health plan that utilized a cost-sharing model at the end of five years. These types of studies will be important for evaluating the new reimbursement paradigms and coverage strategies that will be evaluated as part of the health care reform legislation.

Another type of comparative-effectiveness research doesn't compare two strategies of care, but rather looks at the processes required to implement new strategies. In the early 1990s the standard treatment for a patient with a heart attack was the intravenous administration of a "clot buster" (thrombolytic agent) to dissolve the clot that was blocking the coronary artery. However, these clot busters failed to work in as many as 30 percent of patients; therefore doctors hypothesized that primary percutaneous coronary intervention (PCI)—expanding a balloon in the artery to break the clot and open the underlying artery—might be more effective. Clinical trials in which patients were randomly assigned to receive the clot buster or to undergo PCI showed that primary PCI was more effective. Delays in getting a patient from the emergency room to the cardiac catheterization laboratory negated the benefits that were associated with primary PCI in the real world.[27] People who received a successful angioplasty within ninety minutes of arriving in the emergency department benefited from the procedure, whereas those who underwent the procedure greater than ninety minutes after being transferred from the emergency room saw no benefits. This ninety-minute window of opportunity was referred to as door-to-balloon time and has become a standard for measuring the quality of a hospital's cardiology program.[28]

People fear that the results of comparative-effectiveness research will be used to make capricious decisions about health care services; however, I would argue that these studies will only have value if federal, state, and local regulatory agencies are willing to use the data to make difficult political decisions. If ambulances for example only took patients with acute heart problems to hospitals that were able to meet door-to-balloon times of under ninety minutes, patients would benefit and the overall costs of health care would be less.

Limitations of Comparative-Effectiveness Studies

I strongly disagree with opponents of comparative-effectiveness research who see it as a forerunner of Orwellian medicine, but I do think that we have to be extremely careful designing the studies and interpreting the data. A recent study that compared traditional coronary artery bypass surgery (CABG) with off-pump bypass surgery is a good example of how a study could adversely influence doctor behavior.[29] During traditional bypass surgery, a patient is connected to a machine that takes over for the heart and lungs by oxygenating the blood and then pumping the oxygenated blood through the body. The heart is then stopped during the surgery. Almost two decades ago, surgeons began to develop techniques that would allow them to operate on the heart while it was still beating. The hypothesis was that by not using the heart-lung machine, they could decrease the incidence of strokes, decrease the time it took to perform the surgery, and decrease the risk of changes in cognitive function that we sometimes see in patients after they have surgery.

I have always been a great fan of off-pump surgery and have generally referred my patients to surgeons who routinely do off-pump bypass surgery and who are adept at the procedure. My belief in the benefits of off-pump surgery was more empirical than factual because no large study had compared on-pump surgery with off-pump surgery. I was quite surprised when Dr. A. Laurie Shroyer described the results of a study in which over 2,000 patients at Veterans Administration hospitals across the United States were randomly assigned to have the surgery performed using the traditional approach or to have off-pump bypass surgery.[30] The study showed that after one year, the patients in the off-pump group had worse outcomes than the patients who had received the traditional surgery. Had I been wrong in sending so many patients for off-pump surgery?

I found significant flaws in the study when I took the time to read it carefully. The surgeons who participated in the study were not very experienced—they only had to have performed twenty off-pump procedures before participating in the study. The surgeon who operated on my patients performed over 200 off-pump procedures each year. A cardiothoracic trainee was allowed to perform the critical parts of the surgery at the majority of the hospitals where the study was carried out—again pointing to a lack of experience on the part of the doctors. Another problem with the study was that the patients who are thought to benefit most from off-pump surgery—women and the elderly—were not included in the study. This study teaches an important lesson about comparative-effectiveness research—studies must be carefully designed and analyzed before making decisions that will affect how doctors practice medicine or how hospitals are reimbursed for care.

Another important limitation of the health care reform act is that it does not require the FDA to include comparative-effectiveness studies in the approval process for new drugs and devices. Most new drugs are approved on the basis of studies in which they are compared with placebo—pills that have no active drug. Pharmaceutical companies then market their product as the next generation of drugs without ever having to prove that the new drug is more effective than older and far cheaper drugs that have the same or nearly the same biological properties. The older generic drugs are never advertised, and even older drugs that still have patent protection are not aggressively marketed. By contrast, the newer drugs are aggressively marketed by pharmaceutical sales representatives. Direct-to-patient advertising has become increasingly popular and effective. Just count how many times you see an advertisement showing an attractive couple talking about treatment for erectile dysfunction during any prime-time sports telecast. It is ironic that the cost of comparative-effectiveness studies must be borne by consumers' tax dollars rather than being paid for by the pharmaceutical companies.[31]

A good example of how pharmaceutical companies work to convince doctors and patients that brand-name drugs are preferable to generics is seen with the lipid-lowering agents designed to treat patients with high cholesterol. One of the first drugs in the class of agents called statins was a drug called Zocor or simvastatin that was developed by Merck. This early statin was followed by a very similar statin called Lipitor or atorvastatin—manufactured by Pfizer. The patent covering Zocor expired in 2006, and since that time the cost for Zocor has dropped to between $9 and $20 for a full month's supply whereas Lipitor can cost between $2 and $3 for a single pill.[32] The potential savings with generic drugs is enormous because over 150 million statin prescriptions are written in the United States each year. Robert Seidman, the chief pharmacy officer for the health care insurance company Wellpoint, estimated that wide use of generic simvastatin could reduce the nation's drug costs by $2 billion or more each year, yet doctors continue to prescribe Lipitor.[32] Drug costs will continue to rise until Congress is willing to legislate the use of appropriate studies to assess the benefits of new drugs in comparison with older and less costly drugs.

The story of Lipitor and Zocor is relatively straightforward—two drugs having different costs, but almost identical efficacies. The more difficult decisions that will face regulatory agencies, ethicists, physicians, and patients is how to pay for—or whether to pay for—expensive drugs that work but that have only minimal or modest lifesaving benefits. A good example is the drug Yervoy.[33] It was developed by Bristol-Myers Squibb for the treatment of cancer. Yervoy extended the lives of people with the skin cancer melanoma in a seminal clinical trial, but only by a few months. Twenty percent of the people who received Yervoy lived at least two years, but there is no way to predict who would respond. The conundrum is that Yervoy is expected to cost a patient $120,000. Even more complex issues evolve around incredibly expensive designer drugs, so-called biologics, that improve symptoms of disease but do not influence life expectancy such as etanercept for rheumatoid arthritis. How regulatory agencies deal with these complex issues will have an enormous impact on the ability to decrease rising health care costs.

Another problem with the legislative approach to comparative-effectiveness research is that in an attempt to cater to the pharmaceutical industry and to critics who fear federal rationing, Congress allocated only $1.1 billion for comparative-effectiveness research and almost no money for infrastructure costs. The Institute of Medicine was charged with developing a prioritization for comparative-effectiveness studies. They received over 1,000 suggestions—which they pared down and prioritized to a list of 100 topics. Since most large clinical studies that randomly assign patients to a treatment group cost upwards of $500 million, we will be lucky if the dollars allocated can be used to fund even two or three of the list of 100 topics.

Using Comparative-Effectiveness Research

Rather than fearing comparative-effectiveness research, physicians and the general public should embrace it.[34] I believe that comparative-effectiveness research will be one of the best ways of decreasing health care costs. To be effective, comparative-effectiveness research must develop tools to optimize the dissemination of data to both doctors and patients so that the information can be translated into changes in practice and improvements in public health. This rapid translation of data from the scientific literature to the community physician must be facilitated by a transparent process that allows providers to communicate with researchers and policy makers. Scientists and policy analysts must understand local political and infrastructure constraints and community values that can impair compliance with new guidelines or inhibit the acceptance of new delivery systems. They must also recognize that comparative-effectiveness studies often measure the response of an average patient to a drug or device and that some patients may need an alternative treatment. Community doctors and their patients must at the same time become conversant with the strengths and potential biases of different types of comparative-effectiveness studies and not view recommendations as being capricious or antithetical to good clinical care.

Congress must recognize that comparative-effectiveness research will only improve the way we practice medicine if the commission that oversees the research evaluates a large number of treatments, provides decisions in a timely basis, effectively educates the public and practicing physicians about the processes, deliberates in a transparent fashion, and avoids both perceived and actual conflicts of interest among its membership. Comparative-effectiveness research will only bend the health care cost curve if there is adequate funding to address the large number of questions that exist in the health care marketplace. The Food and Drug Administration must also play a role by requiring the pharmaceutical and device industry to perform comparative studies for drug and device approval—particularly when new drugs are substantially more costly than older drugs and devices.

Congress could learn important lessons about the benefits and limitations of comparative-effectiveness research by studying the processes used by the National Institute for Health and Clinical Excellence (NICE), a regulatory body established in the United Kingdom. NICE has studied an enormous number of new drugs and devices. While the work of NICE has not been without controversy and criticism, most observers would agree that the system for adjudicating the value of new and expensive therapies in the UK is more rational and effective than that in the United States. The Department of Health and Human Services must create a public awareness campaign that will educate the lay public and demonstrate how decisions based on comparative-effectiveness studies can substantially improve the quality of care while at the same time lowering health care costs.

At some point in time we will have to face the difficult issues that relate not to comparative-effectiveness but to cost-effectiveness—something that was not addressed in the Patient Protection and Affordable Care Act.[35] These discussions will be particularly relevant to treatment of cancer where the prices of cancer drugs have been rising faster than their associated benefits.[36] Some patients face out-of-pocket expenses for cancer therapies that threaten their family's financial security.[37] Yet even Medicare has been unable to control the rising spending on these agents.[38] We may at some point have to trade off allocating funds from cost-ineffective treatments for terminal diseases such as late-stage pancreatic cancer to cost-effective treatments for the long-term treatment of diseases such as diabetes.[35] Political pundits have railed against cost-effectiveness analysis, believing that it harms patients with significant diseases such as cancer or heart disease; however, "populations with more impairment typically fare better in cost-effectiveness analyses, because they have more to gain from interventions."[39] Using cost-effectiveness data will be a slow process as over half of physicians express moral objection to using this type of analysis.[40] Discussions of cost-effectiveness will require careful thought and consultation with ethicists and social scientists and must ensure that vulnerable populations are not adversely affected.

Doctors, patients, and regulatory agencies must recognize the inherent value of comparative-effectiveness research. As noted by Kevin Volpp of the University of Pennsylvania,

> CER [comparative-effectiveness research] is a public good that has the potential to greatly inform the decisions of individual clinicians, patients, policy makers, and insurance plans in guiding the American people to preferentially use more effective treatments. The full potential of this effort will be realized only if we define problems broadly and include in those comparisons rigorous testing of behavioral and policy-based approaches to improving the health of populations.[6]

Whenever I read criticisms about comparative-effectiveness research, I look at the rubber heart model sitting on my desk and wonder how many patients would have incurred extra costs and longer surgical procedures if we had not evaluated the Dor procedure in a comparative-effectiveness study.

Notes

1. Athanasuleas CL, Buckberg GD, Stanley AW et al. Surgical ventricular restoration in the treatment of congestive heart failure due to post-infarction ventricular dilation. *J Am Coll Cardiol.* Oct 6, 2004;44(7):1439–1445.

2. Menicanti L, Castelvecchio S, Ranucci M et al. Surgical therapy for ischemic heart failure: single-center experience with surgical anterior ventricular restoration. *J Thorac Cardiovasc Surg.* Aug 2007;134(2):433–441.
3. Prucz RB, Weiss ES, Patel ND et al. Coronary artery bypass grafting with or without surgical ventricular restoration: a comparison. *Ann Thorac Surg.* Sep 2008;86(3):806–814; discussion 806–814.
4. Velazquez EJ, Lee KL, O'Connor CM et al. The rationale and design of the Surgical Treatment for Ischemic Heart Failure (STICH) trial. *J Thorac Cardiovasc Surg.* Dec 2007;134(6):1540–1547.
5. Jones RH, Velazquez EJ, Michler RE et al. Coronary bypass surgery with or without surgical ventricular reconstruction. *N Engl J Med.* Apr 23, 2009;360(17):1705–1717.
6. Volpp KG, Das A. Comparative effectiveness—Thinking beyond medication A versus medication B. *N Engl J Med.* Jul 23, 2009;361(4):331–333.
7. Will G. Stimulus math for the GOP. *Washington Post.* January 29, 2009;A19.
8. Gallagher P, Obama's Fascist "Health-Care Reform" Can be Stopped, Executive Intelligence Review, 6/19/2009, http://www.larouchepub.com/other/2009/3624 fascist_healthcare_stoppable.html.
9. Avorn J. Debate about funding comparative-effectiveness research. *N Engl J Med.* May 7, 2009;360(19):1927–1929.
10. Garber AM, Tunis SR. Does comparative-effectiveness research threaten personalized medicine? *N Engl J Med.* May 7, 2009;360(19):1925–1927.
11. Limbaugh R. *The March to Socialized Medicine Starts in Obama's Porkulus Bill: The Rush Limbaugh Show*; 2009.
12. McCaughey B. Ruin your health with the Obama stimulus plan. *Bloomberg.com.* February 9, 2009;accessed March 30, 2010.
13. Stafford RS, Wagner TH, Lavori PW. New, but not improved? Incorporating comparative-effectiveness information into FDA labeling. *N Engl J Med.* Sep 24, 2009;361(13):1230–1233.
14. Cipriani A, Furukawa TA, Salanti G et al. Comparative efficacy and acceptability of 12 new-generation antidepressants: a multiple-treatments meta-analysis. *Lancet.* Feb 28, 2009;373(9665):746–758.
15. Schoen C, Guterman S, Shih A et al. *Bending the Curve: Options for Achieving Savings and Improving Value in U.S. Health Spending.* New York: The Commonwealth Fund. December 2007.
16. Wilensky G. Reform, regulation, and research—An interview with Gail Wilensky. Interview by John K. Iglehart. *N Engl J Med.* Sep 10, 2009;361(11):1038–1040.
17. Holmberg L, Bill-Axelson A, Helgesen F et al. A randomized trial comparing radical prostatectomy with watchful waiting in early prostate cancer. *N Engl J Med.* Sep 12, 2002;347(11):781–789.
18. Wilt TJ, MacDonald R, Rutks I et al. Systematic review: Comparative effectiveness and harms of treatments for clinically localized prostate cancer. *Ann Intern Med.* Mar 18, 2008;148(6):435–448.
19. Hu JC, Gu X, Lipsitz SR et al. Comparative effectiveness of minimally invasive vs open radical prostatectomy. *JAMA.* Oct 14, 2009;302(14):1557–1564.

20. Barbash GI, Glied SA. New technology and health care costs—The case of robot-assisted surgery. *N Engl J Med.* Aug 19, 2010;363(8):701–704.
21. Washington State Legislature. HB2575-2005-06: *Establishing a State Health Technology Assessment Program.* 2005.
22. Franklin GM, Budenholzer BR. Implementing evidence-based health policy in Washington State. *N Engl J Med.* Oct 29, 2009;361(18):1722–1725.
23. Wang S. State wrestles with health coverage. *Wall Street Journal.* March 19, 2011.
24. Saha S, Coffman DD, Smits AK. Giving teeth to comparative-effectiveness research—the Oregon experience. *N Engl J Med.* Feb 18, 2010;362(7):e18.
25. Office for Oregon Health Policy and Research Policy Brief: The Essential Benefit Package, March 2009. *The Essential Benefit Package Recommendations of the Oregon Health Fund Board's Benefits Committee* Salem 2009.
26. Newhouse JP, Insurance Experiment Group. *Free for All? Lessons from the RAND Health Insurance Experiment.* Cambridge, MA: Harvard University Press; 1999.
27. Nallamothu BK, Bradley EH, Krumholz HM. Time to treatment in primary percutaneous coronary intervention. *N Engl J Med.* Oct 18, 2007;357(16):1631–1638.
28. Naik AD, Petersen LA. The neglected purpose of comparative-effectiveness research. *N Engl J Med.* May 7, 2009;360(19):1929–1931.
29. Peterson ED. Innovation and comparative-effectiveness research in cardiac surgery. *N Engl J Med.* Nov 5, 2009;361(19):1897–1899.
30. Shroyer AL, Grover FL, Hattler B et al. On-pump versus off-pump coronary-artery bypass surgery. *N Engl J Med.* Nov 5, 2009;361(19):1827–1837.
31. Martin DF, Maguire MG, Fine SL. Identifying and eliminating the roadblocks to comparative-effectiveness research. *N Engl J Med.* Jul 8, 2010;363(2):105–107.
32. Berenson A. Lipitor or generic? Billion-dollar battle looms. *New York Times.* October 15, 2005.
33. Pollack A. Approval for drug that treats melanoma. *New York Times.* March 26, 2011.
34. Mushlin AI, Ghomrawi H. Health care reform and the need for comparative-effectiveness research. *N Engl J Med.* Jan 21, 2010;362(3):e6.
35. Weinstein MC, Skinner JA. Comparative effectiveness and health care spending—Implications for reform. *N Engl J Med.* Feb 4, 2010;362(5):460–465.
36. Meropol NJ, Schulman KA. Cost of cancer care: Issues and implications. *J Clin Oncol.* Jan 10, 2007;25(2):180–186.
37. Lee TH, Emanuel EJ. Tier 4 drugs and the fraying of the social compact. *N Engl J Med.* Jul 24, 2008;359(4):333–335.
38. Bach PB. Limits on Medicare's ability to control rising spending on cancer drugs. *N Engl J Med.* Feb 5, 2009;360(6):626–633.
39. Neumann PJ, Weinstein MC. Legislating against use of cost-effectiveness information. *N Engl J Med.* Oct 14, 2010;363(16):1495–1497.
40. Antiel RM, Curlin FA, James KM et al. Physicians' beliefs and U.S. health care reform—A national survey. *N Engl J Med.* Oct 1, 2009;361(14):e23.

Chapter 9

How Will Health Care Reform Change the Way We Practice Medicine?

> Most [doctors] are in practices with five or fewer other physicians. They keep their records on paper in longhand. When they need to consult a colleague, they reach for the telephone. They bill for each visit. They have little idea about how their skills compare to those of fellow practitioners, nor do most know what their patients really think about the care they give.
>
> **David Brown,** *Washington Post,* **May 4, 2010**

In 1978 I was a second-year medical student at the Louisiana State University School of Medicine in Shreveport. The medical school had been started nine years earlier with the goal of increasing the number of primary care physicians in the northwest part of Louisiana. Each Wednesday afternoon we shadowed a local doctor. I spent the year with Dr. Edward Butler, a family practitioner in Haynesville, Louisiana, a rural community of 2,500 people in north-central Louisiana, five miles south of the Arkansas border.

The first time I went to Dr. Butler's clinic, he was sitting in his wood-paneled office, his boots propped up on his desk, enjoying a plug of tobacco. Two stuffed ducks extended from the wall behind his head, and his desk was covered with huge piles of medical journals. He had graduated at the top of his class from the LSU School of Medicine in New Orleans and had scored in the ninety-ninth percentile on the family practice boards, and he devoured each of those journals that sat on his desk. Dr. Butler returned to Haynesville after medical school following in the footsteps of his grandfather, who had been an army surgeon during the Civil War.

The Butler clinic was a long A-frame building nestled in the pine trees indigenous to north-central Louisiana. There was a waiting room at one end and a small emergency care area at the opposite end. A surgeon from Eldorado, Arkansas, came to town once a week to perform elective cases at the local hospital. Patients needing emergency surgery were transported to one of the large private hospitals in Shreveport if they had insurance or to a charity hospital in Shreveport or Monroe, Louisiana, if they didn't have insurance. Dr. Butler shared call with a partner. On some weekends and nights, a surgical or medical resident from LSU-Shreveport would cover the hospital to give Dr. Butler a night off. While some patients had private insurance or Medicare, many of his patients had no insurance, and it was not uncommon for patients to pay for their care with fresh game or produce.

Haynesville has changed little since 1978. The population is largely the same size, most people who are employed work in the oil and gas or the pulp wood industries, and nearly a quarter of all families live below the poverty line. Haynesville is located in Claiborne Parish. The doctors who practice in the parish all have close links to the community. Of the seven primary care physicians who serve the population of 20,000, three are direct descendants of former Claiborne Parish doctors. As a result. Claiborne Parish is the best-staffed rural parish in Louisiana due in large part to the relationship between the doctors and the community.

Sam Abshire grew up in Abbeville, Louisiana, a tiny hamlet in South Louisiana. He exudes confidence and has that ideal mixture of compassion and concern that patients expect and admire. His passions in life are his family, his medical practice, and duck hunting. He joined the Butler Clinic when he finished training, and it is now called the Butler-Abshire Clinic. Sam's practice is much like Dr. Butler's was thirty-some years ago. About 20 percent of his patients have Medicaid, and about 30 percent have Medicare. "In a good year, 15 percent of our patients have no insurance, and in a bad year, it's 22 percent," Sam told me. Patients without insurance pay a fee based on a sliding scale, or sometimes their care is simply written off. Sam told me that this past spring he received "so much produce that we could have filled a truck." A surgeon still visits the clinic two days a week because many patients are unable to travel to Shreveport because of costs or lack of transportation.

Sam makes house calls for patients who cannot get to the clinic because of their health problems or because they lack transportation. The doctors in the parish cover all of the community's acute medical needs as well as preventive care. The hospital recently built a new and expanded emergency room. It is staffed by nurse practitioners during the day and covered from home by a doctor at night. There are four nurses and one nurse practitioner in the Butler-Abshire Clinic (who handle follow-up care and emergency visits). Sam's practice has kept abreast of new technology, installing an electronic health record several years ago, and they have recently moved into a new office. How health care reform works in these rural areas will be as important as how it works in large multispecialty group practices and academic health centers.

In an article in the *Washington Post*, David Brown wrote: "Fifty years from now, it is likely that almost all doctors will be members of teams that include case managers, social workers, dietitians, telephone counselors, data crunchers, guideline instructors, performance evaluators and external reviewers. They will be parts of organizations that are responsible for patients in and out of the hospital, in sickness and in health, over decades."[1] I cannot argue with Brown's vision—but is it realistic? What is health care reform legislation actually going to do to change the way that doctors practice medicine, how they are compensated, how the results of demonstration projects and pilot programs may translate into new health care delivery systems? How can we modify the health care reform legislation to ensure that it works for patients and doctors in both large cities and in small towns like Haynesville, Louisiana?

Physician Compensation

No part of the health care reform act is more politically charged than the bill's failure to address issues regarding physician compensation. As soon as a doctor raises the issue of compensation, the public immediately views us as self-centered money-grubbers. I don't believe that every doctor should see an increase in compensation. We have to develop a more rational system that rewards doctors for the time they spend and for providing high-quality care. The belief that doctors make enormous amounts of money is a myth. This might be true for plastic surgeons, dermatologists, ear, nose, and throat specialists, and some orthopedic surgeons in large metropolitan areas, but it is clearly not the case across the country. The average salary for a primary care physician in the United States is approximately $160,000 per year, and that amount is less than the average salary of most executives, bankers, and other individuals in the financial world. In addition, physicians graduate from medical school with an average debt of nearly $160,000.

How are doctors paid for their services? Medicare and most private health insurers pay doctors a fee for each service they provide—the fee-for-service system. Each billable task receives a CPT code—with thousands of codes assigned to each different specialty. There are over 8,000 CPT codes that apply to cardiology procedures alone. The fee schedule was heavily weighted in favor of tests and procedures, and thus doctors who perform surgical procedures and tests such as ultrasound views of the heart or abdomen receive substantially more remuneration than primary care physicians In 1989, Medicare created the Resource Based Relative Value Scale, a formula to increase its fees on an annual basis to keep up with changes in the cost of living and in the cost of running a doctor's office.

The current fee-for-service reimbursement system impedes the delivery of quality health care and raises health care costs.[3] Physicians are paid almost exclusively on volume and not on value, and there are no reliable mechanisms for controlling overutilization of tests and procedures. Specialists are only paid when they see a patient in person despite the fact that many consultations could be handled over the phone or through e-mails. Payments for some services are exorbitantly high, while payments for other services might be so low that the physician who provides those services actually loses money. Under the current payment system physicians and hospitals are financially harmed when patients remain healthy and are rewarded when patients get sick.

Sustainable Growth Rate

In 1997, Congress determined that total payments to all doctors in the United States per beneficiary should not grow faster than the economy as a whole. Congress set a cap on health care spending to slow the growth in costs and to address the fear that physicians would perform more procedures if reimbursements per procedure decreased. Since total spending equals price-times-volume and since total spending was capped, for any increase in volume there would have to be a corresponding decrease in price. That is, if total volumes increased, the fees paid to doctors would decrease. This formula is called the Sustainable Growth Rate or the SGR.[4]

The SGR is not influenced by the spending (or utilization) of a single physician but links all physicians together. Individual physicians actually have a greater incentive to increase spending, in any given year because nothing they do will affect overall spending and therefore they cannot influence their own reimbursement. Another problem with the SGR is that the targets that were originally set for utilization were far too ambitious—policy analysts expected utilization (spending) to rise at a very slow rate. Spending after 1997 actually rose at an astronomical rate. The SGR was created using a cumulative and prospective formula. If spending in one year exceeded that year's target, spending (including physician reimbursement) in the following year would have to be reduced. If spending in the subsequent year was not reduced to an adequate level, then additional reductions had to come in future years.

When spending continued to increase after 1997 at a rate that exceeded the amount budgeted, the SGR formula required that Congress cut reimbursements to doctors. Congress postponed the cuts in reimbursements to doctors each year because they didn't want to anger doctors. The health economist Bruce Vladeck noted that "every time Congress postpones a formula-determined fee reduction, it compounds the difference between actual and expected fees, making the (theoretical) eventual adjustment that much more severe."[5] In 2010, in the midst of the recession, the Senate finally decided to adhere to the SGR formula and refused to postpone the cuts. As a result, doctors faced a 21 percent across-the-board cut in reimbursement in the summer of 2010. Not wanting to set off a firestorm before the midterm elections of 2010, Congress once again passed a bill that deferred the cuts—but the problem didn't go away.

The SGR remains a point of contention for both Congress and doctors because a considerable amount of money is at stake. Remember that the SGR formula is cumulative and prospective. Aggregate Medicare physician expenditures have only exceeded the budgeted amounts by approximately $20 billion since 1997; however, when the value is compounded by inflation over a period of over ten years, the cost becomes $250 billion. This amount is still a drop in the bucket when compared to the current U.S. deficit of $7 trillion, but is enormous when the cost is attributable just to doctors.[5] Congress is reluctant to institute an increase in health care spending of any size—a view that is even stronger after the 2010 midterm elections. It would have been far easier for Congress to simply "write off" the $20 billion debt, but unfortunately arcane rules do not allow Congress to write off debt. Congress is thus left with a difficult decision: appropriate $250 billion to pay the debt incurred by the SGR formula and anger the voting public or institute an across-the-board pay reduction for all physicians of 21 percent. A cut in reimbursement of this magnitude would be catastrophic not only for a small practice like Sam's but also for a large academic medical center. Can you imagine what the response would be if the government announced that every lawyer or athlete in America was going to have their pay reduced in perpetuity by 21 percent?

How Did the Patient Protection and Affordable Care Act Change the Way Doctors Are Paid?

The Patient Protection and Affordable Care Act does little to change the system other than modestly increasing reimbursement for primary care physicians. The legislation also requires state Medicaid programs to pay primary care physicians at least 100 percent of Medicare's rates in 2013 and 2014—but there are no provisions for physician payment before 2013 and after 2014.[6] The bill does, however, lay the groundwork for a series of demonstration projects and pilot studies that will test a variety of new strategies for reimbursing both doctors and hospitals. How these strategies work and how they are implemented will undoubtedly have a major influence on the practice of medicine and patient care.

The American Medical Association authored a report that described fundamental ways to modify physician payments—many of which are incorporated into the Patient Protection and Affordable Care Act: (1) insurers can pay for certain services that doctors provide that are not currently paid for, such as telephone calls to patients and e-mail contacts with patients; (2) insurers can make payments based on the quality of the service that is delivered—so-called pay-for-performance; (3) the payments to two or more doctors for two or more services can be combined into a single payment to reduce the ability of a single physician to deliver unnecessary services while rewarding doctors for collaborative care ("bundled payments"); (4) payments can be made dependent on the cost of services delivered by other providers; (5) payments can be made that support the development of new kinds of infrastructure or practice structure such as electronic health records and nurse-led disease management programs.[7]

Paying for services that are not currently paid for, such as answering a patient's questions by e-mail, provides an opportunity for doctors to provide better care for their patients and to increase their income; however, if the payment they receive is too low for the amount of time the new service requires, it might make the practice less profitable. Sam Abshire makes house calls on patients he knows well. The house calls are great for his patients because they don't have to leave their homes and worry about transportation, but they are incredibly time consuming for Sam, and he doesn't receive any more compensation for a house call than he does for seeing a patient in his office. He could increase the number of house calls he makes—but only if the level of compensation were also increased. Payments for new services will only work if they do not result in increased physician costs or a decrease in reimbursements for existing services in an effort to ensure budget neutrality.

Pay-for-Performance

Pay-for-performance makes intuitive sense because it rewards doctors for providing better care; however, it has important drawbacks that haven't been considered by health policy analysts. Many private insurers have already instituted pay-for-performance programs. Some pay-for-performance programs reduce the base pay for a service and then reward doctors with a "bonus" when it is determined that the patient has done well or that performance standards have been met. Small or midsized practices may have problems meeting their monthly cash flow needs if payments are withheld. Small practices like the Butler-Abshire Clinic may also be faced with unacceptably high administrative costs to collect the data that is necessary are demonstrate quality performance.

The greatest limitation of pay-for-performance programs is that they only reward what can be measured. It is also more difficult to achieve quality metrics in patients with chronic disease or in those who are socioeconomically challenged. Pay-for-performance may therefore cause doctors to avoid complex patients or penalize doctors who care for a population that is socioeconomically underserved.

Payment Bundling

Payment "bundling" is one of the most popular payment reforms among health policy analysts. The reform act instructs the secretary of HHS to establish a pilot program to evaluate paying a bundled payment for an acute hospitalization for one of eight conditions by 2013. Services that will be bundled include any services provided during the three days prior to a hospital admission, the hospital admission itself, and the thirty days following discharge from the hospital. The secretary of HHS will assess the ability of bundled payments to improve functional status and improve a patient's perception of their care and patient outcomes. Bundling payments reduces the ability of an individual physician to provide unnecessary services since payments remain the same regardless of how many procedures are performed. Economists have predicted that bundled payments can reduce the volume of services and can reduce costs by 5.4 percent between 2010 and 2019.

The level of integration that is necessary to allow a group of doctors and nurses to work collaboratively in both the inpatient and outpatient settings is found at relatively few health centers in the United States. Another limitation of bundled payments is that the bundled payment for the care of a patient will be less than the payment that was historically made to the individual doctors and nurses who cared for a patient with the same group of problems. The hospitals and the participating doctors will, therefore, need an adequate flow of cash to offset any decreases in revenue that come about as a result of bundled payments. For small practices and rural hospitals, bundled payments may be problematic.

Bundled payments will only work if the payments can be judiciously divided among the doctors and nurses who provide care for the patient. Small primary care practices or small subspecialty practices will have little leverage in most hospitals when compared with large groups of surgical subspecialists who are responsible for the lion's share of the hospital's margin. This raises the concern that primary care doctors and medical subspecialists could end up receiving an inappropriately small slice of the health care "pie" if the distribution of the bundled payments is left to hospital administrators.

In 2002, the Butler-Abshire Clinic was bought by one of the large health systems in Shreveport. The relationship fell apart several years later when high overhead costs in the hospital led the hospital's administrator to pass an increasing number of costs on to the two doctors. Drs. Abshire and Butler were able to untangle themselves from their legal agreements with the health system and happily returned to their earlier practice structure—an entanglement that might have been more difficult to unwind if it involved bundled payments.

Payment bundling also presents risks even for large practices. Large practices may not be large enough to provide economies of scale that would make it cost-effective to develop the infrastructure that will allow economic collaboration. Bundled payments also introduce elements of uncertainty for both physicians and their patients. Doctors don't know exactly what they will be paid for any service provided and patients will worry that hospitals and doctors might withhold desirable but higher-cost services to improve their profit margins.

Several models that modify the basic bundling structure will also be evaluated by demonstration projects and pilot studies. Paying for care on a warranty basis is one such model. A health care warranty ensures that neither the hospital nor the physician will charge for services that occur as a result of a preventable error including an infection or a surgical error that occurs during or after a hospitalization. But will patients feel the same way about their health care if it begins to resemble buying a car?

Global Payment

Global payments are another form of payment restructuring. This system was designed to address the concern that payments that are predicated on a single episode of care do not encourage physicians or hospitals to reduce the total number of hospitalizations. In global payments, doctors receive a single payment to cover the costs of all of the care needed for a fixed period of time regardless of the number of acute care episodes. This is the only payment system that rewards doctors for keeping their patients healthy and for avoiding hospitalizations. This is also the only payment system that requires doctors to take medical risk. That is, doctors can make money if they are able to keep their patients out of the hospital or are able to care for their patients without using expensive tests or procedures. Doctors lose money if the cost of the care for a patient exceeds the single payment. Health policy analysts suggest that this disadvantage can be mitigated by adjusting payment levels based on the types and severity of diseases for which an individual is being treated. The global payment system does not, however, account for the fact that patients from underserved areas where people have little access to preventive care are often unable to pay for their medications or that in these areas doctors may be scarce and invariably have higher costs of care. Poverty and poor adherence to medical regimens have long been recognized as substantial roadblocks to gaining improved outcomes for patients. Global payments will only work when health policy analysts can factor both medical and socioeconomic factors into payment formulas. Without careful attention to the many nonmedical factors that influence health care costs, doctors and hospitals will actually have incentives to avoid providing care to individuals who have a high risk because of multiple co-morbidities or because of poverty.

Most of the doctors I spoke with have little confidence that government regulators or health policy analysts sitting at their desks in Washington actually understand the needs of doctors or patients. They point to examples of how both public and private insurers have failed to reconcile these needs in developing new payment system policies. Sam Abshire shared with me a great example of the regulatory conundrum. Medicare pays for physician office visits for its beneficiaries and requires a $117 co-pay. Most of Sam's Medicare patients can't afford the co-pay, but Sam is legally bound to bill his patients for the co-pay regardless of their financial means. In fact, Medicare mandates that he bill the patient at least three times before he can write off the payment. The Butler-Abshire Clinic employs one woman who does nothing but handle government reimbursement and do the complicated bookkeeping that is required to ensure that "we don't go to jail for Medicare fraud," laments Sam.

Health care reform will also have an important impact on the relationships between practicing physicians and their hospitals. U.S. hospitals have begun to respond to what they perceive as the economic threats of health care reform by hiring physicians—both primary care physicians and specialists.[8] A 2010 survey found that 74 percent of hospital leaders contacted planned to increase physician employment within the next twelve to thirty-six months.[9] In the 1990s, hospitals employed primary care physicians because they perceived an opportunity to direct the flow of referrals to specialists who used their facilities. That turned out to be a bad decision as hospitals lost money on primary care, and referrals often went elsewhere.

Hospital economics have now come full circle due in large part to health care reform. Hospitals once again are purchasing physician practices but for different reasons. Hospitals now perceive that by purchasing physicians they will be able to reduce the costs associated with variations in physician practice, maximize asset utilization, control length of stay and patient discharge, utilize information technology, and standardize supplies. Large physician networks provide hospitals with greater power when they contract with health plans in the current fee-for-service system. It is unclear, however, whether purchasing physicians will lower hospital costs or the cost of health care overall. A recent report suggests that hospitals will lose $150,000 to $250,000 per year over the first three years for each employed physician they hire, and losses will persist even after year three.[8] If hospitals can successfully transition through the initial losses, there is the real possibility that large and powerful integrated health systems can actually increase overall health care costs by decreasing competition.[11]

It is less clear how the integration of individual physician practices into large health systems will affect doctors or patients. Doctors will clearly lose a great deal of their autonomy, and they will shift from guaranteed salaries to incentive-driven compensation that is based on productivity and the quality of care that they deliver. There is a real fear that hospitals will place productivity first and quality a distant second. Hospital employment may provide a buffer for physicians against the turmoil of health care reform; however, their options for transitioning from employment back to private practice may be severely limited. Patients will hopefully see only benefits. Greater integration across the health care delivery system, greater use of electronic health records, and more effective quality control will hopefully balance any increase in health care costs.

Integration may not work for everyone. Many large academic medical centers have successfully integrated the many practitioners into the medical center especially when those practitioners are located in close proximity to the hospital. The doctors are then able to take advantage of all of the opportunities afforded to them by an association with a large hospital including home care services, specialty referrals, nursing and pharmacy support, and quality assurance and quality improvement initiatives. For small rural practices like Sam's, integration with a large hospital system that is located at a significant distance would be neither economically nor medically beneficial.

Electronic Health Records

One infrastructure cost that all physicians will face by 2015 is the need to implement an electronic health record. In 2009 in a speech to the joint session of Congress, President Obama noted that "our recovery plan will invest in electronic health records and new technology that will reduce errors, bring down costs, ensure privacy, and save lives." Nationwide utilization of an electronic health record is a cornerstone of health care reform.[12] The Health Information Technology for Economic and Clinical Health (HITECH) Act, a part of the stimulus package, allocated $50 billion over the next five years for implementation of electronic health records.

Physicians point to three important benefits of EHR: the systems can help avoid redundant tests, gather enormous amounts of data for research, and prevent doctors from prescribing drugs that interact adversely with one another.

Advocates for EHR also point to the fact that EHRs can prevent or minimize diagnostic errors by supporting decision making, provide checklists for managing various diseases, and remind doctors when it is time to take preventive steps or follow-up actions. Electronic health records can also provide a communication platform between the numerous doctors who care for a patient and can help the primary care physician track follow-up to ensure that patients keep their appointments with consulting physicians, get their tests, or refill their medications. EHRs provide consultants with ready access to information, maintain a dynamic patient history, track medication changes across different doctors, provide information about new guideline recommendations that apply to a specific patient, and maintain a list of the patient's problems that allows for continuous updating. They can also dump enormous amounts of information into data repositories that can be used to "grade" individual physicians based on how they compare with their peers.

In an article in the *Washington Post*, David Brown envisioned health care fifty years from now: "The records of what they do for a patient—and what every other doctor does—will be in electronic form, accessible from any computer. Software will gently remind them what to consider as they treat and try to prevent diseases. How the patients fare will be measured and publicized and used in part to judge practitioners' performance." Brown's lofty goals are not universally shared. Dr. Thomas H. Lee, president of the physicians' network at Partners HealthCare, noted that the administration's views of electronic health records were based on "unrealistic expectations" and "unachievable timelines."[14]

Only 17 percent of U.S. physicians currently use either a minimally functional or a comprehensive electronic health record system. When systems do exist, they often do not link physician practices with local hospitals much less with health insurers. Dr. David Brailer, former National Coordinator for Health Information Technology and White House information czar from 2004 to 2006, aptly described the current situation when he said, "The hard part of this is that we can't just drop a computer on every doctor's desk. Getting electronic records up and running is a very technical task."[16]

Another major impediment to reaching the goals of the health care reform act is system costs.[17] Large health systems can see a return on investment by using the electronic health record to seamlessly link the health system with regional practitioners.[18] The cost of an electronic health record system can be prohibitive for a small hospital or for a small to medium-sized medical practice—even when factoring in the incentive provided through the American Recovery and Reinvestment Act. For some practices the changes in work-flow required by an EHR might also be problematic.

There is also no proof that electronic health records actually improve patient care. Some experts contend that the time-consuming process of entering electronic documentation can distract the physician from thinking about diagnostic opportunities, can discourage independent data gathering, can cause the physician to pay more attention to the computer than the patient, and can perpetuate errors.[19] Doctors spend too much time clicking boxes and not enough time dictating their evaluations and thoughts to referring physicians. Computer-based documentation is built around billing codes and legal requirements—not on what is going on with an individual patient.[20] Howard Weitz is a colleague and friend who is the director of our cardiology program. Howard has spent his entire life in Philadelphia. Like Sam Abshire, he is an outstanding clinician and a warm and compassionate human being. Sam and Howard used the same adjectives to describe their electronic health record systems—"cumbersome and slow." Howard took it a step further. He did an experiment. He compared how long it took him to see thirty-six patients a day—eighteen in the morning session and eighteen in the afternoon session—with and without EHR. The EHR added seven minutes to the time it took to see each patient—an additional three hours in his day. Not all doctors have the same problem. Some specialists can afford to have "scribes" follow them around in the hospital and in their outpatient offices and fill in all of the check boxes on the computer screen. Unfortunately, neither Sam's practice nor Howard's practice could afford a scribe.

Some health care experts have reported more sinister fears about EHR. The current EHR platforms are built on billing codes because it is the ability to bill expeditiously, accurately, and efficiently that forms the groundwork for the return on investment associated with an EHR. Most doctors—myself included—have a poor understanding of codes, and therefore billing codes are often entered by "coders." Scott Haig pointed out in an article in *Time Magazine* that the opportunity for a coder to change a code with the flick of a button is ominous.[21] He gives the example of a patient who comes to see the doctor because of a "urinary tract infection." If the diagnosis is "pyelonephritis"—an infection involving the bladder as well as the kidneys—the doctor can bill at a higher level than if the diagnosis is a "urinary tract infection." If every time the doctor clicks on the button for "urinary tract infection" the button for "pyelonephritis" also pops up (or is automatically activated), the doctor gets more money and our health care costs go up. How would anyone know that the patient only had a simple infection in the bladder and not pyelonephritis? They wouldn't!

Electronic health records can also allow insurance companies to deny tests and treatments. In the absence of an electronic health record, doctors often order tests with the hope that the insurance company will eventually pay the bill. In an era of instantaneous feedback, the computer may simply refuse to allow the doctor to order a test if there is not enough justification included to warrant it. This type of system could lower health care costs. But who is the best person to decide on a patient's care—the doctor, government regulators, or health insurance company administrators? EHR will certainly improve the practice of medicine despite its current flaws. The important point is that federal regulations and Congress must recognize that the full impact of EHR will be decades away as new generations of the technology will be required before its full effects can be harnessed.

Multispecialty Group Practices

If you look at health care reform from 30,000 feet, it appears that the most effective structure for a physician practice in the future will be the large multispecialty group practice. They have the level of management services, financial management systems, nursing support, and capital resources that facilitate their ability to effectively change their practices in the context of health care reform, and they can use their size to leverage their partner hospitals. Their large number of patients precludes the ability of a single outlier patient to alter the overall statistics of the practice, and the large group has greater leverage in negotiating contracts with private insurance companies and with suppliers.

Many of the practices that are touted as being high-quality and low-cost performers fit into the category of highly integrated multispecialty group practices. These practices include integrated systems such as Denver Health, Intermountain Health Care, Geisinger Health System, and the Mayo Clinic. These systems have health information systems, sophisticated physician compensation systems that recognize the contributions of all physicians, and management and financial systems in place that can effectively link the practice with payers and regulatory authorities. They have the structure and wherewithal to accommodate a bundled payment and, in most cases, are financially linked with one or more hospitals. These organizations are particularly effective when they are physician led as evidenced by the Mayo Clinic, the Cleveland Clinic, the Emory Health System, the Duke Health Systems, Partners Health Care, Johns Hopkins Medicine, and others. Each of these systems also has a long and storied culture of excellence that pervades every part of their operation. They also tend to be the dominant provider in their geographic areas—with little local competition or redundancy in programs.

There are, however, no objective data to support the benefits of a multispecialty group practice or any other practice structure. The structure that works for one practice might not work for another. In large multispecialty group practices, low-performing members may negatively impact high-performing members, and the various members of the group may not have the same practice culture. Multispecialty group practices also have distinct disadvantages when they do not represent the best-performing specialists in the community, or if they do not have all specialties and therefore must contract with specialists who are not part of their practice. A multigroup practice would also be difficult to create in rural Louisiana because there aren't enough primary care doctors or specialists. The great truth that health care pundits fail to recognize is that the structure of the health care delivery system is only one component of insuring high-quality and low-cost care. The physicians and the culture of their practice are the most important elements for the delivery of excellence in patient care.

The Independent Payment Advisory Board

The element of the Patient Protection and Affordable Care Act that is causing some of the greatest angst among physicians is the creation of the Independent Payment Advisory Board. The board will be made up of fifteen members who are appointed by the president and confirmed by the Senate for six-year terms. It replaces the Medicare Payment Advisory Commission (MedPAC). MedPAC submitted annual recommendations to Congress on a broad range of Medicare issues but was not required to achieve budgetary targets and had no independent decision-making authority. Congress was not obliged to follow its recommendations. By contrast, the new board has the authority to recommend proposals to limit Medicare spending growth. If projected per capita Medicare spending exceeds the target growth rate (0.5 percent in 2014 escalating to 1.5 percent in 2018), the Board is actually required to recommend proposals to reduce Medicare spending by specific amounts. The first recommendations are due in 2014 with implementation in 2015. MedPAC will now become simply an advisory body for Congress. The new board has incredible power. The law establishes specific rules that govern how the recommendations of the board will pass through congressional committees, including rules governing the procedures that Congress must follow such as limitations on debate and timelines to ensure fast-tracking through committees. Non-germane amendments are not permitted, and Congress cannot consider any bill or amendment that does not meet the board's targets. Congress can only repeal or change the fast-track congressional consideration process for board recommendations with a three-fifths vote in the Senate. The health care reform bill also limits the board's actions. The board cannot make any recommendations that ration care or reduce benefits; therefore, any cuts must come from physician or hospital reimbursements. Medicare beneficiaries could, however, see decreased access to the kind of care they seek if the explicit limits on Medicare spending growth are unrealistic because of the emergence of new and expensive technologies.

Sam Abshire worries that the new board will not understand the daily problems facing a doctor in Haynesville, Louisiana. Sam loves to tell the story of Medicaid in Louisiana. Each Medicaid beneficiary is permitted to have a fixed number of emergency room visits—whether they need them or not. A visit only "counts" for hospital reimbursement if the patient is seen by a physician. As a result, Sam and his partner must make a trip to the emergency room in the middle of the night not because the patient needs to be seen—but so that the hospital can be reimbursed. Sam points out, "In the thirty years I have been practicing medicine, a state Medicaid administrator has never walked into my hospital or my office in Claiborne Parish. If they had, maybe they would understand the downstream effect of some of their ridiculous rules and regulations."

How Can the Patient Protection and Affordable Care Act Be Improved?

A group of specific and simple changes in how physicians are compensated and practices structured could markedly improve the quality of patient care and lower health care costs. The Centers for Medicare and Medicaid Services should undertake audits of the medical records—including audits of the actual studies— to determine the medical necessity of the procedures and studies. A review of the audits must be performed by a panel of doctors who are in active clinical practice and not by CMS administrators. Second, physicians should only be reimbursed for services that are consistent with consensus practice standards—a step that will substantially decrease overutilization of tests and procedures. The broad implementation of electronic health records will allow both treatment and diagnostic algorithms to be audited on an almost ongoing basis. When there are disagreements, issues should be adjudicated by a panel of practicing physicians—not by administrators or specialists in other disciplines. There must also be opportunities for physicians to appeal the decisions of payers in a timely and cost-effective manner.

We must recognize that the basic mechanics of the Medicare Physician Fee Schedule are flawed.[22] Efforts to increase payments for primary care and decrease reimbursement for procedural and interventional services simply haven't worked.[5] Let's face the facts. There is no mechanism for equitably distributing fees among the many different physicians who care for an individual patient—and if there were, it is certain that "distributional politics" would override any efforts to do so.[5] The lion's share of payments would go to the physicians with the most political clout—not to the physicians who were doing the most work. Even in academic medical centers where physicians are salaried, there are often enormous disparities in salary across the various specialties due entirely to the fact that specialists who provide "high margin" services have far more political clout in the system than do doctors who perform "low margin" services. The most important concept is that we can't change physician compensation and at the same time have budget neutrality—it just won't work!

Arnold Relman, the former editor of the *New England Journal of Medicine*, is one of the few health policy experts who have actually proposed a "system" that would restructure physician payment.[24] Relman envisions a health care system in which medical care is delivered by a national network of community-based, private, not-for-profit, multispecialty, and doctor-managed group practices. Physicians would receive a salary for caring for patients—but the salary would be based on value and not volume. Compensation must be adjudicated to account for the length of training and inherent risks in the specialty (and work hours) in order for this type of system to work. In the health care system that Relman envisions, groups would not be allowed to keep net income. They would compete based only on quality, and groups would be held harmless for losses due to caring for a population of patients that was high risk for expensive conditions. "Capitated prepayment of the groups would allow a central public agency to control the country's total medical expenditures," but patient care would be entirely in the hands of the doctor.[3]

I have worked in highly integrated health delivery systems—and, in general, I agree with his vision of the future—yet I think it is highly unlikely that we will see this type of utopian medical system any time soon. Relman himself notes that without a political awakening, "the economic incentives and organization of medical care cannot be changed and the current slide of the system toward bankruptcy will continue." In the absence of a utopian system we must begin to incorporate the model of an integrated health care system wherever and whenever possible. It will also be imperative that payment reforms and delivery system reforms evolve in a coordinated way. Much like the "chicken and the egg," physicians will be unable to institute reform unless they have the revenues with which to support new organizational structures—but the new revenues will only come with the institution of new structures. Thus payment reform will have to come in stepwise transitions and must be carried out with the recognition that costs will go up before they go down. The final caveat is perhaps the most important. A one-size-fits-all approach will not solve our problems—it will create more of them. Each region of the country and each specialty will have different and unique requirements. A health care delivery system that works in suburban Philadelphia is unlikely to be successful in Haynesville, Louisiana, or urban Philadelphia. For small rural practices like Sam Abshire's, maintaining the present fee-for-service payment methodology will allow Sam and Clint to continue to provide high-quality care at a lower cost than any new or novel payment system. At the end of the day, the structure that works best will be the one that provides the highest quality of care for the people of that particular region.

Notes

1. Brown D. New health-care law might make your doctor more informed, efficient, responsive. *Washington Post.* May 4, 2010.
2. Elliott V. *American Medical News.* March 14, 2011.
3. Relman AS. Doctors as the key to health care reform. *N Engl J Med.* Sep 24, 2009;361(13):1225–1227.
4. MedPAC. *The Sustainable Growth Rate System.* Washington DC. March 2007.
5. Vladeck BC. Fixing Medicare's physician payment system. *N Engl J Med.* May 27, 2010;362(21):1955–1957.
6. Bindman AB, Schneider AG. Catching a wave—Implementing health care reform in California. *N Engl J Med.* Mar 30, 2011.
7. Miller HD. Pathways for Physician Success under Healthcare Payment and Delivery Reforms, Executive Summary, AMA, 2010. http://www.ama-assn.org/ama1/pub/upload/mm/399/payment-pathways-summary.pdf.
8. Kocher R, Sahni NR. Hospitals' race to employ physicians—The logic behind a money-losing proposition. *N Engl J Med—Health Policy and Reform.* March 30, 2011.
9. Cantlupe J. *Physician Alignment in an Era of Change.* Brentwood, TN. September 14, 2010.
10. Kocher R, Sahni NR. Physicians versus hospitals as leaders of accountable care organizations. *N Engl J Med.* 2010;363:2579–2582.
11. Berenson RA, Ginsburg PB, Kemper N. Unchecked provider clout in California foreshadows challenges to health reform. *Health Aff (Millwood).* Apr 2010;29(4):699–705.
12. Cutler DM. Will the cost curve bend, even without reform? *N Engl J Med.* Oct 8, 2009;361(15):1424–1425.
13. Blumenthal D. Launching HITECH. *N Engl J Med.* Feb 4, 2010;362(5):382–385.
14. Pear R. Doctors and hospitals say goals on computerized records are unrealistic. *New York Times.* June 7, 2010.
15. Jha AK, DesRoches CM, Campbell EG et al. Use of electronic health records in U.S. hospitals. *N Engl J Med.* Apr 16, 2009;360(16):1628–1638.
16. Goldman D. Obama's big idea: Digital health records. *CNNMoney.com.* http://money.cnn.com/2009/01/12/technology/stimulus_health_care ed; 2009.
17. Kluger J. Electronic Health Records: What's Taking So Long? *time.com.* http://www.time.com/time/printout/0,8816,1887658,00.html ed; 2009.
18. Shea S, Hripcsak G. Accelerating the use of electronic health records in physician practices. *N Engl J Med.* Jan 21, 2010;362(3):192–195.
19. Hartzband P, Groopman J. Off the record—Avoiding the pitfalls of going electronic. *N Engl J Med.* Apr 17, 2008;358(16):1656–1658.
20. Schiff GD, Bates DW. Can electronic clinical documentation help prevent diagnostic errors? *N Engl J Med.* Mar 25, 2010;362(12):1066–1069.
21. Haig S. Electronic Medical Records: Will They Really Cut Costs? *Time.com.* http://www.time.com/time/printout/0,8816,1883002,00.html ed; 2009.
22. Ginsburg PB, Berenson RA. Revising Medicare's physician fee schedule—Much activity, little change. *N Engl J Med.* Mar 22, 2007;356(12):1201–1203.

23. Wilensky GR. Reforming Medicare's physician payment system. *N Engl J Med.* Feb 12, 2009;360(7):653–655.
24. Relman AS. A second opinion: Rescuing America's health care. *Public Affairs* 2009; New York.

Chapter 10

Will We Ever See Tort Reform in the United States?

> Now, I recognize that it will be hard to make some of these changes if doctors feel like they are constantly looking over their shoulder for fear of lawsuits. Some doctors may feel the need to order more tests and treatments to avoid being legally vulnerable. That's a real issue. And while I'm not advocating caps on malpractice awards which I believe can be unfair to people who've been wrongfully harmed, I do think we need to explore a range of ideas about how to put patient safety first, let doctors focus on practicing medicine, and encourage broader use of evidence-based guidelines.
>
> **President Barack Obama, Address to the American Medical Association, Chicago, June 15, 2009**

Texas, in fact, stands as a good example of how smart, responsible policy can help us take major steps toward fixing a damaged medical system, starting with legal reforms. Just six years ago, Texas was mired in a health care crisis. Our doctors were leaving the state, or abandoning the profession entirely, because of frivolous lawsuits and the steadily increasing medical malpractice insurance premiums that resulted.

Texas Governor Rick Perry,
Washington Examiner, **August 13, 2009**

I received a call several years ago from Steve Smith (not his real name), a friend and colleague in New York. Steve is a Harvard-trained cardiologist who takes care of some of the sickest patients in New York. His patients have heart failure, a disease of the heart muscle that causes patients to have shortness of breath, swelling in their legs, and fatigue. Many of Steve's patients receive heart transplants; Steve cares for them before and after their surgery. His patients sometimes require artificial hearts. He was calling me because he had been sued by one of his patients—and he was distraught. He wanted my help.

The story was interesting. He first met his patient four or five years earlier when his patient was admitted to the hospital with severe symptoms of heart failure. His heart failure was caused by inflammation in the heart muscle—probably due to a virus—an uncommon problem called myocarditis. The patient was given medications and was watched carefully in the cardiac intensive care unit. Many patients who are admitted to the hospital with severe heart failure due to inflammation of the heart require an artificial heart and eventually a heart transplant. A few patients miraculously recover normal or near normal heart function. This patient was one of those lucky few. Although his heart function did not return to normal, the function of his heart improved enough that he was eventually symptom free.

When the patient was first admitted to the hospital, Steve spoke to the patient's family about the possibility of giving the patient an implantable cardio-defibrillator, a pacemaker-like device that shocks the heart when it detects a lethal abnormality in the heart's rhythm. He also spoke to the family about the possible need for a heart transplant. The guidelines published by the American College of Cardiology and the American Heart Association only recommend the use of a defibrillator when the heart function is less than half of what is seen in a normal individual. Patients are also not eligible for a heart transplant unless their heart function is significantly compromised. Steve's patient's heart improved so dramatically that he was not a candidate for a defibrillator or for a transplant.

Steve continued to see his patient several times a year, and each time he measured his patient's heart function, it remained at a level that required only medication. Five years later, Steve's patient died suddenly while shoveling snow. The family was suing Steve because they contended that if he had given his patient a defibrillator or a new heart, he would not have died. The case went on for two years and actually came to trial. I testified at the trial and related to the jury the recommendations of the guideline committee and the fact that Steve had exactly followed those guidelines. The fact that I was an author of the guidelines probably helped as well. The jury found in Steve's favor. Justice was served—but our health system suffered. The hospital spent enormous amounts of money defending Steve, Steve lost countless hours from work attending depositions and meeting with his attorneys, and Steve and his family were put through the uncertainty and anguish of a trial. No good came out of the experience.

It is difficult if not impossible to find a practicing physician in the United States who has not been touched in some way by the debacle that is our tort system. Virtually every doctor has faced the escalating costs of malpractice insurance, and many doctors have moved to communities or states with lower malpractice costs while others have simply left the practice of medicine altogether. Charles Krauthammer succinctly summed up doctors' feelings about tort reform in an op-ed in the July 24, 2009, issue of the *Washington Post* when he noted, "Tort reform would yield tens of billions in savings. Yet you cannot find it in the Democratic bills. And Obama breathed not a word about it in the full hour of his health-care news conference. Why not? It's no mystery. The Democrats are parasitically dependent on huge donations from trial lawyers."[1] In this chapter we will look at the issues regarding tort reform, how our current tort system impacts patient care, and what steps Congress should have taken or can still take to resolve the situation in a way that maintains patient safety and fairness.

Current Tort System

Advocates of tort reform have argued that our current tort system increases the cost of health care by forcing doctors to practice defensive medicine. This concept implies that doctors order tests and perform procedures only to decrease their malpractice exposure and not because it is an important part of caring for a patient or diagnosing their disease. The cost of defensive medicine has been estimated to be anywhere between 1 percent and 5 percent of total health care spending.[2-4] It should come as no surprise that the doctors present higher figures and plaintiff attorneys cite lower figures. Yet even at the lower figures, we are talking about close to $50 billion each year, a significant cost to the health care system.

A major problem in trying to understand the debate over tort reform is that there is an enormous amount of hype and little data. No one enters the debate without bias. Just look at the various entities that fill the Internet with information. You can find websites that will discuss health care reform and also direct you to a lawyer such as injury.findlaw.com, Injury Law Wiki.com, Indiana Medical

Malpractice Attorney Blog.com, Say No To Caps.com, Law Professors Type Pad.com, Legal Info.com, and Lect Law.com. Some organizations have formed to espouse tort reform, including the Texans for Lawsuit Reform, American Tort Reform Association, and For the Defense.org. And then there are the far left or far right organizations that have weighed in on the tort reform issue: the Center for American Progress.com, Every Day Citizen.com, the Heritage Foundation, and People Over Profits.com. Finally, there are a handful of organizations that have actually tried to scientifically address the issues regarding malpractice tort reform, including the Congressional Budget Office and the American Academy of Actuaries.

The health care tort reform debate came to a head in the early 2000s as the median malpractice premiums increased precipitously in many states. Although it was both specialty- and state-specific, malpractice premiums increased anywhere between 15 and 30 percent.[5] The increase in malpractice premiums in Pennsylvania ranged from 26 to 73 percent.[6] Some medical liability insurance companies actually stopped writing policies. The premium hikes led to physician strikes in West Virginia, work slowdowns in New Jersey, the temporary closings of some hospital services, and rallies at state capitals.[7] Doctors pointed to an increase in jury awards, the rising costs of defending malpractice claims, the high contingency fees paid to trial lawyers, and the built-in incentives for filing frivolous lawsuits as causing the marked increase in premium prices. Consumer groups blamed the rising premium costs on lower returns on investments received by the medical malpractice carriers and a downturn in the U.S. economy.

The wind for change was taken out of the sails by three published studies. The first was a report by a group led by David Studdert, from the Harvard School of Public Health.[8] Studdert and his colleagues reviewed 1,452 closed claims from five malpractice insurance companies. The study focused on five areas of medical errors. Each case was reviewed by a group of physicians to determine whether the plaintiff had actually been injured by the care. The study found that almost all of the claims involved a treatment-related injury, and 90 percent involved a physical injury. Seventy-three percent of the claims that did not involve an error did not receive compensation while 73 percent of claims that involved error received compensation. Studdert noted that "overall, the malpractice system appears to be getting it right about three quarters of the time. That's far from a perfect record, but it's not bad, especially considering that questions of error and negligence can be complex." The system, however, wasn't perfect.

The Robert Wood Johnson Foundation also published a report that served as a rallying point for opponents of tort reform. The report, led by Michelle Mello, a coauthor of the earlier report from the Harvard School of Public Health, reviewed existing studies in the area of tort reform.[9] The report concluded that there had been above-average increases in premium costs and volatility in the malpractice insurance market and that malpractice insurance had become less affordable and available. Mello was, however, unable to find evidence that access to high-risk services had declined due to the malpractice crisis, although within crisis states, physicians who were worried about their coverage were more likely to report ordering unneeded diagnostic tests. The report also noted that there was not much direct evidence that access to care had been affected by the malpractice risk in various states. Caps on damages did reduce the average size of awards by 20 to 30 percent and had a modest effect on premium growth and physician supply. Other reforms had little impact. The report also noted that "the liability system does not compensate patients in an equitable way, nor does it effectively deter medical errors or encourage participation in patient safety initiatives such as adverse event reporting. It is also inefficient: only about forty percent of the dollars spent on malpractice insurance go to injured patients."

The third report that influenced Congress and public sentiment came from a 2004 study by the Congressional Budget Office.[10] The Budget Office estimated that malpractice premiums and awards to plaintiffs represented less than 2 percent of overall health care costs. The report stated that "any reductions in medical over-treatment due to 'defensive medicine' would be negligible and that defensive medicine may be driven more by the physician's incentives to increase their income than by fears of liability." It also noted that there was "no evidence that restrictions on tort liability reduce medical spending." Using a different set of data, the CBO also found no statistically significant difference in per capita health care spending between states with and without limits on malpractice torts.

Public opinion has also been influenced by reports in the lay press—but many of these contain far more fiction than fact. For example, Les Weisbrod, president of a Washington-based trial lawyers' group, the American Association of Justice, pointed out that the U.S. Institute of Medicine had found a "decade ago that medical errors kill 98,000 Americans a year." He went on to say, "By taking away the rights of people to hold wrongdoers accountable, the quality of health care will suffer tremendously."[11] He failed to say that the Institute of Medicine report did not blame the 98,000 deaths on individual physicians but rather on systems that existed in U.S. hospitals—many of which were subsequently corrected.

A group of recent studies give pause to the conclusion that there are no economic reasons to support medical liability reform. The first is a study by Jonathan Klick, a professor of law at Florida State University, and Thomas Stratmann, a professor of economics at George Mason University.[12] They used sophisticated analysis to look at the causal effect of medical malpractice reform on the supply of doctors in high-risk specialties. They found that caps on noneconomic damages had a significant effect on the per capita number of doctors in a region and that the effect was concentrated only in those specialties that face the highest litigation exposure: orthopedic surgery, obstetrics and gynecology, and neurosurgery.

William Oetgen, a cardiologist from Georgetown University, published an equally compelling study.[13] Oetgen and his colleagues looked at data from the Physician Insurers Association of America registry of medical professional liability claims that were filed between 2000 and 2007 representing claims from twenty-eight medical specialties. The database holds information from 230,624 closed claims—4,248 of which were cardiovascular medical claims. Eighteen percent of the cardiovascular complaints resulted in payments to plaintiffs—30 percent of the total closed claims were paid, and the average payment was $204,268. The most common allegation among cardiovascular closed claims was diagnostic error, and the most common diagnosis was coronary artery disease. The total amount paid over the time period of the study was $13.9 billion—suggesting that malpractice litigation is both expensive and pervasive.

Two additional reports should cause us to question the views from health care economists and political pundits suggesting that the medical malpractice crisis is a myth. The first is a comprehensive report from Northwestern University's Kellogg School of Management that used a database of employer-sponsored health plans covering 10 million Americans.[14] The report measured the impact of tort reform measures that had been enacted in more than thirty states. The authors concluded that a comprehensive, nationwide reform would lower overall health care costs by 2.3 percent. While this seems like a small amount, 2.3 percent of the $2.5 trillion annual health care cost is $57.5 billion. The second was a report from the U.S. House of Representatives Joint Economic Committee titled the *Perverse Nature of the Medical Liability System*.[15] It noted that the time from injury to verdict averaged five years, only 3 percent of victims of medical malpractice actually file a claim, and more than 80 percent of liability claims don't involve a negligent injury while more than half don't involve an injury at all. In addition, plaintiffs receive less than twenty-eight cents out of every dollar spent on the medical liability system. Unfortunately, all of the large databases from insurance carriers are biased because they don't include information from large practices or academic medical centers—both of which are self-insured. They also do not include the large number of cases that were settled out of court.

Malpractice Caps

Many doctors favor caps on claims for pain and suffering. This is the one area of liability in which juries can make decisions that are purely arbitrary and not based on any predefined guidelines or proven liability. California was the first to limit such awards—a step that doctors credited for stabilizing the medical liability climate there. In 2003, Texas voters approved a constitutional amendment limiting noneconomic damages paid to plaintiffs in medical liability cases to $250,000. Ralph Blumenthal wrote that "doctors are responding as supporters predicted, arriving from all parts of the country to swell the ranks of specialists at Texas hospitals and bring professional health care to some long-underserved rural areas."[16] J. James Rohack, MD, a cardiologist in Bryan, Texas, and former president of the American Medical Association, commented that "this just shows that the answer to the question of 'do caps make a difference' is absolutely they do."[17] Other states followed suit including Wisconsin in 2006 and North Carolina in 2007, with the limit on total awards in North Carolina being $1 million.

A report from the American Academy of Actuaries found similar effects of caps on pain and suffering payments. Liability caps in California led to a decline in premium costs and a stabilization of the physician workforce.[18] Similar changes were not seen in New York; New York implemented tort reforms but did not place caps on awards. The actuarial report also pointed out the importance of instituting a mandatory collateral-source offset rule to ensure that double and triple damages cannot be collected through multiple suits. The chance of instituting caps on noneconomic damages on a national basis had been viewed as highly unlikely until the results of the 2010 midterm elections. A number of states have moved tort reform and malpractice caps onto the forefront of political debate after the midterm elections, and even the Republican Congress has taken steps to move tort reform onto the national debate platform.

Patient Protection and Affordable Care Act Failed to Address Tort Reform

Even President Obama once recognized that our medical liability system is highly flawed. Then Senator Obama and then Senator Hillary Clinton authored an editorial that appeared in the *New England Journal of Medicine* in May 2006.[19] They posited that discussions should focus on the fundamental issue of the need to improve patient safety. They proposed that "the tort system must achieve four goals: reduce the rates of preventable patient injuries, promote open communication between physicians and patients, insure patients access to fair compensation for legitimate medical injuries; and, reduce liability insurance premiums for health care providers." To meet these goals they envisioned the establishment of a National Medical Error Disclosure and Compensation program that would promote open communication between patients and their doctors to reduce medical errors, insure patients fair compensation for medical injury, and reduce the costs of malpractice insurance. The lofty goals espoused by Senators Obama and Clinton were not supported by Congress; however, many of their ideas resurfaced in the debates around health care reform.

Congress had a great opportunity to institute tort reform at the time of the passage of the Patient Protection and Affordable Care Act but it did not mandate change. In fact, it only suggested that states evaluate potential reforms. The bill states,

> It is the sense of the Senate that health care reform presents an opportunity to address issues related to medical malpractice and medical liability insurance. States should be encouraged to develop and test alternatives to the existing civil litigation system as a way of improving patient safety, reducing medical errors, encouraging the efficient resolution of disputes, increasing the availability of prompt and fair resolution of disputes, and improving access to liability insurance, while preserving an individual's right to seek redress in court; and, Congress should consider establishing a State demonstration program to evaluate alternatives to the existing civil litigation system with respect to the resolution of medical malpractice claims.

The bill allocates $50 million for five-year demonstration projects that evaluate potential means of reform. The application states that demonstration projects should "allow States and health care systems to develop, implement and evaluate medical liability models that put patient safety first and work to reduce preventable injuries, foster better communication between doctors and their patients, ensure that patients are fairly and quickly compensated in a fair and timely manner for medical injuries, while also reducing the incidence of frivolous lawsuits and liability premiums." It seems that reducing frivolous lawsuits was just an afterthought. Congress had no intention of formulating national policies on tort reform, and unfortunately the bill prohibits any type of demonstration projects that limit the role of trial lawyers or their compensation.

Medical Malpractice—A Silent Disease

The real reason there is so much contradictory data regarding medical malpractice cases is that medical professional liability could be referred to as a silent disease. Insurance carriers and hospital administrators counsel physicians not to discuss cases with their peers for fear that anything they disclose in a conversation could be discoverable by the plaintiff's attorneys. Cases are often quietly settled with a nondisclosure agreement that forbids either the plaintiff or the defendant from discussing the case or the amount of the settlement.[20] Some of the most frivolous and ridiculous cases never come to light because of these nondisclosure agreements. In states without caps and with a history of unusually high jury awards, the number of cases settled often far outnumbers the cases that actually go to trial, providing a very biased accounting of the number of cases.

Philadelphia County has a national reputation for some of the most capricious jury verdicts. A large proportion of cases are therefore settled. Many cases are settled even when the doctors and their insurance carriers believe that they provided appropriate levels of care because the cost of a trial and the uncertainty of capricious and biased juries often make it more cost-effective to settle a case than to go before a jury. Settlements are recorded in data banks like the National Practitioner Data Bank, but these data banks provide only limited information about the circumstances of each case. The physicians who are involved in these cases experience the same psychological stress that my friend Steve had when his case went to trial, but they don't have the chance to clear their names in a public arena.

Employment Law and the Health Professions

The same tort system that effectively litigates against doctors for perceived malfeasance in the care of patients also protects individual doctors from sanctions that are contemplated by hospitals and physician groups. I have been sued twice during my career. I was sued once when I tried to limit the privileges of a physician who failed to demonstrate the required level of competence when performing invasive procedures. The suit claimed that the supervising physician claimed that the plaintiff was incompetent because he believed that the plaintiff would compete with him for patients. The case was settled out of court—but I was later asked to testify for another hospital when they tried to remove the privileges of the same physician because he had harmed a patient. I was sued a second time when I raised concerns with our hospital's administration that the plaintiff was harming patients. That case too was settled out of court. In each case the physicians who sued me were represented by leading malpractice attorneys who spent the majority of their time representing patients in cases against doctors.

These are just two of many cases I know of where it has been difficult, if not impossible, for hospitals and medical school administrators to deal with unprofessional behavior or incompetence on the part of members of the physician staff. There must be safe harbors for physicians and hospitals that try to deal with impaired physicians or with doctors who simply don't demonstrate the appropriate level of competence required to ensure patient safety.

Congress and President Obama repeatedly espouse the notion that we must improve the quality of care as well as decreasing the cost of care, but they have not provided physician executives with the protections necessary to do so. Doctors are like workers in any other profession or occupation—some are great, some are good, and some were probably at the bottom of their class. Physician administrators must therefore be given the tools to improve quality but also the capability to police their own colleagues without the threat of frivolous employment lawsuits.

It Is Not Too Late—Novel Strategies for Reforming Our Tort System

What could Congress still do to effect change in the tort system? I would like to see a cap on the arbitrary jury awards for pain and suffering, because it is so ambiguous and places physicians at the mercy of capricious juries. But there are other excellent alternatives. Three types of medical liability reforms have recently gained traction—all of which are closely aligned with some of the thoughts put forward by Senators Obama and Clinton—disclosure-and-offer programs, administrative or specialized tribunals, and safe harbors for adherence to evidence-based practices.

Disclosure-and-offer programs provide the opportunity for physicians to disclose unanticipated outcomes to patients and their families and make offers of compensation when appropriate.[4] A study carried out at the University of Michigan found that a program of full disclosure and rapid compensation for medical errors resulted in a decrease in new claims for compensation, a shorter time to claim resolution, and a fall in liability costs.[21] These programs remove the adversarial relationship that can evolve between a doctor and the patient, facilitate transparency, and provide a comfort level for the physician in discussing an unexpectedly poor outcome. They are purely voluntary on the part of the patient. The disclosure-and-offer programs often cut out the need for an attorney and therefore will likely be opposed by the plaintiffs' lobby. Disclosure-and-offer programs do not preclude a patient from filing a lawsuit, and there is no clear evidence that they will reduce costs. Many doctors oppose or at least fear disclosure-and-offer programs because, in some cases, they can make a patient aware of concerns or mistakes that had not even yet surfaced. Complex issues of responsibility also arise when an error is made in a hospitalized patient as the hospital and the doctor may have very different agendas.

The creation of an administrative or specialized tribunal is a far more rational and effective method of reforming our current tort system.[22] Administrative panels or judicial courts overseen by judges with medical expertise make decisions about the merits of a claim and the appropriate level of damages based on a knowledge of medicine and relevant practice guidelines. This approach obviates the risk of a trial by a capricious jury. The medical court system also avoids the battles of the experts that occur when both the defense counsel and the plaintiff's counsel hire knowledgeable experts and makes greater use of practice guidelines disseminated by learned societies. The time between complaint and litigation would be markedly shortened, and in all probability costs could be reduced through the use of judgment guidelines. This type of reform would be very attractive to physicians but would certainly be opposed by trial attorneys and possibly by patient advocates who would see it as a way to lower awards. Tribunals would also be extremely helpful in issues of medical employment law.

Safe harbors are a form of tort law that protects doctors from liability if they adhere to evidence-based practice guidelines.[4] This type of tort reform could stand on its own or work synergistically with administrative panels or specialized tribunals to provide a more effective and fairer medical liability system. The safe harbor would need to be created on the federal level because of the enormous variation in tort laws among the different states. It is both fair and just and obviates the ability of juries to make uneducated or capricious decisions. The care given by physicians could not be determined to be negligent if the practice guidelines were followed or if they practiced in accordance with the findings of comparative effectiveness research. This reform would promote the use of practice guidelines and comparative-effectiveness research, streamline many cases, and avoid many frivolous ones. Some experiments suggest that physicians are able to invoke safe harbors infrequently, but my experience is quite different. The case involving my friend Steve Smith is a perfect example. A simple review of the practice guidelines relevant to the patient who sued Steve would have obviated the case going forward. Safe harbor laws would not affect the size of damage awards.

We live in a health care environment in which there are approximately ninety-five medical liability claims filed each year for every one hundred physicians. Nearly 62 percent of physicians aged fifty-five and older have been sued, and juries continue to award payments to litigants in a highly capricious manner.[23] This is unsustainable if we hope to improve health care costs, retain our physician workforce, and continue to attract the best and the brightest students to the practice of medicine. Some or all of the group of fair, appropriate, and balanced approaches to reforming our medical malpractice tort system that are presented in this chapter must be incorporated into new regulatory policies. Hospital and practice administrators must also receive protection from aggressive trial lawyers when they attempt to discipline compromised physicians or limit the privileges of doctors who don't have the requisite level of competence to perform some procedures.

There is some good news on the horizon—likely due to the results of the 2010 midterm elections. Early in the 112th Congress, representatives Phil Gingrey, a Republican from Georgia, and David Scott, a Democrat from Georgia, introduced H.R. 5, a bill that would bring federal comprehensive medical liability reforms similar to those enacted in California and Texas. Andrew Cuomo, a Democrat and governor of New York, has placed tort reform as a central issue in the state's efforts to deal with escalating Medicaid debt. Tucked into recommendations from New York State's Medicaid Reform task force is a provision that recommends a cap on patients' noneconomic damages at $250,000.[24] The cap has the support of the Greater New York Hospital Association and the union that represents many hospital workers but, not surprisingly, is opposed by the state bar association.[25] The fact that governors and legislators in many states have begun to place tort reform front and center in the health care debate is reassuring and suggests that we might actually see tort reform in the foreseeable future, although the trial lawyers of America are working assiduously to prevent it. It is important, however, that tort reform occur on a federal level so that there is not a migration of doctors from states without tort reform to those with tort reform.

Notes

1. Krauthammer C. Why Obama is failing. *Washington Post.* July 24, 2009.
2. *Medical Malpractice—Implications of Rising Premiums on Access to Health Care*: Government Accounting Office August 2003.
3. Dafny L. *Northwestern's Kellogg School of Management Report.* Northwestern University 2009.
4. Mello MM, Brennan TA. The role of medical liability reform in federal health care reform. *N Engl J Med.* Jul 2, 2009;361(1):1–3.
5. Evaluating State Approaches to Medical Malpractice Crisis. *Health Policy Monitor.* 2004;9(1).
6. *Pennsylvania—State in Crisis.* American Medical Association.
7. W. Va. doctors strike over insurance costs, CNNHealth.com, Jan 1, 2003, http://articles.cnn.com/2003-01-01/health/medical.malpractice_1_medical-malpractice-insurance-surgical-departments-insurance-costs?_s=PM:HEALTH: http://allnurses.com/nursing-activism-healthcare/n-j-doctors-29305.html.
8. Studdert DM, Mello MM, Gawande AA et al. Claims, errors, and compensation payments in medical malpractice litigation. *N Engl J Med.* May 11, 2006;354(19):2024–2033.
9. Mello M. *Medical Malpractice: Impact of the Crisis and Effect of State Tort Reforms.* Robert Wood Johnson Foundation—The Synthesis Project; May 2006.
10. *Limiting Tort Liability for Medical Malpractice.* Washington, DC. January 8, 2004.

11. Nussbaum A. Malpractice Lawsuits are "Red Herring" in Obama Plan *Bloomberg Businessweek.* June 16, 2009 (http://www.bloomberg.com/apps/news?pid=newsarchive&sid=az9qxQZNmf0o).
12. Klick J, Stratmann T. Medical malpractice reform and physicians in high-risk specialties *Journal of Legal Studies.* 2007;36:S121–S142.
13. Oetgen WJ, Parikh PD, Cacchione JG et al. Characteristics of medical professional liability claims in patients with cardiovascular diseases. *Am J Cardiol.* Mar 1, 2010;105(5):745–752.
14. Arranam R, Dafny LS, Schanzenbach MM. *The Impact of Tort Reform on Employer-Sponsored Health Insurance Premiums.* September 2009.
15. *The Perverse Nature of the Medical Liability System.* U.S. House of Representatives; March 2005.
16. Blumenthal R. More doctors in Texas after malpractice caps. *New York Times.* October 5, 2007.
17. Sorrel A. Texas Liability Reforms Spur Plunge in Premiums and Lawsuits. *mednews.com.* September 9, 2008.
18. *Medical Malpractice Tort Reform: Lessons from the States*: American Academy of Actuaries; Fall 1996.
19. Clinton HR, Obama B. Making patient safety the centerpiece of medical liability reform. *N Engl J Med.* May 25, 2006;354(21):2205–2208.
20. Dove JT, Brush JE, Jr., Chazal RA et al. Medical professional liability and health care system reform. *J Am Coll Cardiol.* Jun 22, 2010;55(25):2801–2803.
21. Kachalia A, Kaufman SR, Boothman R et al. Liability claims and costs before and after implementation of a medical error disclosure program. *Ann Intern Med.* Aug 17, 2010;153(4):213–221.
22. Berger J. *Medical Malpractice and Tort Reform.* October 1, 2007.
23. Kane C. *Policy Research Perspectives, Medical Liability Claim Frequency.* American Medical Association. 2010.
24. Hammond B. Thank Dr. Cuomo for taking on N.Y.'s lawsuit sickness: Medical malpractice reform desperately needed. *New York Daily News.* March 1, 2011.
25. Confessore N. Lawyer attack part of Medicaid panel's plan. *New York Times.* February 28, 2011.

Chapter 11
Conclusion

The debate surrounding the Patient Protection and Affordable Care Act has polarized our nation. No one is very happy. The Left has criticized the new legislation for not providing "universal coverage" through a single-payer system, whereas the Right has criticized the new law for increasing the size and power of the federal government. Doctors decry the cuts in reimbursement, while private insurers and the manufacturers of drugs and health care devices argue that the new taxes that are imposed by the legislation are oppressive and inhibit their profitability, yet at the same time they raise the prices for health insurance policies and new drugs. Workers argue that their employers are simply passing their increased costs down to them through lower wages, higher co-payments, and greater cost sharing. Employers wonder whether they will be able to remain competitive in the global market as their cost of health care insurance continues to increase. Some employers intend to simply eliminate the benefit of health insurance altogether.

The schism between Republican and Democrat, Right and Left, and Blue and Red became deeper after the midterm elections of 2010 as Republicans have made efforts to brand the bill unconstitutional and even to repeal the new law. The final arbiter of the health care reform legislation will likely be the Supreme Court—a decision regarding the constitutionality of the Patient Protection and Affordable Care Act likely coming just months before the 2012 election.

The conservatives recognize that if the Supreme Court declares that the bill is constitutional, there is little chance that Republicans could repeal the bill with a Democrat in the White House. They promised instead to "chip away" at the law if they could not dismantle it. Senator Lamar Alexander, a Republican from

Tennessee, was quoted as saying, "If there was a straight bill to repeal the health care law, I would vote for it because I think it's such a historic mistake. If that doesn't succeed, I think we'll go step by step. We can try to delay funding of some provisions and remove some of the taxes."[1] Congress could actually eviscerate the health care reform legislation by simply failing to appropriate funding for critical elements of the legislation. The key parts of the legislation would become problematic without funding, and the country would be left with no health care reform whatsoever, 50 million Americans left without insurance, and an ever-increasing cost of health care that is simply not sustainable.[2] Republican leaders, emboldened by the results of the midterm elections and the growing deficit, have called for major overhauls in Medicare and Medicaid.

Political pundits on the left continue to tout the Patient Protection and Affordable Care Act as one of the greatest pieces of legislation ever passed by a Democratic House and Senate—but still see the bill as just a first step on the way to a Medicare-for-all type program. The president, his advisors, and congressional Democrats continue to point out the benefits of the health care reform legislation: the consumer protections that began to be rolled out in November of 2010, the catastrophic health insurance for those without coverage, the expanded coverage for young adults, the new coverage for preventive services and wellness visits, and the expanded coverage for prescription drugs. Yet many Democrats have buried their heads in the sand—expecting that health care reform will simply happen and that economic recovery will lead to increased voter approval and stability in the White House and in the Senate after the 2012 elections.

I believe that our leaders on both sides of the political spectrum have let us down. The Left is in error when they suggest that the Patient Protection and Affordable Care Act has fixed the problems that permeate our health care system. The bill will not get us to where we need to be in terms of high-quality and low-cost health care for all Americans as it is currently written. Health care costs will continue to rise—a situation that is not sustainable.[3] The number of insured Americans will increase, but so too will the number of underinsured, resulting in an increasing number of health care–related bankruptcies. The specter of a populace that is woefully underinsured is even more alarming. And we have a severe shortage in our physician workforce that raises substantive challenges to our ability to care for the aging U.S. population and the growing number of insured.

The Republicans call for repealing the Patient Protection and Affordable Care Act, and their efforts to declare the mandate for obligatory health insurance unconstitutional are not the answer. We cannot possibly have a health care system without the full enrollment of the entire American populace. The fiscal sustainability of any health care overhaul requires that all Americans have health insurance so that people don't buy insurance only when they become sick. If the young and the well don't purchase health insurance, the cost for the sick will become so exorbitant that individuals will simply not purchase insurance, resulting in their own personal bankruptcy and the demise of the hospitals that care for a disproportionate share of the uninsured or underinsured.

A few states, Oregon and Vermont being perfect examples, have actually taken the heroic step to implement a single-payer health system, but far too many states have done little to improve their health care delivery systems.

But scrapping the Patient Protection and Affordable Care Act is not the answer! We have invested far too much in the bill to go back to the drawing board—we have invested far too much intellectual and political capital. When I wrote the preface of this book, there were 45 million Americans without health care insurance; when I completed the book nine months later that number had increased to 50 million. The health care system we had before the passage of the Patient Protection and Affordable Care Act was neither sustainable nor equitable—and we cannot go backward.

So, how do we go forward? The most expeditious path to constructing a high-quality and lower-cost health care system is to use the Patient Protection and Affordable Care Act as a template. We must initiate changes that will correct its deficiencies and enhance its strengths. The primary focus of reform should be singular—to improve the health care of the American population. By focusing on quality of care first and costs second, we can ensure that the American public will benefit in the long term by health care reform—and the cost curve will eventually bend. The regulatory boards, governmental agencies, and elected representatives at both the state and federal levels that will be given the opportunity to modify the bill must put politics aside and patient safety and quality first. We must all recognize that health care reform is not about whether your political view leans toward the left or the right—it is really about doing what is in the best interest of the people. What must be done to ensure that we fulfill our societal mission to provide high quality of care for Americans?

Regulate the private insurance companies and curb their influence.
- Eliminate "unreasonable" increases in health insurance premiums at the federal level because states are unwilling or unable to do so at the state level.
- Initiate controls on health premiums now—not in 2014.
- Establish national standards that narrowly define what costs are related to patient care and what costs are related to nonpatient care expenses and limit incomes of health insurance company executives.
- The federal government must step in when states are unable or unwilling to regulate the private insurance agencies.
- Restructure the tax on "Cadillac plans" so that it is based on income to minimize the cost to working families.

- Recognize that physicians are more likely to produce cost-effective medicine if they receive an annual fee to care for a defined population
- Require health insurance plans to provide a package of basic comprehensive coverage so that families do not lose their life savings because of skimpy coverage.
- Allow individuals or employers to purchase health insurance coverage across state lines.

Preserve Medicare and expand Medicaid while carefully evaluating new health care delivery mechanisms.
- Eliminate Medicare Advantage programs—they only serve the private insurance industry.
- Develop new health care delivery systems and evaluate them carefully to ensure that there are no unintended consequences that will negatively impact patient care.
- Ensure that health care delivery systems do not create regional or national monopolies that actually increase health care costs.
- Prohibit states from limiting lifesaving Medicaid benefits such as organ transplantation.
- Avoid draconian cuts in fees paid to hospitals and physicians for the care of Medicare and Medicaid beneficiaries.
- Provide reimbursement for care delivery methods that will improve patient care such as house calls, telephone conferences, and e-mail alerts and communication.
- Don't privatize Medicare.
- Recognize that caring for the underserved is the obligation of a democratic society—not an "entitlement."
- Medicaid actually works. It costs less than for-profit insurance plans.
- We should not transfer the financial responsibility for Medicaid to the states—they are ill prepared to manage it.

Eliminate waste and overutilization by creating and utilizing practice guidelines.
- Avoid placing the burden for eliminating waste on patients—they do not have the knowledge to make decisions regarding their own health.
- Compensate doctors based on the value of the services they provide, not on the quantity of services they provide.
- Authorize and fund the creation of high-quality practice guidelines using criteria established by the Institute of Medicine and use these to assess utilization.
- Establish "health care juries" composed of practicing physicians to adjudicate cases where there are disagreements between patients, payers, and providers.

- Establish a commission modeled on the UK National Institute for Clinical Excellence to guide federal payment policies for expensive new drugs and devices.
  - Utilize electronic records to effectively audit hospital reports to ensure appropriate utilization.

Focus disease prevention and wellness on the young and the disadvantaged.
  - Recognize that neither prevention programs nor wellness programs are likely to lower health care costs in the near term.
  - Prevent private insurance companies from directly passing the cost of prevention and wellness programs to the consumer.
  - Restructure the National Prevention, Health Promotion, and Public Health Council to make it smaller and more efficient and its decisions more timely.
  - Focus federal prevention and wellness programs on underserved urban and rural areas of the United States and on America's children, with particular efforts on erasing the epidemic of childhood obesity.
  - Provide medications for individuals with chronic disease such as high blood pressure, diabetes, and heart failure who cannot afford the medications or the co-payments.
  - Set federal limits on sugar and salt in packaged foods and especially foods for children.
  - Screen the homeless, those with chronic psychiatric problems or drug or alcohol dependencies, and illegal immigrants for communicable disease and to prevent the development of chronic disease.

Protect the medically underserved and the safety net hospitals that provide their care.
  - Our federal government has a societal responsibility to provide a safety net for the uninsured and the underinsured and must support safety net hospitals.
  - Many states will be unable to support health care exchanges, and the federal government must therefore be prepared to provide substantive infrastructure, financial, and technical support.
  - States should be encouraged to create and evaluate "single-payer" systems—if they work.
  - Congress must eliminate new administrative requirements of safety net hospitals that increase their operational costs.
  - Congress must continue to fund graduate medical education—hospitals and especially safety net hospitals are unable to do so.
  - Safety net hospitals cannot be judged using the same metrics as are used for hospitals in affluent suburban communities. Patients who receive care from safety net hospitals have higher readmission rates

and longer lengths of stay because they lack social support systems at home and because they are often unable to pay for their medications.

Fix the crisis in the medical workforce.
- The crisis in America's health care workforce will continue to worsen as 35 million individuals gain insurance coverage in 2014, and the federal government must recognize the dire need to increase the supply of both primary care physicians and specialists.
- Congress must fund 15,000 additional postgraduate training positions for graduates of American medical schools while still allowing foreign medical school graduates to continue to train in the United States.
- Congress must recognize that cutting the funding for graduate medical education will decrease the number of postgraduate training positions in the United States and inextricably worsen the workforce crisis.
- The federal government must develop a set of national standards for the creation of new medical schools to ensure that we continue to train a well-informed physician workforce.
- For-profit offshore medical schools must be inspected and regulated by the federal government.
- Congress must create new federally funded programs designed to increase the number of students who pursue careers in primary care medicine by paying back the cost of both undergraduate and medical school education.
- Congress must expand funding for innovative programs that encourage and support the entry of underserved minorities to medical school and the practice of medicine.

Improve the quality of care for all Americans.
- We can decrease health care costs by ensuring that value—not cost—serves as the central focus for all legislative and regulatory efforts to improve our health care system.
- The Department of HHS must develop accurate and sensitive instruments that can measure quality of care and replace the current metrics that only measure processes of care.
- Congress as well as federal and state regulators must recognize that there is no relationship between cost and quality. Some high-cost hospitals deliver excellent care while other high-cost hospitals deliver care that does not meet appropriate levels of quality.
- Hospitals that have low volumes of high-technology procedures are high cost and low quality. Federal regulators can lower health care costs and improve care by instituting volume benchmarks for operators and hospitals that provide services for Medicare and Medicaid populations.

- The largest Medicare expenditures occur at the end of life; therefore, the Department of HHS can only lower health care costs if they address the complex and politically charged topic of end-of-life care. They must create tasteful and respectful programs for palliative care, create pilot educational programs for the lay public, create programs that train patient ombudspersons, and reimburse palliative care experts for their activities.
- Congress can lower health care costs by eliminating reimbursement for new and expensive drugs and devices that provide no benefits when compared with older and less expensive treatments.
- Congress must address the level of profitability that pharmaceutical or device companies can ethically accrue when they develop new and innovative, but costly, treatments.

Expand funding for comparative-effectiveness research.
- The best way to stem our rising health care costs is by utilizing comparative-effectiveness research to identify the best treatment for patients.
- Congress must substantially increase funding for comparative-effectiveness research.
- The Food and Drug Administration must require comparative-effectiveness research as part of the drug and device evaluation process.
- The Department of HHS should initiate a consumer education campaign to teach the public the benefits of comparative-effectiveness research and to allay their fears that this type of research is one step toward "rationing" care.
- Congress should revise the law to allow comparative-effectiveness studies to be used to inform policy decisions.
- Congress should allow comparative-effectiveness studies to assess the cost-effectiveness of new drugs and devices by assessing the relative costs of competing technologies.
- The Department of HHS should consult with physicians and scientists in Europe who have extensive experience in using comparative-effectiveness research to inform policy decisions.

Improve the ability of doctors to practice medicine.
- There is no mechanism for equitably distributing physician fees and we can't change physician compensation and at the same time have budget neutrality. HHS must increase funding to primary care physicians in the short term and worry about equity and cost control later.
- Draconian cuts in reimbursement for hospitals and doctors will have unwelcome consequences and could limit access to health care for our aged and undeserved.
- Eliminate the sustainable growth rate system for physician compensation.

- Health delivery systems that force doctors to take financial risk will be problematic for small practices or even some larger practices and should not become the norm.
- We can lower health care costs by reimbursing physicians only for services that are consistent with consensus practice guidelines and standards.
- The current timelines for electronic health record implementation are not realistic, and the Department of Health and Human Service must redefine them.
- Payment reforms and delivery system reforms must evolve in a coordinated way because physicians will be unable to institute payment reform unless they have the revenues to support new organizational structures.
- The present fee-for-service payment methodology may be the best payment method for small rural practices. A one-size-fits-all approach to payment reform will never work.
- New fee schedules should be flexible enough to reward physicians and hospitals that train medical students and residents and must take into consideration the acuity of illness in a particular patient.

Reform the U.S. tort system.
- The Patient Protection and Affordable Care Act fails to adequately address tort reform.
- Reforming the tort system will clearly lower health care costs, albeit to a modest degree.
- Congress must recognize that physicians spend enormous time and money as well as emotional capital trying to defend themselves in often frivolous lawsuits, dealing with capricious jury awards, and fighting their own insurance carriers or employers who find it expedient to settle even cases with no merit.
- State laws should establish health courts or tribunals and other innovative ways to take the decisions out of the hands of capricious juries and place them in the hands of knowledgeable arbiters.
- Physician administrators should be afforded protection by state legislatures when dealing with physicians who demonstrate inadequate skills or unprofessional behavior.

Surviving Health Care Reform

Throughout this book I have taken the approach that the Patient Protection and Affordable Care Act is an initial step in creating a health care system that takes advantage of America's core competencies in diagnosing and treating human disease and discovering the cures of the future. The bill must now be carefully crafted to ensure that at a time of limited resources, doctors can continue to provide the best possible care for their patients, mitigate the enormous disparities that exist between different segments of our population, and lower health care costs. It is one thing to say that every American has health insurance—it is a far different goal to ensure that every American has a level of insurance that will cover their care for even catastrophic illnesses without leaving their family penniless. Health care has for too long been controlled by the undue influences of groups that can effectively lobby the local, state, and federal agencies and legislative bodies that oversee the system. This undue influence must be stopped. The new health care legislation must be interpreted by federal regulators in such a way that health insurance companies are forced to put the needs of their beneficiaries ahead of the remuneration of their shareholders and executives. The spiraling costs of health care are not sustainable—but neither is a system that rewards corporate America at the expense of the poor and impoverished and passes the cost of health care onto the consumer. Doctors and other caregivers must also be held accountable for developing fair and well thought out mechanisms to restrain the growing costs of health care.

The Patient Protection and Affordable Care Act will unfortunately be a political football that we will see tossed around during the debates leading up to the 2012 national election. It will be a time of enormous rhetoric with far more fiction and gossip than truth. We must avoid listening to the fearmongers who stoke the fires with cries about "death-panels" and "health care rationing" and look beneath the layers of rhetoric to try to understand the complex issues that surround health care reform. It will be a difficult time for all of us who work in the health care field because of the uncertainty, but it will also be a challenging time for those of us who are patients. The continuing debates over health care reform at both the state and federal level will test the fortitude of the American electorate. It will also test the willingness of our federal and local leaders to collaborate, negotiate, and compromise. If our leaders are unwilling or unable to place their societal responsibilities above their politics, we face the specter of falling into the health care abyss.

There is no right or wrong answer to many of the issues regarding the Patient Protection and Affordable Care Act that I raised throughout this book. I have addressed issues that are important to me as both a patient and a physician—a perspective that has been lacking in the robust debates that have taken place among politicians, political pundits, and health policy analysts. I don't by any means believe that I have all of the answers—I don't believe that anyone does. I will have done my job if the information and insights I have provided serve as guideposts for discussions and debate among voters, their elected representatives who will craft health care reform over the years ahead, and the federal and state regulators who will further define and carry out the specifics of the new law. Henry Aaron, the Virginia and Bruce MacLaury Senior Fellow at the Brookings Institute, said it best when he pointed out

> If we got it [health care reform] right the first time, it would be nothing short of miraculous. We will make mistakes whatever we do. And I think by far and away the most important issue is not so much what we do but that we do something, that we move off dead center on the issue of health reform.[4]

We have certainly gotten off dead center—now we need to make sure that we continue to go in the right direction despite the many bumps in the road ahead.

Notes

1. Pear R. Short of repeal, GOP will chip away at health law. *New York Times.* September 20, 2010.
2. Aaron HJ. The midterm elections—High stakes for health policy. *N Engl J Med.* Oct 28, 2010;363(18):1685–1687.
3. Chernew ME, Baicker K, Hsu J. The specter of financial Armageddon—Health care and federal debt in the United States. *N Engl J Med.* Apr 1, 2010;362(13):1166–1168.
4. Epstein AM, Aaron HJ, Baicker K et al. Health care reform in perspective. *N Engl J Med.* Oct 15, 2009;361(16):e30.

Index

A

Abdominal aortic aneurysm screening effectiveness rating, 62
Accountable Care Organization (ACO), 27–31
    anticompetitive behavior, 31
    complexities of accounting, 28–29
    cost-effectiveness, 36
    legal complexities, 30–31
Accountable Health Organization (AHO), see Accountable Care Organization (ACO)
ACO, see Accountable Care Organization (ACO)
Adjudication by physicians, 161
Administrative tribunals for tort reform, 174–175
Adultbasic program elimination, 34
Aging population and health care costs, xvi
AHO, see Accountable Care Organization (ACO)
AIDS patients covered by Medicaid, 23
American health care system
    cost of, xv–xvi
    doesn't work, xv–xvi
    highest cost of developed countries, xi
Annual spending limits removed in health care reform bill, 4
Anticompetitive behavior of ACOs, 31
Anti-trust issues in setting of premium prices, 13–14
"Area" in insurance cost setting, 13
Artificial limbs, 22

B

Bankruptcy due to health care costs, xi
Billing codes, 158
Biologic drugs, 142
Block grants for Medicaid funding, 34–35
Blood disorder specialty funding, 127
Blood pressure control, 67
Blood pressure in children, 57–59
Blood pressure screening effectiveness rating, 62
Body mass index (BMI) awareness, 66
Boston Medical Center, 80
Braddock Hospital, 74–76
    specific needs of population, 85–86
Breast cancer screening
    effectiveness rating, 62
    in reform legislation, 105
Buy-downs to lower-cost insurance policies, 10–11
Bypass surgery study, 140–141

C

CABG, see Coronary artery bypass grafting (CABG)
Cadillac plan regulation, 181
Cadillac tax
    basing on individual income, 14, 16
    drawbacks of, 14
California health insurance exchanges, 86–87
Canes, 22
Capitation payments from medical home programs, 26

189

190 ■ Index

Capricious jury verdicts, 173, 174, 175
Cardioverter-defibrillator (ICD) in end-of-life care, 48
Caribbean Island medical graduates, 123, 127
Cause of health care cost increases, xvi
Cedars-Sinai Medical Center high-performing areas of service, 99
Center for Medicare and Medicaid Innovation, 24
Center for Medicare and Medicaid Services (CMS), 24
CER, see Comparative-effectiveness research (CER)
Cervical cancer screening effectiveness rating, 62
Chemotherapy covered by Medicare, 22
Childhood obesity, 65–67
　funding for reduction of, 61
　need for focus on, 68–69
Children's Health Insurance Program (CHIP), 33
Children's medical care needs additional focus, 68–69
CHIP, 33
Chronic disease
　contribution to high health care costs, xvi
　cost control by reform program, 25
　costs of, 35
　medical home programs for, 27
　nurse practitioners for management, 116
　providers reimbursed for support, 68
　team approach to care, 105
Cleveland Clinic as high-performing center, 99
Clinical services defined by state regulators, 12–13
Clinical trial routine costs denied by insurance during clinical trial, 4–5
"Clot buster" drug use, 139–140
CMS, 24
Cognitive specialty funding, 127
Coinsurance and Medicare fees, 22
Collaborative care networks, 106
Colonoscopy coverage under Medicare, 22
Colorectal cancer screening effectiveness rating, 62
Community health centers, 32–33

Community rating system in insurance cost controls, 13
Comparative-effectiveness research (CER)
　controversy surrounding, 134–135
　cost-reduction through, 138–140
　increased funding needed, 185
　lack of, xvii
　limitations of, 140–142
　need for, 44
　opposition to, xxii–xxiii
　Patient-Centered Outcomes Research Institute, 135–136
　patient need for, 137–138
　SAVER vs. CABG, 144
　uses, 142–144
　value, 136–138
Comparative-effectiveness vs. cost-effectiveness, 143–144
Comparison of service providers not published, 101–102
Computer use and obesity, 66
Congenital heart disease under reform legislation, 105
Co-payments as cost control measure, 49–50
Coronary artery bypass grafting (CABG)
　compared to SAVER procedure, 131–133
　quality-volume link, 107
Cost-benefit analysis, 45–46
Cost control by reform program
　Accountable Care Organization (ACO), 27–31
　burden placed on patient, 49–50
　comparative studies and, 136–138
　Independence at Home Program, 25
　Medical Homes programs, 25–27
　preventive services effects, 63–64
　short-term cost increases, 68
　value increased by improving quality and lowering cost, 108
Cost-effective medical systems, 96
Cost-effectiveness vs. comparative-effectiveness, 143–144
"Costlier care is often worse care," 96
Cost of American health care
　highest of developed countries, xi
　reasons for, xvi–xvii
Cost of health insurance, xx
Cost of medications and noncompliance, 67
Cost-shifting at safety net hospitals, 78, 79

Country doctors, 147–149
Cure Acceleration Network, 106

D

Dartmouth Atlas, 96–99
"Death panels"
 claim repercussions, 48
 comparative research and, 135
 in opposition to reform, xvi
Deductibles
 as cost control measure, 49–50
 increases in, 10–11
Defibrillation programs, 105
Demonstration projects, see also Pilot plans
 under health care reform, 102–103
 need for evaluation, 36
Dental care
 funding for, 60
 under Medicare Advantage plans, 22
Dependent children
 denial of coverage due to preexisting conditions, 4
 extension of coverage to age 26, 4
Depressive disorders under reform legislation, 105
Designer drugs, 142
Diabetes Prevention Program, 69
Diabetes screening recommendations controversy, 63
Diagnostic error malpractice claims, 170
Disclosure-and-offer programs, 174
Disease management program funding, 36
Disease prevention
 in health care reform, xxi, 59
 population health and, 60
Disproportionate-share hospital (DSH) payments, 79
 changes needed to protect safety net, 88–90
 effect of shifting funds, 80
 under health care reform, 80–81
Drug approval process needs comparative-effectiveness study, 141
Drug price contribution to high health care costs, xvi
DSH payments, see Disproportionate-share hospital (DSH) payments
Durable medical goods covered by Medicare, 22

E

ECG, see Electrocardiogram (ECG)
Economic waste, see also Medical waste; Waste
 controlling, 46–47
 definition, 43–44
Egregious error payment cut-off, 50
EHR, see Electronic health records (EHR)
Electrocardiogram (ECG) for, 45
Electronic health records (EHR)
 in ACO systems, see Accountable Care Organization (ACO)
 cost of, 157
 in developing practice guidelines, 53
 funding for, xxiii, 32
 for physician rating, 157
 under reform plans, 156–159
 tied to billing codes, 158
 time burden of, 157–158
 use, 103
Employer-sponsored insurance plans affected by reforms, 11–12
Employment law and physician competence, 173–174
End-of-life effort costs, 47–48
End-stage disease palliative care, 48
Entitlement program labelling, 37
Ethical obligations to provide care, 37
European medical school costs, 126
Evidence-based medicine, see also Comparative-effectiveness research (CER)
 guidelines not used, 95
 lack of comparative studies, xvii
 teaching of, 124
Extenders, see Physician-extenders
Extension program hub, 31–32

F

False economies in cost control, 49–50
Fee-for-service structure
 abuse of, 46–47
 effects of, 95
 parties benefiting from, 51
 perversity of, 44
Firing employees after serious diagnosis, 10
Florida state-funding of medical schools, 122

Foreign-trained physicians, 123
   with postgraduate training in U.S., 127
Funding changes needed for sustainability, xvi–xvii

G

Geisinger Health System
   as cost-effective system, 96
   as high-performing center, 99
Generic drug savings, 142
Geographic variation in medical systems, 162
Global payment systems, 154–156
Government agency rules on health care, xvii
Graduate medical education (GME) payment requirements, 124, 125
Grady Memorial Hospital, 77
Group practices, 159–160
Guidelines for care, 108; see also Comparative-effectiveness research (CER); Evidence-based medicine
   development of, 104
Gym programs in schools and obesity, 66
Gynecology malpractice claims, 169–170

H

Health care exchanges
   scale needed for success, 84–85
   systems for, 82–86
   uncertainties over implementation, 10
"Health care pork," 105
Health care reform, see also Patient Protection and Affordable Care Act
   additional quality needs, 106–109
   changes needed to protect safety net, 88–90
   effect on health safety net, 80–82
   improvements to, 161–162
   influence on quality measures, 101–102
   legislation for specific medical conditions, 105
   lowering costs through, 35–37
   obesity issues, 65–67
   opposition to, xvii
   physician shortage remedies, 116–117
   pilot plan component, 24
   political nature of, 179–181, 186–188
   prescription drug waste reduction, 49
   process of, xvi
   recommendations for, 181–186
   role of Medicaid, 23–24
   state actions in response, xvii
   strengthening of, 15–16
   tort reform not addressed, 171–172
   uncertainty over effects of, xvii
   waste not adequately addressed, 55
   work in progress, 186–188
Health care safety net
   changes needed to protect, 88–90
   components of, 76–77
   efforts to support, xxi
   precarious, 77
Health care warranty, 154
Health Information Technology for Economic and Clinical Health (HITECH) Act, 156
Health insurance
   cost increases of, 3
   history of, 2
   pricing of policies, 3
   regulation of companies, 181–182
Health insurance exchange uncertainties, 10; see also Health care exchanges
Health insurance industry reform, xix–xx
Health insurance mandate
   adverse selection and, 7
   spreading of costs by, 7–8
Health maintenance program (HMO) replacement, 28
Health Technology Assessment (HTA) program, 138–139
Healthy lifestyle promotion funding, 61
Heart failure treatment, 35–36
High-risk patients excluded from insurance coverage, 3
HITECH Act, 156
HIV screening recommendations controversy, 63
Home health cost Medicare coverage, 22
Homeless patients
   lack insurance, 68
   unlikely to use health care exchanges, 85
Hospice care
   cardioverter-defibrillator (ICD) use policy, 48
   Medicare coverage, 22
Hospital closures, 74–76

Hospital costs
  Medicare coverage, 22
  readmission rates and fee structures, 33
Hospital medicine specialty, 119
Hospital Quality Alliance process-of-care measures, 82
Hospitals
  in Accountable Care Organization contracting, 29–30
  in waste control efforts, 49–50
House calls in rural areas, 152
HTA, see Health Technology Assessment (HTA) program

I

ICD in end-of-life care, 48
Illegal immigrants insurance access, 85
Imaging rate, 46–47
IME payments, 118
Independence at Home Program, 25
Independent Payment Advisory Board, 160–161
Indirect Medical Education (IME) payments, 118
Infectious disease specialty funding, 127
Insurance companies
  fees imposed on, 14–15
  lobbying at state level, 15
  responses to health care reform legislation, 8
  use of EHR, 158–159
Insurance costs administrative fraction, 6
Insurance packages in health care exchanges, 83
Insurance plan changes, 11–12
Insurance premiums
  controlled by reform legislation, 5–6
  control of, 8–9, 181
  effect of delayed reform implementation, 9–10
  "reasonable" increase definition, 16
  reporting of fraction spent on qualified costs, 6
  state line crossing in insurance shopping, 13–14
Integrated academic medical center for pilot programs, 36–37
Integrated medical practices, 159–160

Integration of care
  by Accountable Care Organization, 28
  hospital system growth, 155–156
Intermountain Healthcare
  as cost-effective system, 96
  as high-performing center, 99

J

Jackson Health System, 90
Johns Hopkins Hospital, 77–78

K

Kaiser Permanente as cost-effective system, 96

L

Leapfrog Group quality principles, 107–108
Legislation of wellness, 61–62
Lifestyle modification support, 69
Lipid disorder screening, 62
Lobbying
  against health care reform, xvi
  influence on medical care, 63
  undue influences of, 187

M

Maine waiver of reform law participation, 15
Malpractice caps, 170–171, 174
Malpractice claims, see also Tort reform
  capping of, 174
  contribution to high health care costs, xvi
  database study, 170
  heart failure case, 165–167
  highest specialty areas, 169–170
  reviews of, 168
  secrecy surrounding, 172–173
Malpractice insurance costs, 168
Mammography
  effectiveness rating, 62
  Medicare coverage, 22
  screening standards controversy, 62–63
Marshfield Clinic as cost-effective system, 96
Massachusetts health care reform, 87–88
  physician shortages, 121
Mayo Clinic
  as cost-effective system, 96
  as high-performing center, 99

Medicaid, see also Medicaid-Medicare reform; Medicare
  addressing physician shortages, 116–117
  block grant funding of, 34–35
  eligibility changes under reform, 33
  emergency room reimbursement rules, 160–161
  as entitlement program, 37
  hospital reimbursements below cost of care, 75, 77, 78
  lowering costs of, 33–34
  Massachusetts expansion of, 87
  participation rates, 23
  primary care physician compensation, 151–152
  purpose of, 23
  recommendations for reform, 182
  reform of, xx
  role in health care reform, 23–24
  severity of illness consideration, 33–34
  tort reform in addressing debt, 176
  transplant coverage elimination, 34
Medicaid-Medicare reform and state governments, 34–35
Medical education cost
  deterrent to increasing workforce, 126
  recommendations for, 184
Medical error frequency, 94–95
Medical Homes for coordinated care, 25–27
Medical loss ratio reporting, 6
Medical schools
  class sizes, 122
  curriculum changes, 122–123, 124
  new approaches, 122–123
  premed curriculum requirements changes, 126
Medical waste, see also Economic waste; Waste
  controlling, 46–47
  definition, 43
Medicare, see also Medicaid; Medicaid-Medicare reform
  addressing physician shortages, 116–117
  beginning of, 20
  billing requirements, 155
  effective treatments mandated regardless of cost, 135
  as entitlement program, 37
  flawed fee schedule, 161–162
  hospital reimbursements below cost of care, 75, 77, 78
  lowering costs of, 33–34
  not an entitlement program, 21
  Parts A, B, C, D, 22
  primary care physician compensation, 151–152
  privatization proposal, 35
  recommendations for reform, 182
  reform of, xx
  residency training funding, 118
  Resource Based Relative Value Scale, 150
  spending inversely correlated with quality, 96
Medicare Advantage plans
  cost control by reform program, 24
  coverage by, 22
Medicare Payment Advisory Commission (MedPAC), 124, 160–161
Midwives as physician-extenders, 116–7
Modern medical procedure increases, 20–21
Multispecialty group practices, 159–160

N

National Health Care Workforce Commission, 117
National Institute of Health and Clinical Excellence (NICE)
  comparative studies by, 143
National Institutes of Health Diabetes Prevention Program, 69
National Practitioner Data Bank, 173
Neurosurgery malpractice claims, 169–170
New York University Medical Center high-performing areas of service, 99
NICE, see National Institute of Health and Clinical Excellence (NICE)
Nurse-midwives as physician-extenders, 116–117
Nurse practitioners as physician-extenders, 116–117
Nutrition education, 54–55, 68–69

O

"Obamacare," see Patient Protection and Affordable Care Act
Obesity epidemic, 65–67; see also Childhood obesity

Obstetrics malpractice claims, 169–170
Off-pump bypass surgery study, 140–141
Ombudspersons for alternative therapy coverage, 53
Open-ended funding, xvi
Oregon
    plan for single-payer system, 84
    use of comparative-effectiveness research, 139
Orthopedic surgery malpractice claims, 169–170
Outcome must be factored into evaluations, 98–99
Outpatient services covered by Medicare, 22
Overhead cost controls, 12
Overutilization
    reducing, 161
    reduction leading to higher quality, 95–96
Oxygen services, 22

P

Palliative care consultations, 48
Parts of Medicare, 22
Patient burdened with cost control, 49–50
Patient-centered medical home, see Medical Homes
Patient-Centered Outcomes Research Institute, 135–136
Patient Protection and Affordable Care Act, see also Health care reform
    changes to current insurance practice, 4
    constitutionality challenged, xiii
    controversy surrounding, xi
    flaws in, 8–15
    insurance industry controls by, 4
    lack of bipartisan support, xv
    state responses, xvii
    work in progress, xiii
Pay-for-performance
    under health care reform, 102–103, 152–153
    relationship to population covered, 81–82
    unintended consequences of, 102
Payment bundling, 153–154
PCI, see Primary percutaneous coronary intervention (PCI) use
Pediatric blood pressure studies, 57–59
Pediatric emergency care in reform legislation, 105

Pennsylvania state-funding of medical schools, 122–123
Pharmaceutical companies
    fears of comparative research, 135
    influence on legislation of comparative-effectiveness studies, 142
    statin drug promotion, 141–142
Pharmacists as physician-extenders, 117
Philadelphia Urban Food and Fitness Alliance (PUFFA), 67
Physician compensation, see also Pay-for-performance; Payment bundling
    capping of training funding, 150–151
    contribution to high health care costs, xvi
    as cost-effective driver, 182
    under Medicare, 22
    planned changes to, 151–152
    recommendations for, 185–186
    restructuring of, 162
    structure of, 149–150
    waste elimination and, 182
Physician competence and legal actions, 173–174
Physician education debt, xvi
Physician-extenders, 44
    in Independence at Home Program, 25
    physician shortage remedies, 116–117
Physician-led health care organizations, 159
Physician rating by EHR, 157
Physicians conflicts of interest, 106
Physician shortages, xxii; see also Workforce issues in medicine
    across specialties, 120–121
    acute areas, 115
    diversity needs, 125
    education debt and specialty choice, 120
    geographic distribution of doctors, 118–119
    measures to address, 121–123, 125–128
    postgraduate training in U.S., 127
    primary care, 116
    reform legislation approaches, 116–117
    reliance on foreign-trained physicians, 123
Physician support recommendations, 185–186
Pilot plans
    component of reform plans, 24
    for healthy lifestyle promotion, 61
    need for evaluation, 36
Poor populations lack social support, xvi

PPO, see Preferred provider organization (PPO)
Practice guidelines and waste reduction, 52–53
Practice of medicine affected by reforms, xxiii
Practice size affected by reforms, 26–27
Preexisting condition and insurance affordability, xvii
Preferred provider organization (PPO)
  controls costs by excluding benefits, 3–4
  out-of-network costs, xvii
Prescription drugs, see also Lobbying
  coverage under Medicare Advantage plans, 22
  delivery systems and waste reduction, 49
  lack of comparative studies, 142
  Medicare coverage, 22–23
Prescription medication unaffordable, 25
Prevention efforts
  role in health care reform, xxi
  short-term cost increases, 68
Preventive screening tests effectiveness rating, 62
Preventive services
  cost reduction and, 63–64
  focus on young and disadvantaged, 183
  Medicare coverage, 22
  promotion of, 68–70
  reward for meeting standard, 61
Preventive Services Task Force, 62–63
Primary care
  cost effectiveness of, 27
  increase in compensation for, 151–152
  making practice more attractive, 126–127
  physician demographics, 119–120
  setting for practice, 127–128
Primary percutaneous coronary intervention (PCI) use, 139–140
Privatization of Medicare, 35
Process-of-care measures, 82
  distinct from quality measures, 100
Prostate cancer screening recommendations controversy, 63
Psychiatric patients
  lack insurance, 68
  unlikely to use health care exchanges, 85
Public access defibrillation programs, 105
PUFFA, 67

Q

Quality-adjusted life years (QALY) as cost-effectiveness quantifier, 45–46
Quality of care
  compensation based upon, 51–52
  improvement category in legislation, 12
  level of, xxi–xxii
  link to number of procedures performed, 107
  measurement of, 95, 100–101
  metrics for, 52
  recommendations for improving, 184–185
  reform plan efforts for improving, 104–106
  value increased by improving quality and lowering cost, 108

R

RAND Health Insurance Experiment, 139
Rationing of health care
  comparative research seen as first step, 134–135
  and opposition to reform, xvi
Readmission rates and fee structures, 33
Regional variations in service levels, 99–100
Rescinding of coverage due to medical condition, 4
Resource Based Relative Value Scale, 150
Rheumatologic disease specialty funding, 127
Robotic surgery, 137–138
Routine costs covered during clinical trial under reform plans, 4–5
Rural community
  appropriate systems for, 37
  medical organizations, 147–149
  unable to support some practice structures, 159–160

S

Safe harbors in tort law, 175
"Safety net," see Health care safety net
Safety net hospitals, see also Hospital closures
  closures of, 77
  cost-shifting at, 78
  disproportionate-share hospital (DSH) payments, 79, 80

effect of health care reform legislation, 80–82
effects of universal insurance, 76
functions of, 76–77
history of, 77–78
Massachusetts program effects, 87
patients lack support systems, 81
specialty areas for, 89–90
Salt levels in food dictated by food industry, 69
SAVER procedure, 131–133
Second opinion payment by insurance, xvii
Severity of illness consideration
    in evaluating performance, 98–99
    in Medicaid reimbursement model, 33–34
SGR, see Sustainable Growth Rate (SGR)
Shared decision-making programs, 105–106
SHOP, 83
Sick care system, 59
Single-payer universal health care system, see also Universal health care
    not in Patient Protection and Affordable Care Act, xi
    state government systems, 84
Skilled nursing facilities quality measures, 104
Small businesses use of health care exchanges, 83
Small Business Health Options Program (SHOP), 83
Socialized medicine, xi
Specialist care
    contribution to high health care costs, xvi
    demographics of physicians, 119
    education debt and specialty choice, 120
    family-friendly specialties, 119–120
Standardization of health insurance paperwork to reduce costs, 6
Standard summary of benefits mandated by reform legislation, 5
Standby capacity and cost levels, xvi
State actions on health care reform, xvii
State costs for Medicaid, 23
State funding of Medicaid and eligibility changes, 33
State government regulation of health insurance, 9
State government role in insurance reform, 15
    current positions, 86–87
    Medicaid-Medicare reform, 34–35
    politics in, 108
    tort reform efforts, 176
State line crossing in insurance shopping, 13–14
State monitoring of insurance exchanges, 6
State opt-out of health care exchanges, 84
State politics in hospital funding, 79
State waivers of participation, 15
Statin drug promotion, 141–142
Steel industry and health care, 74
Substance abusers
    lack insurance, 68
    unlikely to use health care exchanges, 85
Sudden cardiac death risk identified by ECG, 45
Sugar levels in food and industry involvement, 69
Surgery errors and payment cut-off, 50
Surgical anterior ventricular endocardial restoration procedure, 131–133
Sustainable Growth Rate (SGR), 150–151
Systematic reviews, 108
System reforms needed, 37

T

Tax-free treatment of employer-sponsored health insurance, 14
Team approach to complex patient care, 105
Technology evaluations for waste reduction, 54
Television viewing and obesity, 66
Timing of reform provision implementation and premium increases, 9–10
Tobacco use and insurance premiums, 6
Tort reform, see also Malpractice claims
    estimates of cost savings, 170
    as political issue, 167–168
    reform legislation ignores, xxiii
    safe harbors, 175
    state level efforts, 176
    strategies for, 174–176
Transplant coverage elimination under Medicaid, 34
Tribunals for tort reform, 174–175

U

Underserved populations
    caring for, xxi

need for support, 69
protection of, 183–184
Universal health care, see also Single-payer universal health care system
in developed countries, xvi
legislative option, 7–8
Urban community systems, 37
Urbanization and obesity, 66–67
childhood obesity, 69–70
U.S. medical board (USMLE) evaluations of foreign graduates, 123
U.S. Preventive Services Task Force, 62–63

V

Vaccinations
funding for, 60–61
Medicare coverage, 22
Value-based purchasing, 81
Value increased by improving quality and lowering cost, 108
Vermont plan for single-payer system, 84
Video games and obesity, 66
Vision care under Medicare Advantage plans, 22

W

Walkers, 22
Washington state use of comparative-effectiveness research, 138–139
Waste, see also Economic waste; Medical waste
elimination by cost control, xx–xxi
in end-of-life efforts, 47–48
by inappropriate care, see Universal health care
recommendations for reduction, 182–183
types of, 43–44
unintended consequences of attempts to reduce, 51
Waste reduction
practice guidelines for, 52–54
quality of care and, 52
strategies for, 51–55
Wellness
legislation of, 61–62
promotion of, 68–70
Wellness services
definition, 59
focus on young and disadvantaged, 183
in health care reform, 60
under health care reform legislation, 22
short-term cost increases, 68
Wheelchairs, 22
Workforce issues in medicine, see also Physician shortages
capping of training funding, 118
increasing training slots, 125
medical education cost, 126
multidisciplinary teams needed, 127
recommendations for, 184
use of physician-extenders, 116–117